SAVORY SUPPERS & FASHIONABLE FEASTS

SAVORY SUPPERS & FASHIONABLE FEASTS

DINING IN VICTORIAN AMERICA

SUSAN WILLIAMS

PANTHEON BOOKS
NEW YORK

IN ASSOCIATION WITH THE STRONG MUSEUM

Library of Congress Cataloging-in-Publication Data
Williams, Susan, 1948–
Savory suppers and fashionable feasts.
Bibliography: p.
Includes index.
1. Cookery, American—History—19th century.
2. Dinners and dining—United States—History—19th
century. 3. United States—Social life and customs—
1865–1918. I. Margaret Woodbury Strong Museum.
II. Title.
TX715.W7293   1985   394.1'2'0973   85-42876
ISBN 0-394-54571-0

Book design by Susan Mitchell
Manufactured in the United States of America
First Edition

In memory of Nicky,
who ate every meal of her life
with grace and dignity.

CONTENTS

RECIPES · & ·

INSTRUCTIONS

CONTENTS

· —— ·

viii

PREFACE

This book will tell you what dining was like in Victorian America: what kinds of foods people ate; how, when, and where they ate them; and why. It will help you to see the roots of much of the commonplace behavior we all engage in at the dinner table. Have you ever been to a dinner party and been confronted with more forks, knives, and spoons than you had ever seen in one place, and wondered what the point was—to say nothing of the protocol? Have you ever noticed that fancy restaurants often fold their napkins into elaborate shapes and put them right on the dinner plate, instead of beside it? Did your mother ever bring ketchup to the table in its bottle? Do you feel awkward eating asparagus with your fingers? Who carves your Thanksgiving turkey? Why is French cooking held in such esteem in America? Are some foods more "American" than others? When did bananas first become popular in this country? Would you be able to peel an orange without touching it with your fingers? Do you call your evening meal "supper" or "dinner"? What is French about French dressing? Or Bostonian about Boston lettuce? Why is an apartment with a separate dining room more desirable than one with an eat-in kitchen? To what can we attribute the current resurgence of interest in manners and etiquette in this country?

During the Victorian period, a new class of Americans emerged, people with enough money to be able to live with a certain degree of comfort, often in their own homes, surrounded by an increasing selection of purchased goods and services. The constantly shifting boundaries of this new class, however, generated an unsettling degree of social uncertainty during the last half of the nineteenth century. American families eagerly adopted the rules of etiquette to proclaim and solidify their newly won position in society. Dining rituals—the way these Americans ate, the furniture they bought for their dining rooms, the silver that decorated their sideboards, the pictures they hung on their walls, how they set their tables and dressed for dinner, and the food they chose to serve—were a constant, visible reassurance of an established and secure social position in a complex and changing world.

In addition to offering a detailed view of the intricate rituals of the dining table and of the environment that both supported and shaped those rituals, this book provides menus and recipes for actual nineteenth-century meals. Whether you wish to re-create an elegant Victorian feast or merely examine the wealth and diversity of foods that were consumed by Victorian Americans, the selection of recipes at the end of the book will enable you to do so. A meal-by-meal analysis of many different types of family and company meals is supplemented in each case by actual or ideal menus for those meals. The recipes are grouped topologically to make it easy to locate appropriate soups, fish, entrées, or desserts for each menu. These have been reproduced from popular cookbooks of the last century, and therefore may contain measuring and coding conventions that seem imprecise or strange to us today, such as "butter the size of a walnut" or "a teacup of flour." They all, however, require only the application of common sense to be adapted to twentieth-century kitchens.

I am grateful to the many people who have helped me during the course of this project. At the Strong Museum, the Board of Trustees, and especially William T. Alderson, director, and Lynne Poirier, deputy director for collections, have supported this endeavor from the beginning. Bill Alderson shared with me his enthusiasm as well as his editorial expertise and historical acumen, and Lynne patiently endured the loss of one of her curators for a year while I pursued matters of the dinner table. Many thanks to my colleagues in the collections department: fellow curators Mary Ellen Perry, Patricia Tice, Margaret and Blair Whitton, and Debbie Smith helped supply me with both artifacts and insights; conservator Rick Sherin and his assistant Cymantha Stein made many of the objects illustrated here presentable; and museum librarians Elaine Challacombe and Kathy Lazar patiently dealt with all of my research requests. Extra special thanks to Gretchen Fuller, who kept the wolves at bay while I was writing. Many other museum staff members helped in innumerable ways, but I would like especially to thank Florence Smith, Maria Yannopoulos, Kasey Grier, Jackie Spencer, Anna Wang, Pat Greeno, Gerda Kyle, and Florence Goldstein for their particular efforts.

The volunteer efforts of Rose Garven, Bill and Carol Scheetz, Lew Schuman, Jeanne Wenrich, John Castle, Bobby Rugg, Romie Schickler, Wanda Lodico, Rita Kuder, Mary Hall, Dorothy Harper, Joan Sullivan, and especially Janet Otis— who indexed and annotated the MacDonald diaries—were invaluable to me. Knowledgeable and generous research assistance from librarians Mary Huth, Karl Kabelac, and the late Alma Creek at the Department of Rare Books and Special Collections, Rush Rhees Library, University of Rochester, as well as Ellie Reichlin at the Society for the Preservation of New England Antiquities and Susan Myers at the Smithsonian Institution, greatly enriched the manuscript. Other friends and colleagues who helped me include Jean Callan King, Edward G. Cornwell,

Jane Tucker, Gwendolyn Kelso, and John Kasson, who introduced me to Norbert Elias. I wish especially to acknowledge the graciousness and generosity of Eleanor T. Fordyce, whose extensive collection of nineteenth-century American cook-books provided the core for my recipe research.

Through the talents of the museum photographers Tom Weber and Michael Radtke, collection objects became beautiful images. Melissa Morgan, who served as my left hand throughout that process, used her considerable organizational skills to get the job done. Historian and friend Mary Lynn Heininger helped to transform my early ideas into a workable conceptual framework for this book and continually provided me with wise counsel and encouragement.

Judy White typed the manuscript, some of it several times, and always main-tained her professional objectivity, good humor, and calm disposition, even in the face of rapidly advancing deadlines. I hope she knows how much I appreciated her ready willingness to work far beyond the requirements of her job.

I want also to thank my parents, George and Helen Williams, who first introduced me to the intricacies of manners and the joys of eating; through them, and through their parents, John and Ethel Williams and Edward and Jean Rey-nolds, I have learned to see more clearly the origins of my own history, a process of discovery that was nurtured by the act of writing this book.

Without the guidance and dogged determination of Kathryn Grover, director of publications at the Strong Museum, this book would still be in draft. Kathryn's editorial skills, her sensitivity to the subject matter, and her pursuit of a humorous perspective saw me through to completion, and I am deeply grateful.

Wendy Wolf, my editor at Pantheon Books, was able to see what this book could be, and urged and encouraged me to accomplish that end. Her vision and enthusiasm, her ability to allay the fears of a struggling author by applying just the right amount of humor and hand-holding, as well as her appreciation for good food, were a constant and much-appreciated source of support.

The one person who truly knows what this book means to me is my husband, Harvey Green. His faith in my ability provided me with the primary momentum to attempt a project of this scope, and his constant but loving prodding, in combination with frequent doses of both culinary and intellectual sustenance, helped in great measure to make this book a reality.

S.W.
May 1985

PREFACE

. ——— .

xi

PROPER AND PROSPEROUS 1

THE VICTORIAN MIDDLE CLASS

It's hard to remember a depiction of life among well-to-do Americans in the last half of the nineteenth century that does not include a scene in which people sit down to eat and to drink, whether it's a simple afternoon tea or supper at a large and formal evening party. Think also of an elaborate, multicourse feast, set in a rich scene of silk and damask, attended by a corps of liveried servants who would never allow the brilliant cut-glass decanters on the table to stand empty.

In early March of 1895, thirty men took three days preparing such a dinner in the state rooms of the Waldorf in New York City before the opening of the French play *Mme. Sans-Gêne* at the Ivy Theatre. In the spirit of the play, a Rochester, New York, newspaper society column reported the meal and its setting a "Napoleonic feast throughout"; the walls of the room were hung "in the palest lilac brocade," the furnishings "strictly of the Empire period."

> In the center of the square table was a green silk cloth on which was worked in gold the letter *N* and the Napoleonic emblems, the bees, crown and wreath. Standing on this cloth was a tall column formed of purple violets. At each of the four corners of the table was a candelabrum, with seven burners, each candle covered with a green silk and gold shade marked with the letter *N*. The service was solid gold and white, and the names of the guests were inscribed in gold script on the natural laurel or bay leaves.

First-prize-winning dinner table at the New York Chrysanthemum Show of 1891.

The dinner was given by John W. Mackay, Jr., the son and namesake of the man whose fortune was first made in the gold and silver mines of the Comstock Lode, and whose fortune was made again in the founding of what would later become the International Telephone and Telegraph Company. Mackay invited nine people, including Mrs. William K. Vanderbilt and her daughter Consuelo, and they all sat down to an entirely French menu at the Waldorf: *huîtres* (oysters), *consommé* Talleyrand (soup), *terrapin à la* Bertrand (turtle), *dinde* Brillat-Savarin (turkey), *carré d'agneau de printemps* (roast spring lamb), *petits pois à la française* (French peas), *ortolans à la* Sans-Gêne (a small bird—a bunting—esteemed for its flavor), *asperges froides à la vinaigrette* (asparagus vinaigrette), *mousse des fraises fraîches* (fresh strawberry mousse), and *petits fours* (little cakes). Beverages included two French wines—Château Latour Blanche and La Tache Romanée—Waldorf private stock (probably a sherry or a madeira), *café* (coffee), Apollinaris (bottled water), and liqueurs. "And all of this for ten people!" the Rochester society columnist gasped—"one of those exhibitions of nineteenth century extravagance that make your hair stand on end!"[1]

Certainly the last half of the American nineteenth century witnessed many such parties; but they stand in contrast to other equally common, though less glittery, scenes. At other moments, dinner was not so much a gathering for society as a gathering for sustenance. A great many nineteenth-century American tables were covered with white oilcloth, not with damask, and it was extraordinary fortune rather than ordinary circumstance that brought to them a small bit of butter, jam, or condensed milk for the children to spread on their bread, or cheese and a pint of beer for the adults. One of the foremost American literary realists of the nineteenth century, William Dean Howells, described a meal of this humbler kind in his 1882 novel *A Modern Instance*, as the logging camp cook Kinney prepared his table:

> He went on laying the plates and knives and forks, in silence. These were of undisguised steel; the dishes and the drinking-mugs were of that dense and heavy make, which the keepers of cheap restaurants use to protect themselves against breakage, and which their servants chip to the quick at every edge. Kinney laid bread and crackers by each plate, and on each he placed a vast slab of cold corned-beef. Then he lifted the lid of the pot in which the cabbage and potatoes were boiling together, and pricked them with a fork. He dished up the beans in a succession of deep tins, and set them at intervals along the tables. . . .[2]

At first glance, it may seem as though these meals share no common features, and that the act of dining breaks apart as readily as other acts of its time seem to in the stridently class-conscious society of the post–Civil War era. On the one hand, nineteenth-century Americans of means seemed to pattern their meals slavishly after overly mannered and pretentious European models. On the other, Americans less well endowed sat down to tables, which, if less refined, seemed somehow more genuine.

But in fact, meals along the entire spectrum of means in nineteenth-century America were linked by a common concern with ritual, formality, and schedule. The times at which people ate, the procedures they followed for serving and eating foods, the ways they felt were necessary and proper to dress for meals, the type of environment in which food should be consumed, the kinds of social arrangements for the table—who should sit where, what one should say and how one should say it, who should speak to whom—even the food itself were, in effect, canonized by the end of the nineteenth century in the United States. Behavior at the dining table, even everyday behavior, was governed by an extensive system of rules of genteel behavior encompassed under the general rubric

of etiquette. Etiquette was hardly an invention of the nineteenth century, but it became an institution of almost novel importance at a time when members of a strongly self-conscious Victorian elite sought to distinguish themselves from all other (often newer) Americans. At the same moment, a large class of social newcomers created by prodigious and rapid economic expansion could use such a system of rules not just to affix themselves in a re-forming social structure but to move themselves upward within it.

Etiquette is a legacy of medieval Europe, itself a society of rapid social change. In the sixth through fifteenth centuries, it has been argued, etiquette developed as a formalized social code that served to define and order desirable behavior as a means of identifying a social structure out of a set of fluid circumstances and as a means of maintaining that structure and one's place within it. Underlying these rules is the concept of courtesy, which according to eighteenth-century lexicographer J. H. Zelder, "undoubtedly gets its name from court and court life" and which evolved as individuals seeking esteem and favor from royalty developed an external appearance or demeanor of accommodation and gentility as a means of ingratiating themselves within the court.[3]

The emphasis on "external appearance" is crucial, because it reinforces the inherently artificial (rather than genuine) nature of "correct" behavior. The nagging sense of cultural inferiority that many Americans felt when they compared themselves to Europeans fueled the concern to display correct behavior in the nineteenth century. The society columnist who chronicled John Mackay's "Napoleonic feast" was clearly among those who yearned to find European refinement among his compatriots. He observed in his article that an English translation of *Mme. Sans-Gêne* was playing in New York at the same time that the French performance was being staged at the Ivy Theatre. "Of course the American actress cannot approach the French woman in finish or prestige," the columnist conceded, "but those who know only enough French to interpret a menu, will in their hearts prefer the English play."[4]

Since the day they had begun to think of themselves as members of a new nation, Americans used the concept of artificiality to compare themselves favorably to Europeans on moral grounds. In Europe, as Americans viewed it, feudalism had created a society of artificial constraints and ill-distributed resources: the aristocracy was indolent, supercilious, profligate, and formal; the poor deprived, ignorant, and dependent. American society, by contrast, lacked both extremes of poverty and wealth and was thus an ideal and productive partnership of farmer and pioneer, in which all people had an equal chance to strike out on their own, earn their living honestly from the land, and thence become enfranchised, true democrats, truly independent. Thus, in late-nineteenth-century America, popular understanding of the term "courtesy" had coupled the original idea of ingratiation with the underlying attributes of honor and virtue. "Courtesy is the habit of which the cultivation is recommended by the weightiest and most numerous motives," etiquette writer John Ruth explained in 1883. "We are led to it by the generous purpose of advancing the happiness of others, and the more personal one of making ourselves liked and courted."[5]

The goal of "making ourselves liked and courted" was particularly important in a world of great social and economic mobility, and the burgeoning economy offered a panoply of opportunities for middle-class Americans to reach these goals. The level of affluence was already comparable: families in the 1850s generally lived in their own homes, often with one or two servants who either lived in or came daily. By the 1870s, demographic trends showed for the first time a large number of women engaged exclusively in homemaking and child rearing who made no direct contribution to the household income. The ability of a man to support this degree of leisure in his household was perceived as a distinguishing feature of the middle class. At the same time, declining birth rates and the increased presence of servants afforded these women even more time and capital to invest in leisure activities such as formal dinner parties or ladies' luncheons.

Middle-class homes, increasingly located in newly developed suburbs, were built to accommodate the spatial needs of a prospering family. The plans usually

Charles Dana Gibson's wry vision of the Social Ladder.

provided a balanced arrangement of public and private space—an entry hall, a parlor for formal entertaining, a dining room or family sitting room for both family and company meals, a functionally specialized kitchen or pantry area, and several bedrooms, whose details and furnishings embodied varying levels of fanciness corresponding to the status of their occupants. A home of this sort might have cost as little as $3,000 to build, as did the house built in the 1850s by the architectural firm of Downing and Vaux for the Reverend E. J. O'Reilly of Newburgh, New York. It could also cost as much as $16,000, as did Springside, the country house built for the wealthy Poughkeepsie brewer and college founder Matthew Vassar. If one assumes that the Reverend O'Reilly's house is the nineteenth-century equivalent of a house that might run $50,000 to build today, Vassar's house would then cost $265,000 in the 1980s.[6]

The people who lived in these middle-class houses had personal and household possessions beyond, often far beyond, the bare necessities of existence. It was incumbent upon the wives of heads of households to furnish these homes in a manner that would reflect their family's status, level of education, and degree of cultivation. The job of shopping thus took on a kind of moral responsibility and no doubt inflicted a burden of anxiety upon a woman lest she fail to exercise good taste and prudent economy in her selections. Models of good taste for her to follow were widely available, particularly in the elegant lobbies of large hotels, in the interiors of steamships and railroad cars, and in the homes of her more wealthy friends. Levels of exposure to these grander, more refined interiors increased rapidly as middle-class families used their discretionary income to travel, to attend extravagant parties and balls, and to dine in any of the hundreds of restaurants available in the expanding cities. A woman could also find models in the ever-increasing number of books, popular magazines, and catalogs, all of which offered a detailed vision of the ideal household, artistically furnished.

After the Civil War, a woman who set up housekeeping might have been given a sum of money by her father or husband to buy household furnishings. Popular literature constantly urged women to be careful in the selection of what they were buying. The story of an unfortunate bride was published in the May 1853 issue of *Godey's Lady's Book* as a warning to all. The heroine spent all of her allotted funds buying fancy, showy black-walnut parlor furniture and expensive carpeting and draperies, and then was obliged to go to her husband for extra money to buy pots and pans and other utilitarian necessaries that she had overlooked. The lesson was clearly stated by *Godey's*: "Had the young lady been happy with Kidderminster carpets and tasteful vases of her own making, she might have put $100 at interest!"[7]

Shopping in the second half of the nineteenth century for those living in cities and towns usually meant going to a large "furnishings wareroom" to select wallpaper, carpets, and furniture for the parlor, dining room, chambers or bedrooms, and the kitchen. By the 1860s, these items were readily available in any city in the United States, supplied through large, national mass-production networks. For glass, china, and silver tableware, a woman was apt to have sought out her local crockery and glass or silver wareroom, if she had not been able to find these goods at the larger furnishings establishments. Yet a woman such as Fannie Munn Field of Rochester, New York, came into her marriage in the early 1870s already well supplied with the tools for formal entertaining. She received the customary array of wedding gifts, including a tea set, an ice pitcher, a service bell, a mustard cup, a syrup pitcher, a cake basket, a pie knife, a caster set, a sugar basket, a dessert set, a dozen silver knives, a butter knife and sugar spoon, and a pair of napkin rings.[8]

Miss Lucy Vincent Rice, the daughter of an innkeeper in Grand Haven, Michigan, received similar, if somewhat larger, groups of tablewares when she married Edward Reynolds, a Florida lumber merchant, in 1883. She noted in her journal that she received these items for the table: one pair of silver napkin rings; a fruit spoon in a case; a silver butter dish; a pair of silver and gilt engraved napkin rings; six fruit knives in a case; six nutpicks and a nutcracker in a case lined with scarlet satin; a hand-painted china flower basket; a silver and gilt engraved épergne; a three-piece silver tea service; a chased and embossed gold-lined silver spoon holder; six fruit plates, hand-painted in different colors and designs; six fruit knives in a case; a large gold-lined salad dish; a Chinese fruit dish; a gold- and silver-lined cup and saucer; a gold-lined silver mug; and a solid-silver gold-lined sugar spoon in a case marked R.[9]

Wedding gifts were important, too, to women both above and below the middle class. The wealthy, who could easily have purchased any article of tableware they desired, recorded their wedding presents with the same solemnity, carefully listing each donor alongside the item received. They would then complete the ritual by writing a formal note of thanks. Nineteenth-century wedding lists reveal that a great deal of attention was paid to the number and quality of gifts received, suggesting that they were for many a means of measuring status and social success. They also served as a physical means through which the hopes and values of the giver could be transmitted to a young couple.

For working-class women, wedding gifts may have been the only way to acquire luxury goods, particularly silver. An early twentieth-century account of the eating patterns of the family of a New York City policeman mentioned approvingly that all meals were served in a dining room "with a white cloth on the table, and Mrs. W. has some wedding silver which she uses constantly."[10]

The presence of silver in this home, possibly a gift from someone of a higher social station, was thought (at least by Louise More, a turn-of-the-century social reformer) to have had an elevating effect on this working-class family. Indeed, such gifts were of more than mere display value, as they demonstrated a felt or desired sense of social station; acquiring more was a visibly impressive way of continually proclaiming this sense of rightful place.

Yet this concern to align one's position in the social world of the nineteenth-century United States with one's created domestic space did not spurn a reckless obsession with elaborate interiors and goods with which to fill them. Despite a deep-seated and anxious interest in "civilization" (European, usually) among Victorians, Americans held in common an attitude about their own peculiar history and past, which served as a careful ideological control on the evolution of a national self-image, particularly in the dining room. While Americans continued to look to their European past for refinement, they selectively scrutinized their own colonial past for evidence of moral supremacy, national mettle, and personal ingenuity. Thus "civilization" for them became an amalgam of anything from the past, be it European or distinctively American, that proved useful in ordering their increasingly complex world.

At the same time, the arrived middle class strived to separate itself, psychically and socially, from less desirable aspects of its immediate past, of which the unrefined classes were still a reminder. This reliance on etiquette was identical to an attitude that the Marquis de Coulanges (1633–1716), a well-known literary figure in Europe in his day, expressed a century earlier. "In times past," he wrote, "people ate from the common dish and dipped their bread and fingers in the sauce. Today everyone eats with a spoon and fork from his own plate, and a valet washes the cutlery from time-to-time at the buffet."[11] Coulanges was writing about only the rich—no other social class in the mid-seventeenth century would have had either cutlery or a valet. It is significant, however, that he assumed members of this class ("everyone") to be the only *people*, at least the only people whose behavior was worth observing.

By the end of the nineteenth century, the colonial past was generally revered through a special brand of nostalgia keynoted in colonial furnishings, dwellings, modes of behavior, and cultural vigor; and the ruder, less stylized aspects of those days were carefully forgotten. A story published in 1891 in the *Ladies' Home Journal* entitled "Angels Unaware" made colonial food the object of this veneration and desire among two city "millionaires," who inadvertently became snowbound in the small coastal Connecticut town of Pot Haven. They were generously accommodated during the storm by an "old-fashioned" twenty-three-year-old woman—Berry Savary. Although Berry was observed to have had an empty larder, she was on a moment's notice able to summon up a mouth-watering and millionaire-pleasing supper of hot clams in gravy with toast, fried crumbed oysters, graham muffins (or pop downs, so called by the gentleman whose grandmother—but never his pampered wife—used to make them), baked apples, and coffee. Reflecting somewhat wistfully on this serendipitous bounty, one of the millionaires characterized their good fortune: "There's a girl with a head on her shoulders . . . the kind they used to have in the old colonial days. . . . I only wish they'd take to manufacturing them again in the old patterns, as they do the chairs and the tables."

Ultimately, the millionaires were able to persuade Berry (who was destitute and the sole supporter of her young brother) to come to New York and cook for their club—but on the condition that she prepare only "old-fashioned" food—chicken potpie, "cornbeef" hash, chowder and hoecake, pork and beans with molasses, corn bread, pandowdy, doughnuts, and, of course, pumpkin pie.[12] Berry had been transmogrified by their historical zeal from a woman into a relic; these civilized city millionaires could then venerate the colonial virtues she embodied without compromising their obvious commitment to the social status and capitalist values of an urbane Eastern establishment.

If Berry Savary had cooked for the millionaires' New York City club, she might well have used recipes such as this one for hoecake, first published in 1796 in Amelia Simmons's *American Cookery*:

Johnny Cake, or Hoe Cake

Scald one pint of milk and put three pints of Indian meal, and half pint of flour—bake before the fire. Or scald with milk two thirds of the Indian meal, or wet two thirds with boiling water, add salt, molasses and shortening, work up with cold water pretty stiff, and bake as above.

Much of what we are able to learn about ideal women like Berry Savary and her real-life counterparts—the housewives and hostesses who furnished their dining rooms, planned their menus, and presided over meals in their homes—can be gleaned from sources that are inherently prescriptive: etiquette books, cookbooks, household manuals, women's magazines, and architectural plan books. Such guides were written for a middle-class female readership and spoke directly to their need to appear socially and morally correct in all matters. Yet as evidence they must be approached with caution, because they tend to show us an idealized vision of what life was like, a recommended rather than real view of which attitudes, implements, and practices should compose and surround nineteenth-century dining. Remembering that these guidelines were corrective rather than wishful, we can glean from them the prevailing conditions they ostensibly sought to correct. Literature that endeavors to give advice on the whole tends to focus on areas of disputed authority, on types of behavior that are not yet clearly defined for a particular class or social group from the perspective of another class or social group. Many of the etiquette books were written from the point of view of the upper class, with the goal of retaining a measure of control over those viewed to be below them on the social scale by structuring their behavior.

Certain topics are missing in this domestic literature, behaviors that were probably either so commonplace that they did not need to be debated or that were stigmatized by certain cultural taboos that would make them too embarrassing to write about—notably, anything relating to bodily functions. We know, for example, from architectural plans and existing domestic structures from the nineteenth century that sinks and sometimes water closets were frequently in direct proximity to the dining room, usually located in a connecting corridor with the butler's pantry. Olana, Frederick Church's home in Hudson, New York, had such an arrangement, as did several of the houses illustrated in Calvert Vaux's *Villas and Cottages*. Clearly there must have been social conventions about how and when these facilities were to be used, but there is not a single hint about them in the etiquette books.

Other kinds of written sources—letters, journals, personal memoirs, menus, legal documents, household inventories, wedding-present lists, bills, trade catalogues, and advertisements—as well as the surviving furnishings and implements from nineteenth-century households both confirm and contradict different aspects of the etiquette books' ideal.

The evidence gleaned from all of these sources should always be held against whatever information we have about the culture that produced them and the behavior that prevailed within that context. We know, for example, that extensive dinner services were available to middle-class Americans by the 1860s, but were all meals elaborate exercises in display? Menus abound in cookbooks and etiquette books for fancy dinner parties and even family meals; the "simple" family menus now seem overloaded with courses and food. Did nineteenth-century Americans really eat that much more than we do? Or did they eat more selectively? Diary entries suggest that most family meals probably did not measure up to the expectations of the menu planners, but that a concern about both nutrition and economy escalated during the last half of the nineteenth century and affected the quantity and variety of food found on American dinner tables.

As another example, most nineteenth-century etiquette writers did address the question of how to behave if some foreign object were to become lodged between one's teeth and recommend that refined people never pick their teeth at the table, especially when they are dining at hotels. Even though the practice seems to have been acceptable in nineteenth-century Europe, it was still taboo in the United States, and in 1882 John Ruth warned against attempting to dislodge such matter at the table even with one's hand over one's mouth. "However agreeable such a practice might be to yourself," he cautioned, "it may be offensive

This multitude of special holders suggests that toothpicks were widely used, however much people might protest that they were socially inappropriate in polite society.

to others."[14] The material remains of the late nineteenth century suggest that advice and real behavior were once again at odds. Hundreds of different varieties of toothpick holders, tiny cup-shaped objects whose purpose was to hold a bundle of toothpicks, were available to American consumers. They sometimes took on humorous forms—hats or shoes or animals—but just as often they were designed to conform to fancy tableware. A cut-glass toothpick holder was an expensive object, and if available, would most certainly have been used with pride.

Fiction provides us with another record, particularly in the literary realism of writers such as William Dean Howells, Mark Twain, and Henry James. Reacting against the increasingly formulaic romantic literature that seemed anachronistic in the urban industrial world of late nineteenth-century America, many authors attempted to depict life—especially American life—as it was. For them the timeless issues would best be understood by the reading public if they could be shown to be part of everyday experiences. As Howells himself put it, "Why try to paint the lily or tint the rose?"[15]

Even when all these sources are considered together, they cannot bring back the people of the previous century to answer our questions about their lives and specifically about their eating rituals. They can only create for us a patchwork vision of that world, which, incomplete as it may be, still helps us to recognize and understand better why we eat what we eat, and how, when, and where we do it—today.

THE MANDATES OF MANNERS

2

ETIQUETTE OF THE TABLE

Nothing indicates the good breeding of a gentleman so much as his manners at table. There are a thousand little points to be observed, which, although not absolutely necessary, distinctly stamp the refined and well-bred man. A man may pass muster by *dressing well*; and may sustain himself tolerably well in conversation, but if he be not perfectly "au fait," *dinner* will betray him.[1]

W hen John Ruth wrote about dinner in his 1883 etiquette manual *Decorum*, he loaded into a single meal both tremendous opportunity and dreadful anxiety. By observing the "thousand little points" at the dinner table, it was possible for middle-class Americans pursuing the promise of social mobility to earn and proclaim status. Yet even if there seemed to be no ceiling of the sort that Europe's aristocracy posed to block one's ascent in American social life, neither did there seem to be a floor: the dinner table after the Civil War became the place where one's attention to the thousand little points could lead either to distinction or to disgrace.

He fetched a long sigh of relief when he sank into his chair and felt himself safe from error if he kept a sharp lookout and did only what the others did. Bellingham had certain habits which he permitted himself, and one of these was tucking the corner of his napkin into his collar; he confessed himself an uncertain shot with his spoon, and defended his practice on the ground of neatness and common sense. Lapham put his napkin into his collar too, and then, seeing that no one but Bellingham did it, became alarmed, and took it out again slyly.[2]

For Silas Lapham, a Vermonter who made a fortune on mineral paint and then brought his family down to Boston to live in the style to which their riches seemed to entitle them, the rise through the middle class was a journey that required anxious attention to detail in food, dress, manners, and furnishings. Lapham knew that he must manage these details correctly, even though he believed that intuition was the only true guide in life, and even though he witnessed "old-money" Bostonians like Bellingham relaxing what he took to be the rules. He hired an architect to design his new Back Bay house, and he bought an etiquette book to tell him how to dress correctly for dinner.

Etiquette books by the dozen were written by both men and women in the nineteenth century. Inexpensively printed and widely distributed, they were collectively a kind of social bible to the growing American middle class. John H. Young's *Our Deportment*, first published in 1879, went through seven editions in

OUR

DEPORTMENT

OR THE

MANNERS, CONDUCT AND DRESS

OF THE MOST REFINED SOCIETY,

INCLUDING

Forms for Letters, Invitations, Etc., Etc. Also, Valuable
Suggestions on Home Culture and Training.

COMPILED FROM THE LATEST RELIABLE AUTHORITIES,

BY

JOHN H. YOUNG, A. M.

REVISED AND ILLUSTRATED.

F. B. DICKERSON & CO., Publishers.

DETROIT, MICH., ST. LOUIS, MO., CINCINNATI, O., CHICAGO, ILL.

1883

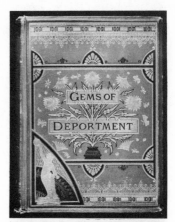

the next three years. Ruth's *Decorum: A Practical Treatise on Etiquette and Dress of the Best American Society* ran to ten editions to satisfy the demand for it between 1877 and 1890. Other much-read manuals included *The Ladies' Guide to True Politeness and Perfect Manners*, by Eliza Leslie, and *Etiquette: An Answer to the Riddle, When? Where? How?* by Agnes H. Morton, who dedicated her efforts to "those who dwell within the broad zone of 'the average.' "[3] All of these authors held objectives similar to those that Ruth expressed: "to impart that information by which anyone may be enabled to acquire gentlemanly ease, or graceful ladylike deportment, so that their presence will be sought for, and they will not only learn that great art of being thoroughly *at home* in all societies, but will have that rarer gift of making everyone around them feel easy, contented and happy."[4] In addition to etiquette books, the articles and stories in such popular women's magazines as *Godey's Lady's Book, Peterson's Magazine*, and the *Ladies' Home Journal* provided their readers with instructive glimpses of upper-class manners (and the fateful lack thereof), as well as with recipes, menus, and patterns for making fancy table linens and appropriate dining room decorations. All of these delineated models of behavior that, if emulated, would provide insurance against the anxiety of possible social embarrassment, would help strengthen the line that separated aspiring members of the middle class from their humble origins, and would assuage the collective uncertainty of a class in transition.

Codes of behavior have of course existed long before popular literature gave them printed form. Prior to the sixteenth century, models and standards were often communicated orally in poetry and mnemonics (organized chants or other verbal devices to aid memorization). The first prose work specifically dedicated to social demeanor, Erasmus's treatise *De Civilitate Morum Puerilium (On Civility in Children)*, was first published in 1530 and was reprinted more than thirty times during its first six years in print. Ultimately, 130 editions of *De Civilitate* were printed; it was translated into English in 1532 and was published in catechism form in 1584 as a text for schoolboys. In sixteenth-century Europe, *De Civilitate* may have been so popular because it successfully articulated a code of behavior that enabled one to anchor oneself safely in a society whose benchmarks and boundaries were continually shifting.

Other writers followed Erasmus in his attempt to rationalize prevailing social values; all of them endeavored to raise the level of consciousness in European court and bourgeois society about what constituted refined or civilized behavior.

Etiquette books and women's magazines (opposite) were the most commonly consulted authorities on manners, social conduct, and dress; they provided insurance against the possibility of social embarrassment.

By what they censured and what they praised, they demarcated good and bad manners—introducing a heightened sense of embarrassment when the rules of acceptable behavior were broken. As the desire for refinement increased, so did distaste for behavioral patterns related to particular bodily functions. As early as the thirteenth century, social commentators had begun to isolate and to condemn certain kinds of activities that had once been common practice as unsuitable for polite society—wiping greasy fingers and lips on the tablecloth, removing inedible food from one's mouth, coughing, or dealing publicly with gastric distress, flatulence, or other eating-related discomfort. Now such unacceptable behavior could cause personal shame or social embarrassment, might lead ultimately to rejection by the members of desirable society, and, etiquette writers warned, could even bring about a permanent decline in one's community status. Erasmus explicitly advised his readers against one behavior that must have been common practice in his time:

> A peasant wipes his nose on his cap and coat, a sausage maker on his arm and elbow. It does not show much propriety to use one's hand and then wipe it on one's clothing. It is more decent to take up the snot in a cloth, preferably while turning away.[5]

As Western societies became more and more conscious of civility and decorum, the degree of explicitness with which etiquette advisers described offensive behavior declined. By the nineteenth century, they were addressing Erasmus's concern euphemistically, if at all; they gently reminded their readers that it was never proper to use one's napkin as a handkerchief, but they never directly mentioned so embarrassing a word as snot. The lexicon of forbidden terms was surprisingly extensive: in 1864, Eliza Leslie warned guests and hostesses alike "that the word 'stomach' should never be uttered at any table, or indeed anywhere else, except to your physician, or in a private conversation with a female friend interested in your health. It is a disagreeable word (and so are all its associations), and should never be mentioned in public to 'ears polite.' "[6]

In nineteenth-century America, the inextricable bond between good manners and social status was keenly felt by people in Agnes Morton's "broad zone of the 'average,' " all members of a massive and ever-widening class above the level of mean subsistence and below the rarefied circle of great wealth. The importance of "good breeding" at the dinner table was compounded by two facts that most Americans readily recognized. Eating, they acknowledged, was a most basic function, common to both man and animal. Only manners could separate man from beast in the act of consuming food and drink. An article in the September

1868 issue of *Harper's New Monthly Magazine* stressed the importance of maintaining this distinction:

> Human nature, perhaps, never appears in a more attractive light than when a brave company of men thoroughly groomed, and of fair women elegantly attired, seat themselves at such a table to enjoy one another's society while partaking of a refined repast. If the act of taking sustenance proves them to be akin to the beasts of the field, the beautiful manner in which the act is performed appears almost to exalt them above mankind. Show me the way people dine and I will tell you their rank among civilized beings. It is a duty we owe ourselves and one another to glorify and refine eating and drinking, so as to place an infinite distance between ourselves and the brutes, even at the moment when we are enjoying a pleasure which we have in common with them.[7]

The publication and instant popular interest in Charles Darwin's *The Origin of Species* in 1859 only fueled such speculative discussions of the critical importance of manners, particularly in the face of increasing ethnic diversity and rapid socioeconomic changes. As social and economic categories multiplied, the level of formality observed at a meal became an important signpost of identification.

The room in which a meal was held, the way a table was set, the people present and where they sat, and even the time of day, the day of the week, or the time of year at which a meal occurred all combined to dictate specific (and clearly understood) behavioral models. Outward appearance—whether one looked the part—suggested a person's origins, but whether one consistently acted the part was thought to be a more reliable indicator of breeding. Many members of the middle class, whose circumstances were constantly changing, felt the constant need to conceal the reality of possibly less "civilized" origins. Working-class people were generally stereotyped by those above them as being not only ignorant of good manners, but almost hopelessly beyond their reach as well: "No more disheartening problem faces the social reformer than the question of how to overcome the bitter hostility to refined manners which marks ignorant 'lower classes,'" Agnes Morton wrote in 1894. "On the other hand, there is no more hopeful sign of progress in civilization than the gradual softening of these hard natures under the influence of social amenities."[8]

Toward the end of the nineteenth century, this society-conscious, middle-class world view became increasingly exclusionary in tone as large waves of southern and eastern European immigrants entered the country—posing a serious threat to the status quo in the minds of more established Americans. Etiquette in all its aspects, and table manners in particular, was one of the most important means by which the middle class defined its boundaries and restricted its membership. There were still limits, though. It was not enough merely to read the etiquette books and follow the rules; the finest decorum still remained a matter of heredity. Bromfield Corey explained the essence of social exclusion in *The Rise of Silas Lapham*:

> If society took in all the people of right ideas and good sense, it would expand beyond the calling capacity of its most active members. . . . Society is a very different sort of thing from good sense and right ideas. It is based upon them, of course, but the airy, graceful, winning superstructure which we all know demands different qualities . . . —which may be felt, but not defined.[9]

Corey's vague specifications of the qualities necessary to enter "society" underscore the fact that, in the end, if a person was not born into the highest social circles, no amount of decorum could guarantee entry.

Americans, particularly the wealthy, had traditionally viewed the dining table as an important social arena. Since at least the fifteenth century in France and England (and centuries earlier in Greece, Rome, the Far East, and the American Northwest among native American coastal tribes such as the Kwakiutl and the Haida), the ability to provide lavish amounts of food and drink for one's guests had signified power, wealth, and status. By the nineteenth century, etiquette books were stressing presentation as much as quantity:

> Perhaps there are few occasions on which the respectability of a man is more immediately felt, than the style of dinner to which he may accidentally bring home a visitor . . . if merely two or three dishes be well served, with the proper accompaniments, the table-linen clean, the small sideboard neatly laid, and all that is necessary to be at hand, the expectation of both the husband and friend will be gratified.[10]

Bartley Hubbard, protagonist of William Dean Howells's *A Modern Instance* (1882)—a fictional account of a young country journalist's ambitions to succeed in Boston—was certainly aware of the social utility of spontaneous hospitality. When two of his friends, Atherton (a lawyer) and Halleck (son of a wealthy Boston family) dropped in unexpectedly one evening, Bartley's wife, Marcia,

> excused herself to Atherton and went out, re-appearing after an interval at the sliding doors, which she rolled open between the parlor and dining-room. A table set for supper stood behind her, and, as she leaned a little forward, with her

Even for simple family dinners, the table was to be set neatly. This dinner table with its starched white cloth (folded in half to fit the table), vase of flowers, and tureen of soup suggests a certain degree of elegance. The napkins rolled in their napkin rings and the bottle of salad dressing on the table, however, confirm that it is not a company meal.

hands each on a leaf of the door, she said, with shy pride, "Bartley, I thought the gentlemen would like to join you," and he answered, "Of course they would," and led the way out, refusing to hear any demur. His heart swelled with satisfaction in Marcia; it was something like, having fellows drop in upon you, and to be asked out to supper in this easy way. It made Bartley feel good, and he would have liked to give Marcia a hug on the spot.

Marcia served oyster stew to her guests from her new white ironstone tureen on a table set with "the glitter of their new crockery and cutlery."[11] Pity the poor man whose wife maintained a slovenly household, for she would ultimately bring disgrace to him and the whole family.

Despite the numerous disclaimers made by etiquette writers that middle-class manners should not imitate those of the wealthy, the model for etiquette conventions has in fact traditionally been the aristocracy, and reference to an aristocracy among Americans meant reference to Europe. The wealthy classes behaved in certain "mannered" ways, particularly when dining. These modes of behavior were quickly observed and adopted by the rising middle class. Ironically, such imitation devalued these styles as measures of social distinction; the wealthy, in turn, further refined (or ocasionally simplified) their codes of behavior.

During the seventeenth and eighteenth centuries, the French court of Louis XIV was the main European courtly model for taste and refined behavior. In eighteenth-century Germany and nineteenth-century Russia, the knowledge and use of the French language became an upper-class status symbol, and French words became incorporated into the German and Russian languages.[12] Nineteenth-century America proved equally susceptible to French forms, as simple vocabulary attests. French words regularly appeared in menus and recipes: *bonbons, blancmange, bouillon, entrées, ragout, liqueurs* (said to have been invented for Louis XIV in his old age, when he could "scarcely endure existence without a succession of artificial stimulants"); as well as in names for table implements: *carafe, tête-à-tête, épergne,* and *bonbonnière*.[13] Elizabeth F. Ellet, a popular etiquette advisor and historian of women in the American Revolution, included a "Glossary of Foreign Terms Used in Cookery" in her 600-page *New Cyclopaedia of Domestic Economy*, which defined more than eighty French culinary and dining terms.[14] Mary F. Henderson, in her popular cookbook, *Practical Cooking, and Dinner Giving* (1878), thoughtfully provided her readers with dinner-party menus in French and English, as well as a French and English glossary.[15]

Popular literature and the actual materials of dining demonstrate that many Americans admired and drew inspiration from French food, French manners, and French styles in clothing and household furnishings. What was commonly referred to as French-style furniture achieved great popularity in this country during the middle years of the nineteenth century. But most of this furniture was designed for the parlor or drawing room, not for the dining room. Perhaps Americans had difficulty reconciling the lighthearted, frivolous, and affected character of French courtly tradition with their need to express piety and family sanctity in the dining room. Americans were willing to partake only selectively of French dining rituals, indulging, for example, their tastes for wine and coffee—both French legacies— by adopting them into today's familiar cuisine. One etiquette writer, describing the proper closing ritual for a dinner party, stated, "We take our manners from Paris instead of London and ladies and gentlemen retire together from the dining table," although it was customary in American elite society for men to remain at the table after the ladies had left.[16] Another writer, however, blurred the distinctions: "If we pattern ourselves after either nation [France or England] in the customs of the table," she argued, "the *genteel* English are far better models than most of their neighbors across the Channel. But the best class of Americans are unsurpassed in the essentials of all these observances." She added that the English attached too much importance to ceremonies merely conventional for which there seemed no motive but the ever-changing decrees of fashion, and that the French, for their part, ate too fast—even faster than the Americans.[17]

While they embraced French courtly manners and practices as a model for polite interaction, Americans were at the same time bothered that French culture was riddled with hypocrisy. In American society, manners above all had to be genuine and constant. "Good manners were perhaps originally but an expression of submission from the weaker to the stronger, and many traces of their origin still remain," John Ruth wrote, "but a spirit of kindliness and unselfishness born of a higher order of civilization permeates for the most part the code of politeness."[18] Anything less would suggest that they were not in actuality "good breeding," but merely sham, which explains why etiquette books continually threatened potential backsliders with the eventuality of the unexpected visitor. "Etiquette is not so much a manifestation *toward others* as it is an exponent of *ourselves*," Morton wrote in 1894. "We are courteous to others, first of all, because such behavior only is consistent with our own claim to be well-bred."[19] Prescribed form rather than the uncertainty of individual fancy was to be the governing agency that controlled food and its service, table settings, linens, dining room furniture, and a woman's role in selecting and organizing all of these aspects.

The sentiment of hospitality served for many as a foil to the potential hollowness of refined behavior. The importance of hospitality was discussed over and over in many different guises. Middle-class families were encouraged to entertain in a generous, friendly, and loving manner. "In all essential points, the laws of etiquette controlling the conduct of [the] simple dinner of an American democrat are the same as those observed in the ceremonious banquet of the ambitious aristocrat," Agnes Morton argued. "The degree of formality varies; the quality of courtesy is unchanging."[20] Through the agency of hospitality, the broader cultural impulse to affirm Christian morality and ethics in American society was brought directly into the domestic sphere, specifically into the dining room. Miss Leslie instructed her readers that hospitality was expected of those who had achieved a certain social and economic station: "If you are known to possess the means of living well (as evidenced by your costly furniture and elaborate dress), you ought to do so; and to consider a good, though not an extravagantly luxurious table as a necessary part of your expenditure."[21]

The financial demands on families who wished to "keep up" socially could be considerable, as *Godey's Lady's Book* reminded its readers in 1885: "The elegant requirements for fashionable hospitality have multiplied so rapidly of late that people of moderate means have to economize if they want to keep up with society." The author of this article went on to discuss various means of economizing, including the recommended option of using paper flowers instead of fresh flowers on one's table.[22]

The impulse to be hospitable, however, was never to be confused with ostentation. Etiquette books and domestic periodicals constantly warned hostesses against extravagance, a tendency that would endanger the sanctity of the home by threatening both its harmony and its economy. "Hospitality shares what it has," Agnes Morton explained. "It does not attempt to *give* what it *has not*. The finest hospitality is that which welcomes you to the fireside and permits you to look upon the picture of a home-life so little disturbed by your coming that you are made to feel yourself a part of the little symphony. . . ."[23] An overly extravagant dinner party that exceeded in people or splendor the limits of the host's ability to orchestrate or provide for adequately would not be enjoyable for either the guests or the host. Stories abounded in popular literature about hostesses, particularly inexperienced brides, who attempted too-ambitious *soirées* with disastrous results, bringing shame and disgrace upon themselves, their families, and their husbands. "The Third Bridesmaid," for example, published in *Godey's Lady's Book*, described young Harriet Ronaldson's attempts to give her soon-to-be-married friend, Julia, a brilliant evening party in spite of the fact that her mother ran a very modest boardinghouse. Harriet cut corners on everything—the food, the lamp oil, and the servants—but she borrowed china, cut glass, silver, even a replacement for her mother's shabby carpet, to create an illusion of wealth for the affair. Predictably, the bargain, store-bought cake was stale and rancid, the jellies and ice cream were melted, one hired servant tripped over the newly laid carpet and dropped a trayful of borrowed cut-glass dishes, and another stole a set of borrowed silver spoons. Two of the guests were overheard to remark cattily, "But that is their way; when people who have not the means, attempt to make a show, their friends must be the sufferers."[24]

Extravagance beyond the realm of reasonable generosity was considered a sure sign of the absence of good breeding, and Christian humility and commitment in the domestic sphere. Protestant Americans had linked extravagance or luxury to vice since at least the 1820s, when no less a cleric than Lyman Beecher warned that "our republic is becoming too prosperous . . . to be governed by any power but the blessed influence of the Gospel."[25] Each household was to entertain and live according to its station and income, and the home itself was to be the "sanctuary," complete with decorative and behavioral references to the ecclesiastical world. Religion was never to be too far—either visually or behaviorally—from everyday life.

Self-restraint, a crucial indicator of piety, was expected not only in matters of hospitality, but also while eating. Americans had difficulty reconciling their admiration of French cuisine with this cultural imperative for self-restraint and neurosis about gluttony. Robert Laird Collier, an expatriate American who had lived in England for seven years (long enough to have acquired a dissenting viewpoint) and who had written the widely popular *English Home Life* in 1885, argued: "France is the best fed, the most economically fed, and the most aesthetically fed nation on the face of the earth." He disparaged his own countrymen for their lack of interest in good food, a failing due, he felt, to an overdose of piety. In America, Collier wrote, "it is thought to be self-pampering and self-indulgent to care considerably for what one eats and drinks," but in France, he said, "the preparing and serving of food is universally deemed a fine art, and no individual is either so pious or otherwise so absorbed as not to be concerned about his diet." Indeed, many advice books recommended to potential dinner-party goers that they "praise the food, but not too effusively."[26]

This reluctance to seem overly self-indulgent or interested in food is curiously expressed in the diary of a thirteen-year-old schoolgirl named Fannie Munn Field. During her first two weeks of boardinghouse life, away from home at school in Rochester, New York, she kept detailed records of all meals. On Friday, 17 September 1886, for example, she recorded having eaten these foods: for breakfast, potatoes, warmed-over veal, an omelet, graham muffins, peaches, and coffee; for lunch, dried beef, stewed potatoes, bread, and peach shortcake; for dinner, lamb chops, mashed potato, tomato, eggplant, and tapioca pudding. She also mentioned that at about 4:00 P.M. "We went downtown. . . . We had ice cream and cake at Graves store. [I]t was good we laughed lots and giggled too, then we took a long walk up the avenue. . . ." But after the second Sunday-visit home, a cryptic note appeared at the end of her entry: "Fannie [her aunt] and I quarrelled over what I should write in here." Following that entry, the girl never mentioned food again in her diary.[27]

For many families grace, the short prayer said before meals to thank God for the food He had provided, sanctified the act of eating. Margaret E. Sangster in *Good Manners for All Occasions* offered several examples of graces commonly used during the late nineteenth century:

> Bless, O Lord, we beseech thee, this food to our use
> and us to thy service. For Christ's sake.
> Amen.

> We ask thy blessings on our food, and return thee, O Father,
> our hearty thanks for these and all thy mercies.
> Amen.

> Some hae meat and cannot eat,
> Some can eat and hae not meat.
> We hae meat and we can eat,
> May the Lord be thanket.[28]

The well-mannered guest was never to begin eating without waiting to see whether grace would be said. The courteous host, however, rarely recited grace at a dinner party or at family meals when guests—even clergymen—were present, lest he or she run the risk of offending those of a different religious inclination. If the host insisted on carrying out the ritual, then grace was to be kept as brief as possible for the guests' sake.

Guests, of course, must be treated with decorum at all times. Social procedures with regard to a guest's reception, activities, conversation, length of stay, and departure were clearly spelled out in etiquette books and other sources. The social intimacy implied by the act of embracing outsiders and introducing them within the family circle was offset by the formality with which that act was accomplished, a formality mandated by the acute self-consciousness and uncertainty among middle-class Americans about their own social position. Any undue presumption of social equality, if misdirected or misinterpreted, could instantly reduce an offender to the level of social pariah.

The degree of formality for a particular event could be indicated in several ways, beginning with the invitation. An invitation to a simple evening party could be both issued and accepted verbally. More formal events—teas or dinner

For many families, table rituals reaffirmed religious values, as well as minimizing the potential hypocrisy of highly mannered behavior. A family that began its meals with a humble grace was less likely to appear to "put on airs." Breaking bread was also a traditional act of Christian hospitality, and the motto on this bread tray clearly links consuming food and taking communion.

parties—required a handwritten note, phrased either in the third or, at an intermediate level, in the first person. Elsie Smith's note to her friend Mrs. A. Ericson Perkins, the wife of a prominent lawyer in Rochester, New York, mixed staid formality with humor:

My dear Mrs. Perkins:

When I thank you for the exquisite roses, I thank you not only for their beauty and fragrance but also for the kindly thought of my pleasure—what good fairy prompted you to think of me during this happy, busy season? Thank you many times.

I was thinking of you when the flowers arrived for I wish to ask you and Mr. Perkins to dine with us New Years evening at six o'clock and go to hear Col. S. Russell in the evening—I am very sorry that Mr. Perkins has an engagement for that evening, and we are tempted to set fire to the Club but I hope we shall surely see you.

I expect Mr. and Mrs. Danforth and Miss Danforth besides two or three others.

Will you please send an answer to Arthur's office.

Again I thank you and I am

Very sincerely,
Elsie Smith[29]

The New Year was a traditional time for socializing during the nineteenth century, as it is today, and Mrs. Smith's note appears to be for a dinner party of a less than grand scale. Because the group was to be going out to a lecture after the meal, rather than dancing or otherwise celebrating at home, the invitation took a relatively casual tone. In addition, Mrs. Smith was courteous enough to let her friend know who the other guests were to be, which alerted her to the social level of the gathering. Creating the guest list was a job over which many hostesses agonized, since the composition of a party was an important means of expressing social aspirations and of communicating degrees of social acceptance to others. One had to guard against inadvertently implying too much familiarity, mistakenly assuming social equality, or admitting an unsuitable person into one's social circle.

An engraved invitation, always written in the third person, was required for weddings, balls, and dinner parties given in honor of a noted person, and other such formal or ceremonial events, usually the highest forms of social activity. An engraved invitation dictated an appropriately high level of behavior on the

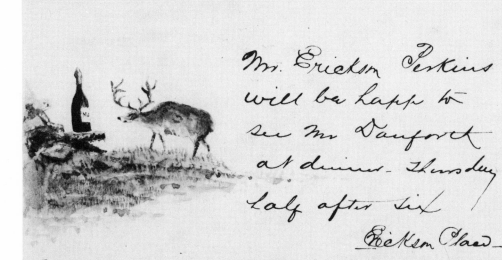

Handwritten invitations were often sent by hostesses giving informal dinner parties.

Mr. & Mrs. Erickson Perkins

will be pleased to see you at

Erickson Place, the evening of

Monday, September the twenty-

fourth, at eight o'clock.

Sept. 18/88

A formal evening dinner party—for which
an engraved invitation was sent—would require
a special "company" dress as well.

part of the invited guests: their responses were to be written in the third person, and dress was to be costly and elaborate, so that it would reflect both an appropriate degree of display and an appreciation of the host's and hostess's efforts and expense. Even for simple family dinners, a woman was expected to dress somewhat more formally than she had during the day in the event of unexpected callers. Although she was not advised to wear artificial flowers, she was to wear a ribbon in her hair and at her neck; restrained lace, jewelry, or other simple ornaments were also encouraged. Miss Ethel Rafter, a twenty-year-old student at the Brockport, New York, Normal School wrote one Sunday in 1897 to her future husband in Utica that she had not dressed yet that day, but that she had to terminate her letter so that she could go dress for dinner in the boardinghouse where she lived. Thirteen-year-old Fannie Munn Field of Scottsville, New York, noted in her diary in 1886 that she "wore [her] silk dress to dinner [and] had veal, boiled potatoes, gravy and dressing, stewed tomatoes, corn and custard. . . ."[30] Even for ordinary people in ordinary circumstances, the notion of dressing was embraced as an integral part of the overall dining ritual.

For a dinner party at which she was hostess, a woman was advised to wear a dress "rich in material, but subdued in tone, in order that she may not eclipse any of her guests." If she was young, she might wear a dress of black or dark silk, with a lace collar and cuffs and plain jewelry (or glittering gems in gaslight); older hostesses would wear satin or velvet, with lace. This emphasis on restraint in the attire of the hostess reinforced the broader issue of hospitality: humility was a further gift to her guests.

Dinner party guests had a much wider choice of color, varying from light pearl or camel to black, purple, dark green, garnet, dark blue, brown, or fawn. Female guests were not to expose their neck and arms (as they did in England), and although the dress was to be less showy than for "evening," it was to be "rich." Male guests were reminded by *The Successful Housekeeper* that they were expected to wear dress coats, light trousers, and light kid gloves. In all of these arrangements a carefully structured system of reciprocity was implied. Preparation of the house, the table, and the meal by the hostess was to be acknowledged by personal preparations made by the guest, as well as by conformity to accepted standards of behavior while inside another's household. Would-be guests were reminded of the importance of grooming: bodily cleanliness was stressed, and clothes were to be neat and clean (if not necessarily expensive); "hands and fingernails require especial attention."[31]

Nineteenth-century literature provides an amusing insight into the social neurosis that surrounded the issue of appropriate dress. *The Rise of Silas Lapham*, William Dean Howells's 1885 novel about a Vermont bumpkin who rose to become a self-made Boston millionaire, is richly embellished with the details of middle-class and upper-class social practices. When Silas, his wife, and their two daughters were invited for dinner by the Coreys, an upper-crust Boston family whose social acceptance Silas dearly desired, the household was thrown into a panic over what to wear. Mrs. Lapham exclaimed nervously, "I don't know what I'm going to wear; or the girls, either. I do wonder—I've heard that people go to dinner in low-necks. Do you suppose it's the custom?" Silas replied, "You needn't fret about it, you just go round to White's, or Jordan Marsh's, and ask for a dinner dress. I guess that'll settle it; they'll know," confirming as he spoke the importance for the middle classes of the department store as a relatively new arbiter of taste. Trying to put to his wife's aid his vague awareness that high occasions were characterized by European (especially French) forms, Silas suggested that she "get some of their imported dresses. I see 'em in the window every time I pass; lots of 'em." In the end, after a flurry of dressmaking, Mrs. Lapham abjured a "low-neck" and "intrenched herself in the safety of a black silk, in which she looked very handsome. Irene [her daughter] wore a dress of one of those shades which only a woman or an artist can decide to be green or blue.... If it was more of a ball dress than a dinner dress, that might be excused to exquisite effect."

Silas's costume deliberations were equally fraught with anxiety. Initially he determined that "he should not wear a dress-coat, because, for one thing, he considered that a man looked like a fool in a dress-coat, and, for another thing, he had none—had none on principle. He would go in a frock-coat and black pantaloons, and perhaps a white waist-coat, but a black cravat, anyway." His wife and daughters, however, entreated him to reconsider.

> Irene reminded him that he was the only person without a dress-coat at a corps-reunion dinner which he had taken her to some years before, and she remembered feeling awfully about it at the time. Mrs. Lapham, who would perhaps have agreed of herself, shook her head with misgiving. "I don't see but what you'll have to get one, Si," she said. "I don't believe they *ever* go without 'em to a private house."

Silas's initial convictions thus duly undermined, he went to his tailor the following day to be measured for a dress coat. To resolve his conflict about the propriety of a waistcoat, Silas was moved to purchase an etiquette book, "which settled the question adversely to a white waistcoat." After being very explicit in telling them not to eat with their knives, and above all not to pick their teeth with their forks—a thing that he said no lady or gentleman ever did—the author was still far from decided about the kind of cravat Colonel Lapham ought to wear.

> Shaken on other points, Lapham had begun to waver also concerning the black cravat. As to the question of gloves for the Colonel, which suddenly flashed upon him one evening, it appeared never to have entered the thoughts of the etiquette man, as Lapham called him. Other authors on the same subject were equally silent, and Irene could only remember having heard, in some vague sort of way, that gentlemen did not wear gloves so much any more.
>
> Drops of perspiration gathered on Lapham's forehead in the anxiety of the debate; he groaned, and he swore a little in the compromise profanity which he used.
>
> "I declare," said Penelope, where she sat purblindly sewing on a bit of dress for Irene, "the Colonel's clothes are as much trouble as anybody's. Why don't you go to Jordan Marsh's and order one of the imported dresses for yourself, Father?"[32]

Once having responded to an invitation, having dressed properly, and having arrived at the stated time, hosts and guests then engaged in a ritualistic procession from the parlor into the dining room. Generally led by either the host or the hostess, the procession served to establish social ranking of the guests: the host offered his arm to the highest-ranking lady, and the hostess was escorted into the dinner by the highest-ranking gentleman. Silas Lapham "had never seen people go down to dinner arm-in-arm before, but he knew his wife was distinguished in being taken out by the host. . . . Lapham was startled . . . by Mrs. Corey's passing her hand through his arm, and he made a sudden movement forward, but felt himself gently restrained. They went in the last of all; he did not know why, but he submitted. . . ."[33] John Ruth pointed out that the procession into the dining room was completed when "having arrived at the table, each guest respectfully bows to the lady whom he conducts, and who in her turn bows also."[34] This formal sashay came directly from the court of Louis XIV in the late seventeenth century, not from any precedent in America in the late nineteenth century.

Seating at the table was an obvious index of rank. The positions of honor were at the right and left of the host and hostess, with the more important person on the right. Seating was also an effective means of nurturing genteel conversation, one of the standards by which the success of a dinner party was determined. Men and women were usually seated alternately, and relatives or business associates were to be separated—lest they engage in private conversation. These

"Served Him Right"

Fast Youth, who has been asked to dine at half-past five, and arrives at half-past seven: *"Aw! how d'ye do, Mrs. Jones? I hope you have'nt waited Dinner for me."*

Mrs. Jones: *"Oh! dear me, no! We dined two hours ago. Would you like a cup of tea?"*

seating rituals extended to solely family meals as well. As soon as he or she was old enough to dine with the adults, each child was assigned a place at the table, according to rank. Mother and Father were generally at the head and foot of the table, with the children who needed the most supervision closest at hand. Children were introduced to the concept of "dinner partners" at least as early as nine years old, as one diary makes clear: "Henry's 9th birthday—a party of 12 from 5 to 8—a *cobweb* to draw partners for supper."[35] A cobweb consisted of several long strings, in this instance six, that were draped around a room, crisscrossing each other to create a web effect. Each child was supposed to find one of the twelve free ends and start untangling the web. At the end of this unraveling, each child would be connected by a single string to a dinner partner. This procedure was a great deal more democratic than the one adults followed, but it instilled a sense of the formality they would surely encounter as they matured and became subject to, if not the perpetrators of, the tyranny of adult social strictures.

At the table, the refined consumption of food was the trial by fire of etiquette. Any well-bred person was expected to manage elegantly all varieties of serving utensils, carving dexterously if requested to do so, using a knife, fork, and any variety of spoon properly, coping gracefully with cherry stones, fish bones, corn on the cob, unpeeled fruits, uncracked nuts, and using napkins and finger bowls correctly. The underlying principle appears to have been to avoid having one's fingers make direct contact with food, and by the middle of the nineteenth century, the widespread availability of pressed glass, transfer-printed earthenware, bone china, and Britannia metal (an improved form of pewter) or silver-plated tableware provided middle-class Americans with new and enticingly complex ways to keep fingers and common foods apart. By the 1880s, an entire array of special tools had been developed for this purpose. Serving spoons and forks were ubiquitous, as were sugar tongs, salt spoons, butter knives, and lemon forks. Grape shears, oyster ladles, sardine tongs, Saratoga chips servers, and ice cream knives were less common, but were certainly among the tools of dining in many nineteenth-century households. Miss Leslie told her readers that "fish must be carved with a fish slice: you may carve it more dexterously by taking a spoon in your left hand."[36]

A silver fish slice.

"The dish upon which the article to be carved is placed should be conveniently near to the carver, so that he has full control over it; for if far off, nothing can prevent an ungracefulness of appearance, nor a difficulty in performing that which in its proper place could be achieved with ease" (A Practical Housekeeper, Cookery As It Should Be, *1856).*

ON CARVING

One of the most important acquisitions in the routine of daily life is the ability to carve well, and not only well but elegantly. It is true that the modes now adopted of sending meats, &c., to table are fast banishing the necessity for promiscuous carving from the elegantly served boards of the wealthy; but in the circles of middle life, where the refinements of cookery are not adopted, the utility of a skill in the use of a carving knife is sufficiently obvious.[37]

In families without servants, or at informal meals—breakfast, lunch, or perhaps supper—guests or family members generally passed the dishes to one another around the table, serving themselves. The intricacies of serving oneself from the common bowls and dishes were governed by the widespread feelings of delicacy about having the fingers of others touch one's food, sentiments that must have arisen in part from the desire to separate oneself from a ruder colonial past in which tableware was scarce, and from a stereotyped frontier past, which imputed a certain barbarism to Americans in general. These taboos also, no doubt, related to a growing awareness in the nineteenth century of the origins and modes of communication of diseases. The urban societies of the nineteenth century were prone to epidemics; cholera, typhoid, scarlet fever, and typhus were especially prevalent. By the 1880s, the reading public had begun to learn that these diseases resulted from germs; table manners thence became justified, not only as evidence of refinement, but also as one way to prevent the spread of sickness.

To avoid the potential indelicacy of contaminating food, Miss Leslie instructed that "in helping, wherever a spoon can conveniently be used, it is preferable to the use of a knife and fork."[38] Serving spoons, with large bowls, were a basic element in any set of flatware. The delicacy of a situation in which many people were taking food from the same vessel prompted the following stern warning from Eliza Leslie:

> Always keep your own knife, fork, and spoon out of the dishes. It is an insult to the company, and a disgrace to yourself, to dip into a dish anything that has been even for a moment in your mouth. To take butter or salt with your own knife is an abomination. There is always a butter knife or salt spoon. It is nearly as bad to take a lump of sugar with your fingers.[39]

Once having successfully transferred food from serving bowl or dish to plate, a person was expected to eat with a minimum of noise or extraneous activity, using

Butter knives, sugar tongs, and salt spoons helped to preserve feelings of delicacy where many people were serving themselves from a common bowl.

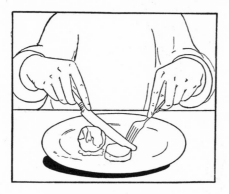 

Use of Dinner Knife and Fork   *Use of Fork and Spoon in Eating Certain Dishes*

the fingers only when absolutely necessary and never under any circumstance eating from knives. A constant stereotype of barbarous Americans at the table depicted them eating from their knives, a common practice in eighteenth-century England, when forks were scarce. Knives were designed with round instead of pointed ends to facilitate that practice. Its persistence among Americans was reported with particular frequency by European travelers, who no doubt did observe this behavior at less refined American tables. To counter the habit, Americans were continually reminded, "Always feed yourself with the fork; a knife is only used as a divider. Use a dessert spoon in eating tarts, puddings, curries."[40] To accommodate those who might be unfamiliar with the correct use of a knife and fork, Eliza Leslie provided specific instructions:

> Many persons hold silver forks awkwardly, as if not accustomed to them. It is fashionable to use your knife only while cutting up the food small enough to be eaten with the fork alone. While cutting, keep the fork in your left hand, the hollow or concave side dominant, the fork in a very slanting position, and your forefinger extended far down upon its handle.[41]

After cutting, one was to switch the fork to the right hand, put down the knife, and take a piece of bread in the left hand. For soft foods, the fork was to be used bowl up, and readers were continually reminded, "Never hold your knife and fork upright on each side of your plate while you are talking."[42]

Bread was one of the few foods that was permitted to be eaten with one's hands; like everything else, however, there were special rules that governed its consumption. "Bread should be broken, not bitten," and one was never to dip bread into the gravy or preserves on one's plate and then bite it. The proper procedure for achieving that end was to break (never cut) the bread into bite-

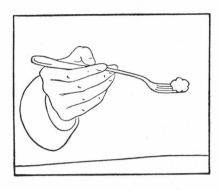

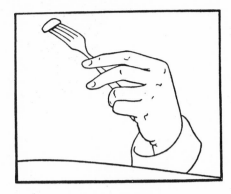

Fork Held in Right Hand   *Fork Held in Left Hand*

sized pieces and then to dip the bread into the desirable liquid with a fork. Under no circumstances was one to use a slice of bread to wipe one's plate clean. In fact, it was generally considered bad manners to scrape a plate clean in any way, since this behavior might suggest uncertainty about the source of one's next meal.[43]

If diners did happen to soil their fingers, the convention of the finger bowl provided a remedy. But it also was to be used in a specified way, as Miss Leslie suggested:

> When the finger bowls are sent around, dip a clean corner of your napkin into the water, and wet round your lips with it, but omit the disgusting foreign fashion of taking water into your mouth, rinsing and gurgling it round, and then spitting

The finger bowl was usually brought out prior to the fruit and dessert course of a dinner party, so that guests could freshen up between courses. The finger-bowl doily provided a convenient place to wipe fingers or lips after this cleaning ritual.

THE
MANDATES
OF
MANNERS

•——•

4 1

it back into the glass. . . . Dip your fingers into the glass, rub them with the slice of lemon, or the orange leaf that may be floating on the surface, and then wipe them on the napkin.[44]

American etiquette writers did display some humor and objectivity about the proliferation of rules for eating. It often took the form in the popular literature of a kind of middle-class self-critique, perhaps as a safeguard against possible conceit or ostentation. Eliza Leslie captured this somewhat dubious tone in her comments about the proper method of eating pie:

It is an affectation of ultra-fashion to eat pie with a fork, and has a very awkward and inconvenient look. Cut it up first with your knife and fork both; then proceed to eat it with care, the fork in your right hand. Much of this determined fork-exercise may be considered foolish. But it is fashionable.[45]

By the 1880s, silver flatware manufacturers included a pie fork, with a special cutting tine that eliminated the need for a knife at all in eating pie. Despite the availability of this utensil, however, many people, particularly in rural areas, continued to use a knife as an all-purpose eating utensil, as is suggested by an exchange in William Dean Howells's *A Modern Instance* (1882) between would-be gentleman Bartley Hubbard and Andy, a hotel ostler in rural Maine:

[Andy] was not without his disdain for the palate which must have its mince-pie warm at midnight; nor without his respect for it either: this fastidious taste must be part of the splendor which showed itself in Mr. Hubbard's city-cut clothes, and in his neck scarf, and the perfection of his finger nails and moustache. The boy had felt the original impression of these facts deepened rather than effaced by custom: they were for every day, and not, as he had at first conjectured, for some great occasion only. . . . Andy pulled his chair round so as to get an unrestricted view of a man who ate his pie with a fork as easily as another would with a knife. . . . "Bring you anything else?" he asked, admiring the young man's skill in getting the last flakes of the crust on his fork: the pie had now vanished.[46]

At the dinner table, ill fortune could strike unexpectedly, and the well-mannered person had to be prepared for any eventuality. The napkin provided a social defense against the effects of such bad luck. As Agnes Morton wrote, ". . . the napkin partially unfolded is laid across the lap. It is not tucked in at the neck or the vest front, or otherwise disposed as a feeding-bib. It is a towel, for wiping the lips and fingers in emergencies, but should be used unobtrusively—

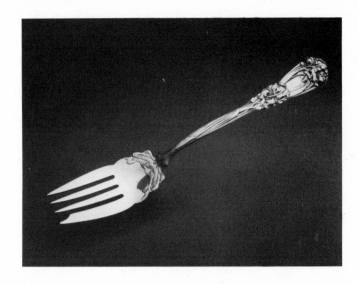

Sterling silver pastry fork.

not flourished like a flag of truce."[47] The napkin could be used to remove unfortunate grease from one's lips, to cover the mouth during removal of a fish bone or fruit pit, or to wipe the juice of pared fruit from the fingers. It was never, however, to be used as a handkerchief "by wiping the forehead or blowing the nose with it."[48] The napkin was only temporarily assigned to a guest; it was in reality the property of the hostess, and using it for such personal activities was considered somehow a depreciation of that loan. An implicit principle of reci-

Boardinghouse or hotel napkin rings, available in sets of six, enabled transient guests to distinguish and reuse their own napkins over the course of several meals.

procity demanded that the hostess provide scrupulouly clean, "snow white" linens and that the guests treat them with respect. After the meal, ritual demanded that the guest return the napkin in a specified way: "Fold your napkin when you are done with it and place it in your ring, when at home. If you are visiting, leave your napkin unfolded beside your plate." Napkin rings were commonly used, but only when the napkin would be reused by the same person—for family, boardinghouse, or servants' dinner tables, never for parties.[49] The act of not folding the napkin reinforced the notion that the hostess would not reuse it, but that it would be laundered for the next guest, which provided simultaneous and subtle assurance that the same courtesy had been extended to you.

Drinking, as well as eating, was saturated with complicated rituals. Tea drinking had a long tradition of formal procedure that migrated with it from China to the West. The custom of taking tea required that the drinkers use established signals to indicate whether they wished to continue to partake. By the nineteenth century, these signals carried over to coffee drinking as well: "If a person wishes to be served with more tea . . . or coffee, he should place his spoon in the saucer," John Ruth advised. "If he has had sufficient, let it remain in his cup."[50] These signals enabled a person to be discreet about requesting more— an act which, if done directly, might be interpreted as a presumption. It also saved a guest from the possible embarrassment of having to refuse a gracious offer of more beverage from the hostess, and thus was a convenient dual-purpose convention.

These systems of nonverbal signals also enabled the diner to let a servant or waiter know when one was finished eating, without having to speak to the servant directly. *The Successful Housekeeper* in 1883 directed its readers that "when a guest wishes to have his plate removed, he is supposed to rest his fork on the plate" as a sign that the plate could be cleared way. If one did not wish to drink whatever was being offered—wine, in particular—it was perfectly acceptable to turn one's glass upside down, to indicate that wish to whoever was pouring.[51]

Based on the material evidence, another tea and coffee drinking practice must have been somewhat common despite admonitions in the etiquette books—the custom of pouring the hot liquid from the tea or coffee cup into the saucer to cool, and then drinking from the saucer. This practice originated with the Chinese method of brewing tea in the tea cup, using the saucer as a lid during brewing. When the beverage had brewed sufficiently, it was poured off from the cup into the saucer for drinking—hence the term "a dish of tea." This was not an uncommon practice during the eighteenth and early nineteenth centuries, but it began to be considered old-fashioned by the mid-nineteenth century. Manufacturers supported the practice by providing small saucers called cup plates, often made of pressed glass or transfer-printed earthenware, to match a tea service. The cup plates served as a coaster to protect the tabletop from the damp bottom of the hot tea or coffee cup while the drinker was imbibing from the saucer. These cup plates survive in hundreds of mass-produced patterns, and although most of them were produced between the 1830s and the 1860s, their use was still sufficiently widespread in 1883 that John Ruth felt compelled to warn, "Tea and coffee should never be poured into a saucer."[52]

Glass or ceramic cup plates served as coasters to protect table linens from the damp bottoms of tea or coffee cups while the drinker was imbibing from the saucer—a common, if not always approved, practice.

Ritualistic ceremonies abounded during the consumption of other types of beverages, particularly wine. Since it was usually imported (mainly from France), wine was expensive and was therefore generally associated with the wealthy classes—unlike some of its more high-spirited cousins, whiskey, rum, and cider. It was improper as a rule for women to drink in public, but there were certain socially acceptable exceptions. Eliza Leslie supplied women with specific protocol for the public consumption of wine, particularly when men were involved: "When both glasses are filled, look at him [your drinking partner], bow your head, and taste the wine. . . . It is not customary, in America, for a lady to empty her glass."[53] In a hotel women were permitted to drink wine when dining and were also permitted to imbibe in mixed company during dinner parties and evening social events. When dining in a hotel, however, a woman had to beware, since she was on public display. A lady was never to take wine with the same gentleman more than once, "for wine is expensive, and no lady should every day place herself under the same obligation to the same gentleman, even for a single glass."[54] The principle of reciprocity is implicit here, with unspoken sexual overtones. Eliza Leslie warned against the dangers of champagne. One glass was permissible, but

> on no consideration let any lady be persuaded to take two glasses of champagne. It is more than the head of an *American* female can bear. And she may rest assured that (though unconscious of it herself) all present will find her cheeks flushing, her eyes twinkling, her tongue unusually voluble, her talk loud and silly, and her laugh incessant. Champagne is very insidious, and two glasses may throw her into this pitiable condition.[55]

A woman's virtue was threatened by the economic and psychological power of a relationship that an expensive and intoxicating gift established. If Americans, women in particular, were going to drink alcoholic beverages at all, social occasions—dinner parties, suppers, evening parties, dances, and balls—were the most likely times to do so. Historian Norman H. Clark interprets drinking as a release from the "rigid canons of success ideology (achievement, self-reliance, self-restraint)"—indeed, the presence of wine on a dinner table might have acted as an unconscious tempering of the formalized behavior required of all dinner-party participants.[56] Moreover, drinking wine may have been proper for some normally temperate members of the middle class in the early nineteenth century because it was thought to be alcohol-free, and also because it did not have the associations with violent, abusive behavior that were attached to stronger spirits.[57]

Conversation was an integral part of any meal. Whether at a family meal or a formal dinner party, conversation expressed a degree of civilization and literacy that was essential to the success of the meal. Guests were expected to be conversant about a variety of illuminating (and socially acceptable) topics, and hostesses were warned to develop a dinner-table seating plan that would eliminate the possibility of any embarrassing lulls in the conversation. It was a hostess's responsibility to promote and sustain an interesting or "lively" level of conversation throughout the meal, at the same time avoiding the many conversational taboos—particularly references to any bodily functions. One was also not to discuss food being eaten by others, or to refer to the "American disease"—dyspepsia, or indigestion—which was deemed "vulgar and disgusting." Other "painful or disgusting subjects" included medical ailments, gossip, "political or sectarian controversies . . . sicknesses, sores, surgical operations, dreadful accidents, shocking cruelties, or horrible punishments."[58] The majority of these topics were expected to invoke a level of emotional intimacy that was unacceptable in the public realm of decorum. Such topics were appropriate only for the private sphere of people's lives, a sector in which bodily functions and sexual intimacies could be discussed under close and careful guard.

Directing conversation at the family dinner table was especially important because children were often present. American children customarily joined their parents for meals as soon as they were old enough. There they could be conditioned to sit quietly and not make disruptive noises, to wait to be served without grabbing at the food, and, in the words of one child-rearing expert, "to be able to see delicacies without expecting or asking to partake of them."[59] The family dinner was a place of spiritual as well as physical nourishment and a training ground for children to become civilized adults—in words as well as in deeds.

The final level of conversation that was codified by the rules of etiquette was that between hostess or guest and servant. This type of exchange was unique in its blatant assumption of social inequality. Servants were never to speak unless directed to do so, and anyone who spoke to a servant was exhorted to proceed with great care. Two reasons were commonly given for such stern advice. Servants were generally characterized as being vindictive, emotional, and unreliable—to speak roughly or carelessly to a servant usually resulted in some form of retaliation, ranging from having soup spilled on one's coat to having one's servant quit. John Ruth provided a second reason for maintaining a careful level of cordiality with servants—yours or others—when he advised guests always to *request*, never to *command*: "To speak to a waiter in a driving manner will create, among well-bred people, the suspicion that you were sometime a servant yourself, and are putting on *airs* at the thought of your promotion."[60] This reason might have had particular meaning to many members of the middle class, among them those who had invested heavily, and in diverse ways, in concealing their humbler origins.

Whether dining was structured by such fixed rules in all situations and among all people is a hard question. It seems that specific meals, particularly breakfast and other everyday meals that took place among members of the family, were less rigid. Breakfast, the first meal of the day, was less encumbered with special tools and rules than any other. In some families, it was eaten not in the dining room but in the kitchen. If dinner did not occur at noon, lunch, a much less formal meal, occurred in its place. Often lunch was taken by women and children only, or by women alone among their peers. In either case, the tyranny of high etiquette was somewhat relaxed, and much less emphasis was placed on environment and display. During the late afternoon or early evening (six o'clock), many families who did not eat dinner at that time had a light meal, which they called tea or supper. Like dinner, it was often transformed into a social event, with a corresponding elevation of behavior, but not to the height required for dinner. Tea might have even been taken in a room other than the dining room. Such license would never have been accorded to dinner.

Dinner, the main meal of the day, was usually set in the dining room, a place whose furnishings and visual references to religious values seemed to mandate proper behavior. Dinner was generally at midday until the latter half of the century, when the routine absence of men from the home during the day necessitated moving it to early evening. It was the most important family meal, serving to communicate and reinforce family values, and was typically highly formalized. More than any other meal, dinner would have been held at a special table reserved just for that purpose, and frequently in its own room—the dining room. In addition, if outsiders were to be invited for any meal, it would most likely be for dinner. Their presence made it imperative that the rules of etiquette be followed, lest a family be exposed as socially unsuitable because of its table manners.

It is also clear that special meals, such as Sunday dinner for many families, Thanksgiving, Christmas, or a New Year's celebration, were conducted with a greater degree of formality. (An exception seems to have been the Fourth of July, which was often a less formal, outdoor meal.) The rules of etiquette could be relaxed slightly once outside the sanction of the dining room. Dining in a public place, however—such as a hotel, where the participants might be exposed to both the criticism and social indelicacies of strangers—gave rise to clear distinctions between public and private behavior. At home, sheltered from prying eyes, one might feel less constrained about eating a drumstick with one's fingers; but in public, "no lady looks worse than when gnawing a bone, even of game or poultry. Few *ladies* do it. In fact, nothing should be sucked or gnawed in public; neither corn bitten off the cob, nor melon nibbled from the rind."[61] Miss Leslie's animalistic imagery sent a strong message to the middle class, consumed as it was by the continual struggle to separate its behavior from those they considered to be beasts, whether animal or human.

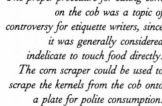

The proper procedure for eating corn on the cob was a topic of controversy for etiquette writers, since it was generally considered indelicate to touch food directly. The corn scraper could be used to scrape the kernels from the cob onto a plate for polite consumption.

THE 3 ALTAR OF GASTRONOMY

DINING ROOMS AND THEIR FURNISHINGS

he highly ritualized dining practices of the second half of the nineteenth century not only dictated a stardardized code of behavior, but also required a specifically ordered domestic space and the accumulation of a supporting array of utensils and furnishings.

> The floor of this room should be hard wood. The table and chairs must be well made and of generous size. It is impossible to arrange a narrow table in an elegant manner, and nothing is more uncomfortable than small, unsubstantial chairs. When the sideboard is built into the side of the room, the table and chairs will be all the necessary furniture. . . . Growing plants and pictures are always a pleasing addition to this room, which should be one of the pleasantest in the house.[1]

In America, the dining room first appeared as a separate architectural space in the late seventeenth century, when the wealthy began to add special rooms to their homes for dining. Most people still ate either in the hall—at that time a large room rather than the passageway it has become—or the parlor (the two major rooms in most houses), or sometimes in an upstairs chamber or bedroom, if there was one. Utility, warmth, and convenience seemed to be the main criteria in determining where people ate, as well as where they stored their eating and serving utensils. During the eighteenth century, household spaces were increasingly rationalized so that by the American Revolution, separate dining rooms, furnished with dining tables and storage units for dining utensils, were common in the homes of wealthier individuals. These rooms were often multipurpose and might have included additional furnishings for activities unrelated to dining, such as a desk or a reading chair.[2]

Those at wealthier levels of the middle class, especially city dwellers, probably had dining rooms during the first quarter of the nineteenth century. Urban row houses cropped up in great numbers after 1800 in cities such as Boston, New York, Philadelphia, and Baltimore. Typically between 15 and 20 feet wide by 30 to 40 feet deep, these houses stood three or three-and-one-half stories high. The ground floor, or basement (usually at street level or a little below grade), contained a kitchen in the back and a "combination family dining room/sitting room/nursery" in the front, both of which were the centers of informal family activity and production. Above them, on the first floor, were more formal public spaces—the parlor and dining room—used for entertaining. The upper floors contained bedrooms, with servants' quarters in the unheated attic.[3]

This layout clearly suggests how domestic spaces now fell into three separate spheres of activity: private, public, and productive, and rooms within each had special characteristics according to their functions. This ideology of domestic spatial organization was widely promoted and reinforced during the 1840s and 1850s by ministers, architects, and domestic writers, all of whom believed strongly in the power of environment to shape the character of an individual, a family, or a nation. The importance of dining as part of that doctrine of progress was stressed continually:

> If the truth must be known, all affectations and pretense aside, the dinner, the world over, is the symbol of a people's civilization. A coarse and meanly cooked and raggedly served dinner expresses the thought and perhaps the spiritual perception of a nation or family. A well-cooked and a prettily-served dinner will indicate the refinement and taste of a nation or family.[4]

Nation and family are equated deliberately: the virtue and dignity of America was thought to depend on the domestic qualities of individual citizens and of their family units. A woman was charged with the responsibility of creating a household environment that would nurture taste, civility, and Christian ideals in her husband and children, thereby influencing them to be moral and productive members of society.[5]

Because of dining's key role as an educational and social family function, the dining room—a separate space where the dining rituals were to take place —commanded growing attention even in middle-class homes by the second quarter of the nineteenth century. Townhouses often had two separate spaces for dining—one close to the kitchen for informal family meals and another for formal, public dining, separated by a floor from the noise, smells, and informality of the kitchen.

There were, of course, probably many exceptions to the rule. An 1853 auction catalogue of New York City auctioneer Henry H. Leeds provides a room-by-room listing of the contents of a townhouse to be dispersed, thus offering a detailed look at the layout and function of the entire house. All dining furnishings were listed in the "front basement," a room that had in it yards of ingrain carpet, a black walnut extension table with leaves that would extend it to sixteen feet, a mahogany sofa with haircloth upholstery, six black walnut cane-seat chairs, two black walnut cane-seat rockers—one a "sewing" rocker—a mahogany desk, an airtight stove, a spittoon, a gas pendant or hanging light, a cherry tea table, a worsted table cover, yards of drugget, an oil cloth, and miscellaneous china, glass, and silver—including a silver-plated tea or coffee urn.[6]

This room must have been used not only as a formal dining room but also as a family sitting room—given the sofa, the rocking chairs, and the tea table, much like the combined family sitting room, dining room and nursery of the eighteenth-century townhouses. But there is no mention of a second, more formal dining room upstairs. On the first floor two richly furnished parlors are found, but no table large enough for dining was included in either. The whole tone of these two rooms was much more elaborate and opulent than that of the dining room below. The contrast was apparent even in the lighting fixtures: a "very rich ormolu gas chandelier" and a "splendid 6-light ormolu chandelier" were found in the parlors, while the dining room below was furnished merely with an unadorned "gas pendant." The grand opulence that was deemed necessary for the parlors—rooms whose purpose was strictly limited to entertainment— was not appropriate for a room that had to serve not only company but family as well. There the potentially corruptive presence of rich, showy materials was virtually eliminated, replaced instead by materials like ingrain instead of "rich tapestry" carpet, and black walnut instead of imported rosewood furniture. The former, though certainly not inferior in quality or expense, was generally more restrained in character.

This attitude toward household furnishing echoes the advice about certain styles for the dining room given by Mrs. William Parkes more than twenty years earlier. "Every room should be furnished in a style not inconsistent with the use for which it is set apart," she advised. "The dining-room, the place of rendezvous for the *important* concerns of the table, should not be furnished in the light and airy style which you may adopt in your drawing room. . . . there, no other attraction is desirable, nor scarcely anything requisite, beyond the well-arranged table, and the chairs that surround it."[7]

As the century progressed, so did the dining room's formal and functional distinction, although some homeowners still kept a sofa or maybe even a piano in their dining room throughout the late nineteenth century. Photographs of dining rooms, particularly those in middle-class homes, often show a *recalmier*, or small sofa. As both a public and a private space, the dining room was an appropriate family gathering place in the evening, to read or play games or merely to sit and talk, particularly if they had no other room that presented an alternative to the formality of the parlor.

Perhaps the most prevalent architectural feature that transformed an ordinary space into a specifically dining area was a niche or alcove for a built-in or brought-in sideboard. "In the *dining room*," wrote architect Calvert Vaux in 1857, "several useful features may be architecturally managed. The sideboard, for example, may be arranged in a recess . . . with a door to a private closet on one side, and a pantry or service room on the other. This idea admits of numberless modifications, and always has a rich effect if well managed." Vaux also suggested that the dining

The presence of a small cozy sofa and several comfortable chairs contradicts the formality of the imposing sideboard and suggests that the family may have done a variety of things besides eat in this room.

room include a "plant cabinet, or small conservatory" in a bay at one end of the room, adding that "the glass doors of communication [between the two spaces] are fitted with slightly ornamented glass, so as to decrease the monotony of effect that would otherwise occur, while enough clear glass is left to give a good view of the flowers . . . when the sliding doors are closed."[8]

More and more members of the upper and middle classes moved from the cities to newly developing suburbs after the Civil War for the amenities that one prominent architect described in 1866: the suburbs were "ten to fifteen miles away from the unceasing noise and hurry of the city," he wrote, "where the business of the day is forgotten, and fresh air, fresh milk, butter, and eggs, fruit, flowers, birds, etc. are luxuries unknown in town."[9] As this transfer of population took place, the functional specialization of middle-class housing accelerated. In 1863, Americans could build houses ranging from a "simple cottage" for between

$800 and $1,000 to "an old English seat" for $28,000. The simple house plan included a porch, hall, sitting room, dining room with china closet and dumb-waiter, veranda, basement kitchen, three second-floor bedrooms, and a linen closet.[10] The dumb-waiter appeared frequently in plans of the 1850s and 1860s, serving as a communications link with the basement kitchen. It was a small, cupboard-sized elevator that was usually operated by means of rope pulleys. It was used to carry both food and utensils from the basement food-preparation center to the first-floor food-consumption area. Within a decade, however, further refinements in spatial organization provided a more efficient cluster of food-related spaces, placing the dining room and kitchen together on the first floor. By the 1880s, the basement kitchen, a holdover from the early nineteenth-century town-house plans, had disappeared from "modern dwellings."

More expensive middle-class houses had more options in the food service–food preparation areas. A butler's pantry commonly might have included a built-in "dresser for table linen and china"[11] and a sink with hot and cold running

A built-in sideboard was the main architectural feature that distinguished a dining room from other household spaces.

water. A washroom, storeroom, milk room, and sometimes even a separate "breakfast room" might have been added to the kitchen section. With the luxury of running water and rationally organized spatial arrangements—adjacent food-preparation and food-service areas, and a second floor restricted to private functions—this plan would have created what was considered a modern and very desirable middle-class house.

Only the least expensive houses lacked a separate dining room. In those cases, either the kitchen expanded functionally to become a dining-sitting room as well, or there was a multipurpose "living room" adjacent to the ktichen that could be used for dining. The layout of urban working-class houses around 1850 usually had two main rooms—a small formal parlor used for company occasions and a larger kitchen for family sitting, cooking, and eating.[12] The practice of eating in the kitchen was viewed with increasing disfavor as the nineteenth century progressed. As early as 1857, Calvert Vaux commented in his description of a plan for a farmhouse:

> The accommodation in the main part of the house consists of a hall with a staircase in it, a parlor communicating with the general living-room, and a bed-

As household dining spaces became increasingly specialized, the dining area itself expanded to include a china closet or perhaps a butler's pantry. In some houses, the china closet was directly linked to the kitchen by means of a small pass-through window.

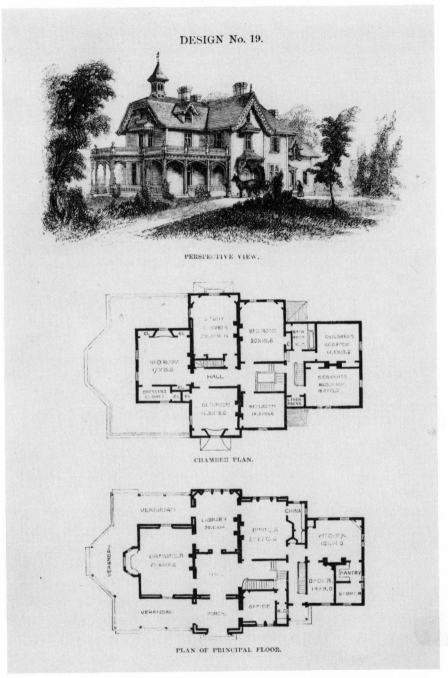

DESIGN No. 19.

PERSPECTIVE VIEW.

CHAMBER PLAN.

PLAN OF PRINCIPAL FLOOR.

The dining room in this suburban house has both a china closet and a special niche for a sideboard.

THE
ALTAR
OF
GASTRONOMY

5 7

room connecting with this apartment and the kitchen wing. It is not thought necessary to provide a separate passage to the kitchen from the front door, and it is calculated that the family-room will be used as a dining room. It is the custom with some farmers to make a constant practice of taking all meals in the kitchen; but this habit makes a low state of civilization. The occupation of farming is the natural employment of a human being, and it ought to be made a refined and noble pursuit, not a mere way of earning a rude subsistence.[13]

This attitude continued to gain momentum among the middle class. Working-class people, however, continued to eat in the ktichen. Calvin Coolidge (1872–1933) was born and raised in rural Plymouth, Vermont, where his family lived in a small addition tacked onto the rear of the general store. Even after the Coolidges had prospered to the point of purchasing a larger, separate house across the street in 1876, the dining table remained in the kitchen, close to the stove and the center of all indoor family activity. The tradition of eating in the kitchen remained strong for both American-born and immigrant members of the working class well into the twentieth century. Margaret Byington, in her 1910 study *Homestead: The Households of a Mill Town*, wrote that

in five-room houses we find an anomaly known as the "dining-room." Though a full set of dining room furniture, sideboard, table and dining chairs, are usually in evidence, they are rarely used at meals. The family sewing is frequently done there, the machine standing in the corner of the window; and sometimes too, the ironing, to escape the heat of the kitchen; but rarely is the room used for breakfast, dinner, or supper. The kitchen is the important room of the house.[14]

Furnishing a nineteenth-century dining room was a task of far-reaching social significance, since an entire complex of ideals and aspirations were made manifest within that room. The dining room—scene of one of the most important family rituals—was to be furnished in an appropriately inspiring manner, with visual cues to institutions or activities of a noble and uplifting character. The popular prevalence of this faith in the ability of home environment to shape character is implicit in this indictment of hotel dining by popular late-nineteenth-century cookbook writer Marion Harland:

> Have you ever thought how large a share the kitchen and dining-room have in forming the distinctive characteristics of the home? It is no marvel that the man who has had his dinners from an eating-house all his life should lack a word to describe that which symbolizes to the Anglo-Saxon all that is dearest and most sacred on earth.[15]

Women had such a wide range of choice of available furniture, carpets, draperies, lamps, silverware, dinner sets, and any other furnishings they might need for a dining room that the mere act of *choosing* could produce true anxiety. Shopping, especially to those for whom a purchase represented months of saving, could be a treacherous adventure. The tempting qualities of a glamorous Brussels carpet over a more practical ingrain led more than one naive Victorian man and woman astray, especially when encouraged by a slick city salesman. The warerooms were full of options, created to satisfy the popular demand for a stylish Renaissance, Eastlake, Gothic, artistic, Elizabethan, Jacobean, or colonial dining room. Kate Taylor of Norwalk, Connecticut, wrote to her mother in Mandarin, Florida, of the colonialization of her dining room in 1880:

> . . . this week we expect to have up in the dining room a genuine old Franklin stove. Jim has found one at last, w/brass pieces on the top, and brass trimmings in the front. I don't think he can ever pay for the wood to burn in it, but he is delighted w/his purchase, or trade. . . . With our old clock and spinning wheel, the dining room will have quite an antique appearance.[16]

In choosing one's furnishings, the dining-room floor could be treated in several ways. In earlier nineteenth-century houses, the floors were usually soft pine covered with wall-to-wall carpeting. During the 1860s, Katherine E. Bragdon, wife of a Rochester, New York, newspaper editor, used a rag rug on her floors. On March 21, 1861, she wrote in her diary, "Am very busy preparing my rag carpet for weaving." A week later she reported that she had colored the warp for her carpet "and also a few rags—my first experience in the business. It left my hands black, blistered, stiff and sore." On the first of April, a Monday, she took all the material for her carpet to a weaver to complete—more than forty pounds of woolen and cotton rags in more than a dozen different colors.[17]

By the 1870s, when improvements in woodworking machinery had made planing hardwood a simpler and less exorbitant task than previously, hardwood floors grew in fashion. They were still expensive, however, and although she recommended them for dining rooms, etiquette advisor Maria Parloa conceded that hardwood floors had several disadvantages: "Noiseless service is more difficult on the polished floor," she observed, "and there is danger of accidents from slipping."[18] On the other hand, wall-to-wall carpets absorbed odors and were difficult to clean; they were less popular as fashionable floor coverings by the 1880s, although they continued to be used by people of moderate means. by 1881, Ella Rodman Church's *How to Furnish a Home* stated that rag carpet was still "most agreeable and suitable" and therefore best for either the kitchen or the dining room. Batavia, New York, farm wife Julia Amanda Cook was thus furnishing her dining room in acceptable fashion when she wrote in her diary in August of 1880, "Put down sitting room carpet, our rag carpet we have been so long waiting for." Church also recommended area rugs or Japanese matting as preferable coverings for bare hardwood floors, and in carpeted dining rooms, a drugget or crumb cloth of woven cotton or of oilcloth was laid over the carpet to protect against spills.[19]

Proper lighting for a dining room was one topic in Sarah Josepha Hale's 1853 discussion of dinner-party procedures. "For a small party," she wrote, "a single lamp in the center is sufficient; but for a larger number, the room should be lighted with lamps hung over the table. . . ."[20] According to Maria Parloa, "There is one point in the dining-room that may be regarded as the center. The chandelier is usually this point. The center of the table should come exactly under the center of the chandelier."[21] Many of these lighting fixtures were produced with counterweight mechanisms, so that they could be raised and lowered over the table, thus making them both easier to fill and clean, and capable of satisfying the artistic whims of a hostess. Hosts and hostesses could select that illumination which was most flattering, romantic, or practical for a particular occasion.

The floor, its carpeting, and the lighting were all meant to flatter and to call attention to the focal point of the room—the table. According to Mrs. Mary Jane

Since carpeting was usually one of the most expensive household acquisitions, crumb cloths (like this one advertised in Jordan Marsh and Company's catalogue) or druggets were often laid under the dining table to protect against spills.

Anderson Loftie, author of *The Dining-Room*, a dining-room table had to have two requisite features: "Many people seem to imagine a dining-room table ought to differ in some mysterious way from any other table. But the indispensable quality is one which all tables should share. It should have perfect steadiness." Her second requirement for the table was that it "be capable of variation in size."[22] The introduction of the gate-leg table in the seventeenth century was an important step toward varying the size of dining tables. These tables had a movable leg that could be unfolded to support a hinged semicircular leaf, transforming the table in shape as well as in size. Large drop-leaf tables, with one or preferably two movable legs, which could be engaged to support large, hinged, rectangular leaves on each side of the table—thereby doubling or tripling the size—came into fashion during the first half of the eighteenth century in the dining rooms of the wealthy. Other attempts to vary size included tables that were produced in sets (with a square center and two D-shaped ends that could be added on) and, the most common form in the nineteenth century, the extension table, developed about 1830, when both wood and metal mechanisms were designed to expand the size of the table through the insertion of leaves. An improved

The gate-leg table, developed during the seventeenth century, helped make it possible to vary the size of dining tables. Both this and the drop-leaf table, introduced during the early eighteenth century, utilized the principle of a hinged leaf that could be supported by a movable leg when necessary to double or triple the capacity of the table. Extension tables with wood or metal mechanisms that supported added leaves first appeared in the 1830s.

extension table designed by George Henkels, a Philadelphia furniture maker, was praised in *Godey's Lady's Book* in 1850:

> Its advantages are obvious to those who were once obliged to place two square tables, sometimes of unequal height, side by side, if company was to be entertained. In this improvement, the mechanism is managed by rope and small windlass concealed under the rim of the table which also obviates the necessity of screws to fasten the different leaves together . . . they may be tightened by a turn of the windlass. When entirely shut up, it has the appearance of a beautiful oval center-table, with a heavy base. We commend it to the consideration of "heads of large families."[23]

Dining tables were usually made of fine hardwoods; mahogany, cherry, and black walnut were especially popular. New York State farmwife Julia Holmes Cook wrote in her diary in 1881 that she and her husband, Irving, had come to Batavia one afternoon to order "a bl. walnut extension table of Dailey," a local furniture dealer. Two weeks later she wrote, "Julia [her daughter] and I go to Batavia. Get some house plants and bring home our black walnut ex. table we ordered. It is satisfactory."[24] The top of a dining table was to be kept gleaming, whether or not it was going to be covered. "Heat rings" were the enemy of conscientious women, and all household manuals contained formulas for polishing dining tables. Mrs. Loftie advised her readers to avoid wood that was subject to heat rings, although she remarked that "of late years, since the habit of taking off the cloth after dinner has gone out, it does not much matter except on high moral grounds, whether the top is mahogany or deal [pine]."[25] Sarah Josepha Hale, editor of *Godey's Lady's Book*, recommended that her readers rub their tables with cold-drawn linseed oil, using a piece of linen to spread the oil all over the surface. They were then to rub for ten minutes, using a clean piece of linen, and finally to rub until dry with a third linen cloth. If done every day "for some months . . . you will find your mahogany will acquire a permanent and beautiful lustre, unattainable by any other means, and equal to the finest French polish, and will protect the table, when covered with a cloth, from hot vessels." For those with less time or patience available, "if the appearance must be more immediately produced, take some Furniture Paste," Mrs. Hale advised.[26]

Chairs for the dining table were to be "comfortable, with backs that are almost straight, and they should be absolutely trim and strong."[27] Chairs also had to accommodate women's clothing fashions. Mrs. Loftie reminded her readers that the fashion in chairs varied very much with the fashion in ladies' dresses. "The wide spreading skirts which were supported by crinoline needed a different kind of chair from that on which the well 'tied back' lady of the present day can sit comfortably."[28] The most efficient woman had chairs that were easy to clean. Cane-seat chairs were often recommended because they could be wiped clean with a cloth or washed with soap and water. "A Practical Housekeeper" provided directions for doing so in 1856:

> Turn up the chair bottom, and with hot water and a sponge wash the cane-work well so that it may become completely soaked; should it be very dirty, you may add soap. Let it dry in the open air if possible, or in a place where there is a window draught, and it will become as tight and as firm as when new, providing that it has not been broken.[29]

Upholstery except leather was discouraged, because washing it might damage the fabric. "Such a piece of good fortune has happened to us today," a Rochester woman named Alcesta Huntington wrote to her mother, Annjennett, in February 1868. "Uncle Charles . . . went with Sue this morning and selected a set of 14 chairs for our dining room oak, half arms and cane seated—one of the set is an arm chair with a cushion for the head of the table . . ." all of which could be wiped with a damp cloth.[30]

The sideboard, whether free-standing or built-in, was the most prominent piece of dining-room furniture and served multiple functions, including storage, service, and display. Common elements in middle-class dining rooms beginning around 1860, sideboards were usually the single most expensive item purchased for a dining room (or possibly for the entire house, second only to carpets). They were specific to the dining room, replacing the more multipurpose cupboard as the place where dishes and silver were stored and displayed.

Dining-room chairs had to be comfortable, sturdy, and easy to clean. They were usually purchased in sets of eight or twelve and often had seats of cane or leather which, unlike upholstery, could be wiped with a damp cloth.

What the Sideboard Is For

Several people have asked about the uses of the sideboard. The drawers are for the silver and cutlery, the closets for wines, if they be used, and often for such things as preserved ginger, confectionery, cut sugar, and indeed, any of the many little things that one likes to have in the dining-room, yet out of sight. The water pitcher and other silver and pretty bits of china can be placed on the sideboard. Cracker jar and fruit dish also belong there. At dinner time the dessert dishes are usually arranged upon it.[31]

Sideboards, such as these advertised in the Paine's Furniture Company catalogue, varied in quality and price to appeal to a broad range of homeowners.

Fashion and stylistic variations were as evident in sideboards as in any other furniture form, but they retained their basic shape and structural features regardless of their surface ornamentation. Sideboards were tall rectilinear forms, usually with open shelves and possibly a mirror above and a cabinet below. The cabinet held plates and serving utensils, and the upper shelves displayed glass, silver, china, or artistic bric-a-brac. The top of the cabinet doubled as a serving board.[32]

In a society strongly influenced by Christian religious ideology, the sideboard took its place within a distinct series of parallels between dining rituals and religious rituals. The Eucharist is, after all, a ritual of eating and drinking, and the prescribed settings and order of service at the table all have liturgical over-

The similarities between the domestic modern Gothic dining room (right) and its ecclesiastical counterparts (above) were striking and far from coincidental.

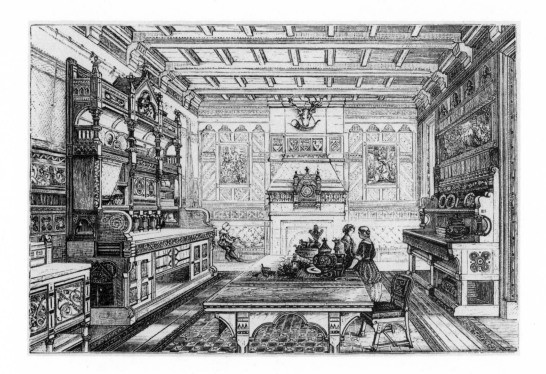

tones. In this religious context, the sideboard took on the guise of an altarpiece, its form obviously derived from church architecture. During the 1870s and 1880s the popularity of Gothic-style sideboards and other dining-room furnishings did much to enhance the churchlike aspect of the dining room and dining rituals.

The sideboard, with its imposing size and its numerous shelves and mirrors, also testified to artistic and economic status. "Ladies and gentlemen that have splendid and costly articles," a butler's manual published in 1827 advised, "wish to have them seen and set out to best advantage."[33] Silver articles, of course, were a main sideboard item. With the combined discoveries of the Comstock Lode—a wondrously rich silver mine opened in 1859—and the process of electroplating, the cost of silver tableware dropped considerably during the second half of the nineteenth century. Silver serving dishes, tea and coffee services, drinking vessels, trays, and a host of other silver items once affordable only to the wealthy were suddenly available to the middle-class consumer. The American silver industry, happy to accommodate this rapidly growing new market, introduced a wide variety of new forms—tilting ice-water pitchers, elaborate caster sets, butter dishes, ice-cream stands, or revolving fruit-knife holders—all of which were exhibited proudly on the sideboard. A typical late-nineteenth-century sideboard would also have displayed cut glass, examples of hand-painted French or German porcelain, "antique" German or Italian glass, a German beer stein, a brass samovar, or a decorative piece of pottery—possibly Delft or majolica.

This imposing oak sideboard comes complete with carved images of fruits, fish, fowl—and even rabbits.

. . .

By the late 1870s, middle-class Americans were beginning to buy their dining-room furniture in "suites" (sets)—usually a table, chairs, sideboard, and possibly a server, which was a less imposing version of the sideboard. This piece was used during a meal to hold dishes and platters of food between courses, a stack of extra plates, the coffee cups and saucers, and a pair of lamps or candlesticks. "If there is no sideboard, and the expense of one cannot be incurred," Maria Parloa suggested, "a side-board table, which may be covered with a pretty cloth, will do to hold the odd bits of tableware one always wants in the dining-room."[34] Other, smaller tables might also be found in nineteenth-century dining rooms in addition to or in place of a server. In 1878, Mrs. Loftie remarked on the utility of having a small table from which to serve and at which to eat breakfast, lunch, or tea. Their small size, she said, made it possible to move them nearer to the fire in winter or into the "bow window" in summer.[35]

Supplementary storage for eating utensils could be provided by one or more china cupboards, which might have been part of a dining set or purchased separately. "One or two cupboards give an opportunity of displaying pretty bits of porcelain and glass to the best advantage," according to home economist Maria Parloa. "Nothing one may put in the dining room will add such brightness and charm as closets and cabinets, through the glass door of which the brilliant glass and china may be seen."[36]

Further artistic decoration of the dining room was encouraged, but with certain restrictions. It was assumed that the main focus during a meal would be the food and conversation at the table, rather than the art in the room. Accordingly, as Charles Wyllys Elliott wrote in an 1876 issue of *Art Journal*, "the objects which decorate the dining-room . . . should speak to the finer sense, but they should be such things as speak simply and to a divided attention."[37] Prints and paintings on dining-room walls were encouraged, as long as they did not detract from the room's primary purpose of social interaction. A specific genre of dining-room pictures revolved around themes of food and drink, fruit, flowers, and game, although some nineteenth-century writers found visions of dead game depressing and inappropriate. Boston fine-art publishers L. Prang & Co. included a category of "Dining-Room Pictures" in its 1883–1884 catalogue. The listing included a set of four fruit prints, a pair of fish pictures after George N. Cass, *Our Kitchen Bouquet* after William Harring, *Dead Game* after G. Bosset, two pairs of dessert pictures, a pair of game pieces, and a pair of still lifes that depicted lobster, eggs, celery, trout, grouse, and tomatoes, after R. D. Wilkie. The fish pictures were the most expensive, at $5 each, and the rest ranged in price from $1 to $3 each.[38]

Mirrors also were frequently suggested, for they added a touch of brightness and gaiety to the dining room. Yet care in hanging mirrors had to be exercised, it was advised, so that they did not become a distraction for those seated at the table.

Table linens, once a luxury only for the wealthy, became essential elements in any civilized life style by the late nineteenth century. Because of the amount of labor involved in their production, textiles had always been expensive. In the

China cabinets, usually with mirrored backs and glass doors, could be purchased separately or as part of a dining-room suite, to serve as additional storage and display space for a family's glass and porcelain tablewares.

This pair of paintings, with their themes of fish and game, are typical examples of mid-nineteenth-century dining-room art. These graced the dining room of Joseph Curtis, a prominent Rochester, New York newspaperman, who died in 1883.

seventeenth, eighteenth, and early nineteenth centuries, textile working was extremely tedious and time consuming and was one of the jobs a family purchased if they could afford to do so. Major technological innovations in spinning and weaving dramatically changed the availability of textiles by the middle of the nineteenth century, as mass-produced fabrics for clothing, bedding, window coverings, and tables rolled out of the mills and into the homes of middle-class Americans.

In 1840, the author of *The Workwoman's Guide*, a household manual widely read by American women, listed these table linens as "necessities" for an English "gentleman's" house: eight to ten damask breakfast cloths in four sizes; eight to ten common damask tablecloths in five sizes; one to three large fine damask cloths; "table linen in the piece, per yard," eight different widths, both damask and diaper (a type of patterned cotton cloth); three to six dozen fine damask dinner napkins; three to six dozen damask breakfast napkins; three to six dozen "Doyleys" of white or colored damask, six nails (or 13.5 inches) square; six to twelve dozen large tray cloths in damask or diaper; six to twelve dozen small tray cloths in damask or diaper.[39] Although this seems like a huge supply by current standards, it was the normal amount advocated by home economists. Elizabeth F. Ellet's *The New Cyclopaedia of Domestic Economy*—written in 1873 and "adapted to all classes of society"—recommended an inventory of linens that included three dozen napkins; two and one half dozen tablecloths of various sizes, "including breakfast, dinner, etc."; six servants' tablecloths; three dozen towels; six round towels; two dozen napkins for fish, vegetables, and fruits; six pudding cloths; two dozen damask "d'oylies"; and one dozen Berlin wool "d'oylies."[40]

Except for the doilies, most of these items would probably have been purchased by a woman as uncut, unfinished yard goods, and then cut and hemmed to specification, either by hand or, by the 1850s, on a sewing machine. Most household management books provided directions for making tablecloths, carving and tray cloths, dinner napkins, and other table linens, and young women spent many hours prior to marriage preparing these necessities for their hope chests. The term "d'oyley" (now "doily") derives from the famous late-seventeenth-century London draper D'Oyley, who was a supplier of the materials for the inexpensive woolen mats or small, often fringed, napkins that were used during the fruit and dessert course to wipe one's fingers after the dinner napkins had been removed.[41] *The Workwoman's Guide* further defined the term. Doilies, it suggested, "may be either white or colored, and are sometimes open, of six nails square; they are generally fringed."[42] The idea was to protect the white dinner napkins from fruit stains.

By the late nineteenth century, doilies were often brought out with the finger bowls and were used either as napkins or to protect the bare table after the tablecloth had been removed prior to the fruit course. Mrs. John Logan, who wrote *The Home Manual* in 1889, stated that the finger bowls were to be brought out on china or glass plates, with a fruit napkin or doily (which could be embroidered) in between.[43] Doilies were still being mentioned as late as 1894, but they seem by then to have taken on a different function. "Small fringed napkins of different colors are used with a dessert of fruits," Agnes Morton wrote in 1894;

The preference for bare, polished tables opened the way for sets of plate, dessert, fingerbowl, tumbler, carafe, and center doilies, to be used in lieu of a single tablecloth.

"fancy doilies of fine linen embroidered with silk are sometimes brought in with the finger bowls"—not for utility, but for "dainty effect."[44] "The popular use of polished tables has created a demand for complete sets of doilies for table service, whereas formerly those for the finger-bowls were almost the only ones employed," the *Ladies' Home Journal* observed in 1893. "Lace doilies are particularly effective, being both rich and dainty in appearance." The magazine went on to enumerate the sorts of doilies a woman might have bought in sets or might have received as wedding presents:

> Cover doilies, used over a table-cloth, should measure about twelve inches, but if laid upon the polished table may be as large as sixteen inches square. Dessert doilies average seven inches in size, and tumbler doilies about four or five inches. At present round doilies are decidedly popular, and where they are so made the centre mat should be also round. As a general rule these latter are from twenty-four to twenty-seven inches in size, and are exceedingly artistic.[45]

Because linens in general were so expensive in the nineteenth century, a woman would often keep detailed inventories that noted the conditions of her linens, how long they had been in use, and what evidences of wear they had begun to show. Martha Buell Munn, the wife of a medical examiner for the United States Life Insurance Company in New York City, noted in her 1889 diary that she had "27 square & 3 round Doylies."[46] Another such inventory, found in a Munn family ledger from 1886–1887 recorded 36 round doylies, 36 square doylies, and 24 "new" square doylies.

Tablecloths varied according to the occasion. For an ordinary family dinner, the table was always covered with a white tablecloth, often over a piece of double-faced cotton flannel or an old tablecloth to improve the smoothness and appearance of the cloth and help protect the table from hot dishes. Smaller carving

cloths or napkins might also have been used on a family table under a bird or roast to protect the tablecloth from spills. Even working-class families with very little extra money felt it was important to cover the table with a white cloth for dinner. This pattern was followed by a New York oysterman and his family, which included seven children. "The meals [were] served regularly at the kitchen-table, which is covered with a white oilcloth," an analysis of wage-earners' budgets observed, although, it noted, "there is not room for all the family to sit at the table at once." Another New York household included a truckman, four children, a nephew, and the truckman's wife, who was described as "accustomed to a much higher standard of living then she has had since her marriage." In that household, "the meals were served regularly on a dining-room table in the kitchen, with a white tablecloth on it." For both families, neither of whom had a dining room, the white tablecloth seems to have been an important part of their dining ritual, a visible emblem of their social and cultural aspirations.[47]

In the nineteenth century, the process of laundering table linens—or anything else—was a difficult burden. They often had to be boiled and scrubbed hard. Although good manners demanded that table linens be always "snowy white," no doubt most middle-class housewives tried to make that snowy quality last through as many dinners as possible. "The handsomest damask linen cloths for

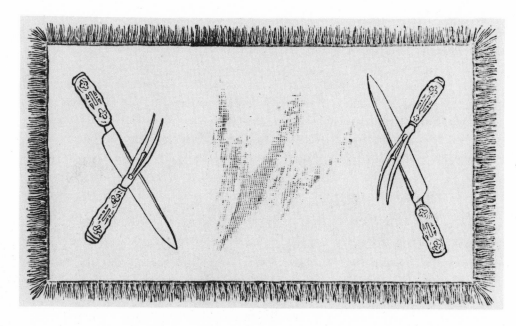

Design for a carving cloth from the Ladies' Home Journal.

party dinners, or company dinners, despite innovations, retain their pure white-ness," *The Successful Housekeeper* observed in 1883, "while colors are introduced in the smaller cloths for breakfast, supper, and lunch tables."[48] The constant usage table linens received, coupled with rather harsh techniques for washing and ironing, meant that they wore out more rapidly than today. Martha Munn kept an active listing of table linens "In Use," noting when specific tablecloths, napkins, towels, and doilies were used. Because the laundry was no doubt sent out, her marginal notations probably served her as a receipt. In January 1886, for example, she noted that her stock of "13 napkins fine" had been "returned . . . worn out 11."[49] In that same January, she recorded that she had twelve square doilies; when she sent these out to be cleaned, she noted in October that one that was returned was worn out.

In 1858, Catharine Beecher's *Domestic Receipt Book* described the traditional procedure of putting not one but two or even three cloths on the table for a dinner party. "If the tables are handsome ones, put on two white tablecloths, one above the other. If the tables are not handsome, cover them with a colored table-cloth, and put two white ones over."[50] The cloths would then be removed successively between courses as the meal progresssed, the uppermost after the meat course and the second after the pudding, cheese, and pastry course. The final course of fruit and coffee could be served either on the colored cloth or on the bare table—protected by doilies. By the end of the nineteenth century, how-ever, the practice of removing the tablecloth had diminished, as is indicated by Foster Coates in an 1891 issue of the *Ladies' Home Journal*:

An old time expression, "When the cloth was removed" is going into disuse, as the cloth is never removed at the present time. In the olden days of polished tables, the cloth was taken off and fruits with coffee were served on the bare table. Later side-slips were used which could be taken off after the game and thus save crumbing; but all that has been changed, and now the same table-cloth remains throughout the entire dinner.[51]

The table would have been further protected throughout the meal by "table" or "place" mats. Used from the mid-eighteenth century on, table mats were made of straw, willow, or cane and were imported from India, Africa, and the Phil-ippines. Miss Beecher stated in 1858 that they were placed on the table "where the dishes are to be set." Apparently these mats went out of fashion toward the end of the century; according to one etiquette writer, "Small table mats for the purpose of protecting the cloth are not fashionable at present," though some families, she conceded, still used them. *Good Housekeeping* wrote in 1889, "The use of mats is optional; they are useful in keeping the cloth clean, and, when dishes are brought in hot, they save the table from marks."[52] In 1892, Maria Parloa called table mats "useful but not fashionable. . . . Where one finds the most elegance such mats are no longer used, and nothing is substituted. But housekeepers who must economize in laundry work still employ them." Parloa advised that even though using mats on a table set only for family was "not wholly objectionable," they should not be used for "ceremonious meals," during which a centerpiece alone should occupy the middle of the table.[53]

Napkins were ubiquitous on nineteenth-century tables, at all meals and for both family and company. They were a crucial tool for maintaining the standards of neatness that good manners demanded. Napkins were generally white and large—often as much as a yard square. They usually matched the damask tablecloth. At dinner parties, a guest might be supplied with two or three different napkins during the course of the meal. Upon arriving at the table, he or she would find a napkin at each place, "folded square, with one fold turned back to inclose [sic] a thick piece of bread; or, the napkin may be folded into a triangle that will stand upright, holding the bread within its folds."[54] The same basic napkin procedure had been described fifty years earlier in *The Workwoman's Guide*: "Dinner napkins are folded in various ways, and are generally put upon the plate, enclosing the roll or bread." The author described the "modes . . . usually adopted": a half-pyramid, a diamond shape, and a diamond within a square.[55]

Although fresh napkins were always used when setting a table for a dinner party or for company, such was not the case for family dinners. Napkin rings were the common symbol of the family or boardinghouse dinner. The impracticality of laundering family table linens on a daily basis made the use of napkin rings a popular, and perfectly acceptable, alternative. Their sometimes elegant and often whimsical forms added an artistic touch to the family table. Napkin rings were most frequently made of silver plate, which gave them a certain degree of status and dignity alongside the other tableware. Their sentimental themes—depictions of children and animals predominated—were perfectly suited to the emotional intimacy of the family circle but would have been out of place in a more formal social situation.

By the middle of the nineteenth century, most homemakers aspired to own matched sets not only of linens but of tableware as well. This impulse drew its inspiration from several sources. Eating with utensils has been identified as a hallmark of civilization since the eighteenth century and was manifested in the highly specialized and large silver, glass, and porcelain services in the French

THE PRINCE OF WALES'S FEATHER.

The Prince of Wales's Feather is a perfectly new design, invented especially for the present work. It is simple in effect and very handsome in appearance. It requires a very stiff crisp serviette. Lay the damask on the table, ironing it

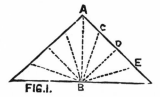

FIG.1.

FIG.2.

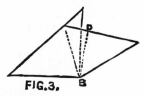

FIG.3.

damp. Fold it from fig. 2 in the Crown, from A to B, using the hot iron to crease it. Without disturbing this fold, crease in half again the reverse way, from C to D, thus reducing the size to a quarter. Smooth it with the iron. Next fold this in half diagonally, like fig. 4 in the Crown. Observe fig. 4, in the

FIG.4.

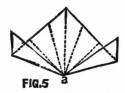

FIG.5

FIG.6.

illustrations on the present page, carefully. Fold it in half from A to B, using the iron; this will produce fig. 2. Make the fold C to B, on one side only, in the manner shown in fig. 3. Then fold it back again at the dotted line D, and it will resemble fig. 4. Fold the other side to match, always using the iron to press every fold. Open it and it will resemble fig. 5, with the folds A, C, D. Make the folds, E, as shown in fig. 5, taking care not to flatten the other

FIG.8.

FIG.7.

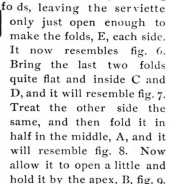

folds, leaving the serviette only just open enough to make the folds, E, each side. It now resembles fig. 6. Bring the last two folds quite flat and inside C and D, and it will resemble fig. 7. Treat the other side the same, and then fold it in half in the middle, A, and it will resemble fig. 8. Now allow it to open a little and hold it by the apex, B, fig. 9. Keep it very much indented

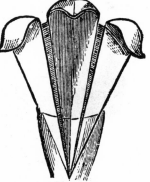

Fig. 10.

FIG.9.

in the centre (A to B); bring the wings or side feathers rather forward, and curl over the three tips of the feathers by bending them with the fingers. Place it upright in a wine glass or a slender single flower glass in the same manner as the Fan is placed. Fig. 10 shows the Prince of Wales's Feather complete.

court. By the time of the French Revolution, eating utensils as we know them today were fully developed in form and function, although they were limited in their distribution and use to members of the wealthy class.[56] Poorer people in both eighteenth-century Europe and America generally used a few common serving spoons and forks, a knife, possibly a steel fork, and one plate—usually of metal, wood, or rough pottery.

By the nineteenth century, in tableware as in other matters of etiquette, French courtly tradition exerted a powerful influence in both Europe and America. The desire for order and symmetry, a legacy of eighteenth-century rationalism, reinforced a preference for harmonious and coordinated tableware. Complexity was understood by the middle class to be emblematic of a heightened level of civilization, as was apparent in all observable rituals of Victorian life—furnishing the home, calling and visiting, and serving and conducting meals.[57] Around 1850, this cultural value manifested itself in an impulse to own services that were larger and more functionally specific. Technological innovations, such as the processes of machine-pressing glass, mechanically decorating earthenware by means of transfer-printing, and electroplating silver onto inexpensive base metals, both accommodated and reinforced these preferences by dramatically lowering the cost of tableware, as well as widening the range of both form and decoration. Between 1850 and 1900 the glass, ceramic, and silver manufacturing industries greatly expanded their production capacities and distribution networks: by the end of

the century, a wide choice in the selection of dinner, tea, glass, and flatware services was available at all socioeconomic levels.

The 1895 Montgomery Ward mail-order catalogue offered dinner and tea services to please any purse. At the top of the line was Haviland & Company's "Carnot" pattern, "artistically hand decorated with delicate sprays of cornflowers in soft tints of pink and blue. The handles are richly finished in gold clouded effect." The fortunes of the Haviland factory paralleled those of the American middle class. Haviland china was by far the most desirable tabletop symbol of success between 1870, when Charles Field Haviland began exporting decorated porcelain to New York, and the end of the century; indeed, even today the name Haviland carries with it a connotation of elegance and desirability. "Carnot" was available in thirty-four different forms, for serving dinner or tea. For everyday use, or if a family could not afford Haviland, Montgomery Ward offered Doulton & Company's "Yale" pattern in "English decorated semi-porcelain" for less than half the price; it was described as "a handsome design of blackberry blossoms and vines in a neutral or slate blue color," available in "new graceful shapes [with] neat gold trimmings [and] scalloped edge plates." At the bottom of the price range was the "Dove Genoa" pattern from Smith & Ford of Staffordshire, England, which included the same functional array as the Doulton service, at 63 percent of the cost.[58]

Tableware manufacturers made many different sets available to fulfill the varying requirements of all of the different dining rituals. Dinner, tea, breakfast, and dessert wares formed the basis of a family's china closet. The inventory of glass and china recommended by Mrs. Ellet to her readers in 1873 included three dozen wine glasses, two dozen champagne glasses, two dozen claret glasses, three dozen goblets, six water carafes, six decanters, one liqueur stand, twelve liqueur glasses, two glass pitchers, one celery glass, one trifle bowl, eight dessert dishes, one full dinner service, one common set for kitchen, one common tea service for kitchen, one "good" tea service, one breakfast service, and one "good" dessert service.[59] Throughout the second half of the nineteenth century, the "kitchen" sets— probably used for both servants and everyday family dining—were most often imported English earthenware, either white ironstone or "graniteware," either plain or decorated with molded and blue-painted edges or all-over printed designs in blue, green, brown, pink, purple, or yellow. "Good" china for the middle class was generally French porcelain. A service for twelve in 1877 could cost as much as $500 for finely decorated French porcelain (probably Sèvres) or as little as $35 for ordinary French china. Sèvres, Dresden, and fine Oriental services cost at least $300, and sets of decorated English and French earthenware ranged between $70 and $125.[60] Sèvres was the most luxurious ware one could imagine and was well beyond the economic grasp of most Americans.

By the 1850s, a complete dinner service was made up of a fairly standard array of components regardless of its style, although the numbers of pieces would have varied considerably from family to family. In 1848, a letter written by a pottery manufacturer to his agent described a shipment of light-blue printed dinnerware, which included twelve dozen flat plates (ten-inch dinner plates), twelve dozen soup plates, eight dozen "twifflers" (smaller plates, about eight inches in diameter), six dozen "muffins" (plates smaller yet, between four inches and seven inches in diameter), twenty-four hot-water plates and stoppers (plates similar to a modern child's feeding dish, with a receptacle for hot water to keep food warm), two root dishes (probably open serving bowls), four "cover dishes" (covered serving bowls), eighteen "dishes" (this term was used for platters) in seven different sizes, ranging from nine to twenty inches long, two "gravy dishes" (platters with a recessed well-and-tree to collect the juices from a roast), two bakers (rectangular serving dishes for baked entrees), two soup tureens "complete" (with lid, ladle, and underplate, or "stand"), two sauce tureens complete (smaller tureens for serving sauce), and finally two "boats and stands" (gravy boats).[61]

This was an enormous number of pieces—514 in all—and no middle-class family would have found it necessary or possible to have so many. Many more plates than today, however, were required to accommodate the elaborate ritual of the Victorian dinner party, with its seemingly endless succession of courses. Catharine Beecher advised her readers in 1858 to have on hand these pieces for a dinner for twelve people: one dozen forks, one dozen tumblers, two dozen wine glasses, twelve soup plates, twelve silver spoons, two dozen large knives, and four dozen plates. This service, she noted, "is to allow one plate for fish, and two for two changes of meat for each guest. Some would provide more," she added—three dozen dessert plates, two dozen dessert forks and knives, one dozen saucers, and one dozen dessert spoons.[62]

This French porcelain dinner service from the 1860s includes a formidable array of tureens, platters, serving dishes, plates, cups, saucers, custard cups, pitchers, gravy boats, and relish dishes—161 pieces in all—enough to accommodate any level of entertaining.

An 1850s invoice from the Boston merchant John Collamore, Jr., & Co., who advertised his firm as "Importers and Dealers in China, Glass, and Earthenware," listed what is probably a much more typical dinner service. In November 1858, he sold to Captain Richard H. Tucker, of Wiscasset, Maine, this dinner set:

1½ doz Plates Dinner
1½ doz Breakfast Plates
1½ doz Tea Plates
1 doz Soup Plates
2 Sauce Tureens
2 Sauce Boats
1 Soup Tureen
4 Oval Covered Vegetable Dishes 2 sizes
7 Oval Meat Dishes Assorted sizes
1 Round Pudding Dish
2 Oval deep Dishes
1 Butter Plate
1 doz Custards
1 Gravy Dish

This set, for which Collamore charged Captain Tucker $22.56, was blue-and-white English earthenware. Porcelain or "China," as it was commonly called, would have been much more expensive.[63]

Breakfast services were also available but were much less common. More often, breakfast plates were included in a dinner set, as they were in the one that Captain Tucker purchased. Inexpensive Chinese export porcelain breakfast sets, popular during the first half of the nineteenth century, commonly included twelve cups and saucers (breakfast teacups were generally of a larger size than for other meals), a "sugar dish and stand," a milk pot, a teapot, a slop bowl (into which dregs or cold tea could be poured before a cup was refilled), and plates. The set might be expanded by the addition of a coffee pot, a "butter boat and stand," and a cake plate.[64] By the end of the century, Maria Parloa described a standard breakfast of fruit and mush (a hot cereal made of boiled cornmeal, oatmeal, or other grains), which required a fruit knife and teaspoon, a fruit plate, and a mush bowl for each person. In addition, there were to be cups and saucers, a sugar bowl and cream pitcher, a coffee pot, a hot milk pot, a butter dish, butter knife, and small butter plates on the table.[65] Her description sounds much like that of sets of the early nineteenth century. Because breakfast was usually an informal meal, special breakfast sets were probably the exception rather than the rule. The middle-class breakfast table was more likely to be set with odd plates, cups, saucers, and silverware.

At the same time that he ordered his dinner set, Richard Tucker also ordered a "White China tea set," which included a teapot, sugar bowl, creamer, waste bowl, two cake plates, one dozen cups and saucers, one dozen plates, one dozen

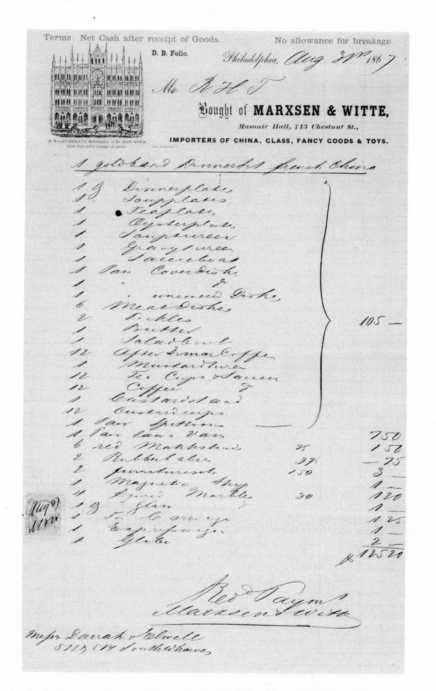

A decade after buying an entire set of blue-and-white English earthenware, Richard Tucker bought a second service—a "gold band" French china dinner set—for $105.

preserve plates, one dozen cup plates, and a butter plate, for which he paid $7.[66] Often a tea set also included a waiter or tray, hot-water urn, spoon holder, and sometimes a syrup or molasses pitcher. Silver-plated tea services became popular during this period and began to displace the hold that English pottery teaware had had in middle-class homes prior to 1850. The plates and cups and saucers, however, continued to be made both of pottery and porcelain, and certain items, such as the syrup pitcher, butter dish, sugar bowl, and creamer, were also commonly available in glass.

Dessert services, intended to be used for fancy dinner or dessert parties, were usually ornately decorated (often with gilding or painted and enameled fruits and flowers) and made of the most expensive materials a family could afford—porcelain, bone china, or fine earthenware, silver, or glass. Imported English and French

This six-piece set sold for $60 hammered and engraved, $56 engraved or engraved satin, or $48 in plain or plain satin.

porcelain dessert services were available to people with a little (or a great deal of) extra money to spend on them. These services were often composed of a series of compotes of varying heights, two or more cake plates, and twelve dessert plates. Glass vessels were often used on the dessert table because their transparent quality offered a view of the brightly colored fruits, cakes, candies, truffles, and bonbons that were the mainstay of the dessert table. Agnes Morton, while extolling the virtues of "artistic" glassware, offered confirmation of its use on the dessert table: "the serving of fruits and bonbons gives the opportunity to display the most brilliant cut-glass, or its comparatively inexpensive substitutes [pressed glass] which are scarcely less pretty in effect." Mrs. Ellet, writing in 1873, also encouraged the use of glass on the dessert table, specifically mentioning "compotes in glass dishes; frosted fruit served on lace paper, in small glass dishes; preserved and dried fruits, in glass dishes. . . ." If a family could not afford cut

Matching "services" of glass dessert wares were available in many different patterns by the 1860s. Typical components included compotes (covered or uncovered) of several sizes and heights, cake stands, pitchers, bowls, "nappies" (small serving bowls), and sweetmeat dishes.

glass, which was quite expensive, or wanted an alternative for less formal occasions, pressed glass was perfectly acceptable. Sarah Josepha Hale mentioned it specifically as early as 1853 with this caveat: "glass dishes and stands made in molds are much cheaper than others, and they have a good appearance, if not placed near cut glass."[67] The manufacturers' trade catalogues of this period and later mention a rich assortment of plates, finger bowls, compotes, jelly glasses, bowls, dishes, decanters, molasses "cans," wine, champagne, and cordial glasses, and footed sweetmeat dishes with covers, intended as vessels for "liquid confects"; the lids would have kept flies out of the sticky syrup.

Accompanying this array of dinner, dessert, tea, and breakfast wares were all of the specialized silver flatware implements required for the service and consumption of food. Recommended "plate" in 1873 included three dozen "prongs" (forks), two dozen tablespoons, a dozen and a half dessert spoons, two dozen teaspoons, six salt spoons, one cheese knife, four butter knives, one asparagus tong, two sugar tongs, two soup ladles, four sauce ladles, two gravy ladles, two sugar ladles, a fish slice (to serve fish), cheese scoops, and grape scissors (for cutting a small bunch of grapes for oneself from the fruit bowl).[68]

Though table knives don't appear in this list, they would certainly have been necessary, along with dessert forks and knives. They were no doubt excluded because knives were not always considered part of a flatware service before the 1890s. A set of flatware in its original box, given as a wedding present to Mary C. Reigart in the 1860s, included forks and spoons, but no knives. Knives, with mother-of-pearl, silver, ivory, or plastic handles, were often sold separately, although they could be obtained with a set. As late as 1894, Agnes Morton noted that the "best dinner knife is of steel, of good quality, with handle of ivory, ebony, or silver." She went on to say that "silver-plated knives are much used; they do not discolor so readily as steel, and are easily kept polished," and thought them "fine for luncheon, but not sharp enough for dinner or breakfast."[69] The meats served at breakfast or dinner—usually beef or pork—required a sharper blade; luncheon, by contrast, did not often include meat. Some advisors warned their readers against the pretension and false economy of "plated ware"—a reference to silver plate. Martha Buell Munn, who could well have afforded sterling silver, listed Lorne flatware—a well-known silver-plate pattern that was introduced in 1878—in her household inventory. Since she was married in 1881, this service, which included 22 dinner knives, 12 dessert knives, 23 dinner forks, 17 dessert forks, 12 tablespoons, 13 teaspoons, and one mustard spoon, may well have been a wedding present to her.[70]

New flatware forms were continually introduced in the latter half of the nineteenth century, and were often related to the introduction or sudden fash-

ionability of certain foods. Asparagus forks and tongs first appeared in the early 1850s, orange spoons around 1880, ice-cream forks also around 1880, ice-cream spoons in the 1860s, and ice-cream knives were available in the 1870s. Individual oyster forks had been available since the 1840s, but during the 1880s both an oyster server and a fried oyster server were introduced, and in 1875, an oyster fork and spoon combination turned up in the marketplace. Not all of these flatware forms were essential for the well-bred hostess; as Agnes Morton explained, only "fruit knives are required, and ice-spoons, orange spoons, and other unique conceits may be provided . . . if one happens to own them."[71]

Most people, excluding the wealthiest members of the upper class—the Vanderbilts, the Mackays, and the Rockefellers—did not have the enormous numbers of place settings, serving utensils, and linens that were recommended by the

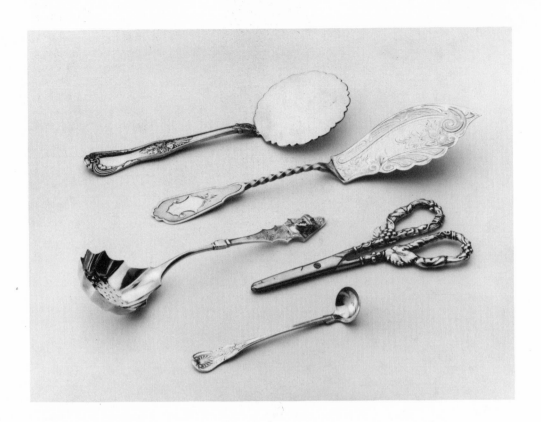

household manuals. Wedding lists, invoices, and household inventories reveal that a middle-class family usually had the capability of serving dinner to somewhere between six and twelve people. Certain kinds of items—dinner plates, dessert spoons, tea spoons—were desirable in greater quantity, since they might be used for entertaining when greater numbers of people were present or a course structure required that one have fresh utensils available for each course. The kinds of wedding presents a bride received were often indicative of the style of life she would be expected to lead after her wedding. Sets of nutpicks, fancy serving spoons for berries, soup ladles, sugar spoons, cake baskets, pie knives, and syrup pitchers would outfit an ordinary middle-class woman adequately for the type of entertaining she would most probably be doing. It was only the more wealthy brides who typically received a wide variety of the more specialized utensils—strawberry forks and horseradish spoons—appropriate to their more frequent and elaborate style of entertaining.

Consider the contrasts in these two Rochester, New York households. When

Buckwheat-cake servers, ice-cream knives and forks, sugar sifters (used to sprinkle sugar on fruit or cakes), grape shears, asparagus tongs, lemonade sippers, oyster forks, cheese scoops, orange spoons, and sardine servers were among the many new flatware implements introduced in the Victorian era, often in response to new or suddenly fashionable foods. Their novelty made them popular wedding gifts.

shoemaker Jonathan C. Babcock died in 1858, his estate included six knives, forks, and spoons, "a lot of" crockery—apparently not important enough to describe further—six plates, six tea cups and saucers, a sugar bowl, and a milk pot, as well as assorted cooking utensils. While these items would have enabled Babcock's family to entertain in a modest manner, they certainly would not have supported the types of meals that can be inferred (from the record of possessions left after he died in 1879) to have taken place in the home of Henry T. Rogers, the treasurer of the Rochester Gaslight Company. Rogers's flatware alone included sixteen salad forks, ten plated tablespoons, eleven plated teaspoons, three silver tablespoons, six silver teaspoons, one silver gravy spoon, one pair of silver sugar tongs, eighteen knives, twelve knives and forks, and twelve silver spoons. His dining room was furnished with a carpet, a gas fixture, and a dining table with eight chairs and a table spread, while Babcock's will contained no mention of any dining-specific furniture beyond eight chairs.[72]

Consider, now, the artifacts in Babcock's and Rogers's inventories, individually and cumulatively, in context. Jonathan Babcock's dining room indicated—as indeed did all of his household furnishings—to himself and all of his peers that he had risen to and was firmly anchored somewhere in the civilized realm of the middle class. Although what he had may have been considered minimal to some, to him those items were the essential components of a civilized existence. Above and beyond that fundamental purpose, his possessions took on the additional function of displaying his economic status: for Babcock and other less affluent members of the middle class, the ability to own goods and the levels of complexity that characterized his domestic environment were an important means through which he could proclaim his middle-class status. For men like Henry Rogers, already firmly rooted in upper regions of the middle class, there was less concern about elevating oneself socially; the complex array of items included in his inventory reflect an inherently formalistic and formulaic world view that had been codified and was readily identifiable in the material world of his dining room.

Jonathan Babcock and Henry Rogers both accumulated, to differing degrees, sets of matching items. In so doing, they affirmed their faith in the power of science and rational thought to transform the world through the products of an industrial society. Matching tableware no doubt satisfied their mutual desire for order and symmetry, values which had been a prevalent inheritance from the Enlightenment, and which helped shape popular thinking about the forms and structures of daily life. The marketplace helped Babcock and Rogers realize these values by providing replicable goods of consistent quality, thereby reinforcing the essential dynamic of capitalism—the accumulation of property.

THE BOUNTIFUL PANTRY

4

FASHIONS IN FOOD AND DRINK

How often do we see the happiness of a husband abridged by the absence of skill, neatness, and economy in the wife! Perhaps he is not able to fix upon the cause, for he does not understand minutely enough the processes upon which domestic order depends, to analyze the difficulty; but he is conscious of discomfort. However improbable it may seem, the health of many a professional man is undermined, and his usefulness curtailed, if not sacrificed, because he habitually eats *bad bread*.[1]

The highly refined manners, tools, and environment of late-nineteenth-century dining provided structure and definition for an age-old—indeed, primal—social activity among animals—eating food. In the nineteenth century, and particularly between 1850 and 1900, not only did the elements of the process of eating change, but the food itself also was altered. Mechanization had transformed all aspects of food production. Small-scale farmers were joined by huge "bonanza" farms, and both sold their goods to mechanized food processors, who flooded the marketplace with ready-made products. Refrigeration made more fresh foods available. Large-scale, efficient transportation networks brought out-of-season foods to consumers, and the rapid expansion of the publishing industry produced a multitude of cookbooks and

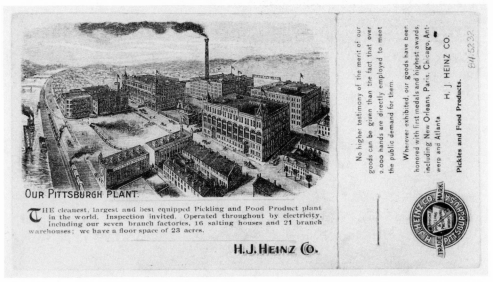

The food-processing empire of Henry J. Heinz began in 1869 with pickled horseradish. By the 1890s, the company had expanded to encompass the now famous fifty-seven varieties of convenience foods.

household manuals to guide the American housewife "scientifically" through the complex tasks of food preparation for family and guests.

The choices people made about what to serve and eat, however, were not completely based on the appeal of new products or the desire for social acceptability. Concerns about nutrition also exerted a powerful cultural influence in the last half of the nineteenth century. Beginning as early as 1832, food reformers, such as Sylvester Graham, were preaching the benefits of nutrition and proper diet as a means of disease prevention. Graham was something of a romantic, who, in the tradition of the eighteenth-century back-to-nature philosophers, wished to reaffirm the relationship between man and nature through the vehicle of nutrition. He asserted that bread, made of unrefined flour and ground from wheat that grew in the earth, was the embodiment of that relationship. He also advocated the consumption of raw fruit and vegetables and was convinced that "food should not be robbed of its most important values in the course of preparation."[2] Mastication, or chewing, was an important aspect of his nutritional scheme; thus, "mushy" foods like mashed potatoes (which he deplored) were to be avoided, as was any bread less than a day old.

Graham and his vegetarian contemporaries were often extreme in their nutritional preachings, but they and some less dogmatic reformers—Catharine Beecher and her sister, Harriet Beecher Stowe, in particular—held a certain amount of appeal for middle-class women. A woman's sphere of influence was limited to husband, home, and family, and within that structure of responsibility, food was a means by which she could effect health and happiness directly. Her role as meal planner became charged with moral overtones, since many of the writers she read and believed in directly linked the condition of her family to the condition of the nation. The popular belief that good health encouraged a Christian soul and ultimately a moral and strong nation led one cookbook author to the conclusion that "the system of morals therefore becomes identified with that of cookery."[3] Throughout the next fifty years, the connections between moral values, health, and food were evident in the introductions and prefaces to numerous cookbooks, in which writers emphasized the need for nutrition and properly prepared meals.

New methods of food processing not only produced new foods for the marketplace but also expanded the access of the middle class to delicacies and prepared foods that had traditionally been available only at considerable cost. In purchasing products, consumers had to pay not only for raw materials, but also for the labor required to process them, which added a certain degree of status as well as convenience to their appeal. Late-nineteenth-century grocers advertised a wide variety of ready-made foods, ranging from ketchup, mustard, and anchovy and soy sauces, to tinned meat, fish, vegetables, fruits, crackers, macaroni, confections, and ice cream. These foods helped diversify the choices for those planning and preparing meals.

The trend toward convenience foods was perhaps yet another bit of evidence of popular faith in the scientific rationalism that had its roots in the Enlightenment, and which by the mid-nineteenth century was one of the most pervasive aspects of American culture. The same scientific principles that had built the foundations of the American factory system during the first half of the century were being applied to domestic activities during the second fifty years. Striving for household efficiency, American women re-evaluated their daily routines and adopted a burgeoning variety of labor-saving devices—carpet sweepers, vacuum cleaners, sewing machines, meat grinders, and cast-iron ranges—that would (they hoped) make their homes run more smoothly. The rhetoric of the household manuals reinforced the image of the household as a well-oiled machine. In the words of one, "A woman's workshop ought to be as well supplied as her husband's is."[4]

In 1809, a French inventor, Nicholas Appert, developed a vacuum exhaust process to seal glass jars hermetically. Within fourteen years, Thomas Kensett, of New York, had taken out his first patent for the tin can. The canning industry began in the East Coast fishing trade as an attempt to overcome the difficulty of transporting highly perishable fish. Lobster, salmon, and oysters were the first foods canned. These early canned goods were undoubtedly expensive, which elevated them from plain food to high-status comestibles. In a world in which social aspirations were becoming a crucial factor in shaping the marketplace, manufacturers responded quickly to the voice of the consumer, elaborating on the successes of their initial product and expanding the range of options. As demand for these canned foods grew, vegetables—corn, tomatoes, and peas—were added, as were fruits and cooked meats, fowl, fish, and shellfish. Canners processed vast quantities of the abundant American harvests. In 1855, Mills B. Espey & Company, of Philadelphia, canned "ten tons of cherries, five tons [of] strawberries, ten thousand baskets of peaches, tomatoes, and pears, and four thousand bushels of plums, gooseberries, and quinces."[5]

A tomato-processing plant in New Jersey, described in the book *Ten Acres Enough* by Edmund Morris in 1864, was packing 50,000 cans each season. Three hundred employees processed 150 bushels of New Jersey-grown tomatoes a day. During the winter, when there was no crop to process, tinsmiths who were employees of the company busied themselves making the cans. Generally, food processors hired their own tinsmiths to make tin cans during the early years of commercial canning, and a skilled tinsmith could produce about fifty cans a day. By 1849, Henry Evans had developed a machine that made bottoms and tops of cans (the most difficult part of the process). Shortly thereafter, a mechanical method of soldering the side seam was developed. Mr. Morris continued his description of the tomato-canning factory:

> The building in which the business is carried on was constructed expressly for it. At one end of the room in which the canning is done is a range of brick-work supporting three large boilers; and adjoining is another large boiler, in which the scalding is done. The tomatoes are first thrown into this scalder, and after remaining there a sufficient time, are thrown upon a large table, on each side of which are ten or twelve young women, who rapidly divest them of their leathery hides. The peeled tomatoes are then thrown into the boilers, where they remain until they are raised to a boiling heat, when they are rapidly poured into the cans, and these are carried to the tinmen, who, with a dexterity truly marvellous, place the caps upon them, and solder them down, then they are piled up to cool, after which they are labelled, and are ready for market. The rapidity and the system with which all this is done is most remarkable, one of the tinmen soldering nearly a hundred cans in an hour.[6]

By 1876, the most advanced canners sealed their cans on an assembly line. So rapidly did technological change overtake the industry that by the 1880s, the makers of tin cans were no longer employed by the food producers but had become a separate packaging industry. The canned-food industry grew explosively in the middle decades of the nineteenth century. In 1840 two skilled tinsmiths could produce 120 cans per day; in the 1850s two unskilled workers could manufacture 1,500 per day. Five million cans of food were produced in 1860; in ten years, 30 million entered the marketplace. The value of the output of the food-canning industry increased by 200 percent during the next decade.[7]

Much like today, the most popular canned foods in nineteenth-century American homes were tomatoes, corn, beans, and peas, but quite a range was actually available. The 1882 edition of the *Philadelphia Cash Grocer*, a trade journal, listed at least fifty-one different types of canned goods, including asparagus, okra, succotash, apples, applesauce, blackberries, pears, pie peaches, oysters, lobster, salmon, corned beef, roast beef, and condensed milk.[8] Fabens & Graham, a Boston food dealer, advertised in the same year a comparable variety of foods, including plums, cherries, quinces, grapes, pineapple, strawberries, raspberries, blueberries, gooseberries, apricots, cranberry sauce, squash, green corn, pumpkins, baked beans, French mushrooms, veal, lamb, mutton, turkey, chicken, goose, lambs' tongues, pigs' feet, tripe, sausage meat, shrimp, clams, deviled crab, and mackerel.[9]

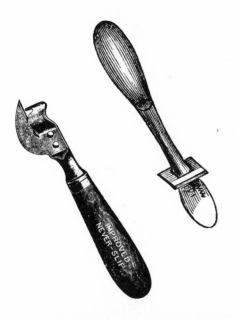

The first American patent for a can opener (left)—a device necessitated by the rapidly increasing use of canned foods—was issued to Ezra J. Warner of Waterbury, Connecticut, in 1858. The ready availability of canned foods threatened, in some minds, a deterioration in home cooking skills, and ultimately, the decline of family life in general.

For middle-class housekeepers, many of these canned goods were new and exotic foods. French mushrooms or pineapple—which must be grown in a tropical climate—were certainly not staple items in the diets of ordinary families before mass canning, nor were lobster or deviled crab, except on the coast. Canned foods added novelty and variety to everyday American menus. Boston housewives could also buy "Huckins' Hermetically Sealed Soups," including tomato, mock turtle, oxtail, julienne, pea, beef, chicken, macaroni, vermicelli, consommé, mutton broth, okra or gumbo, mulligatawny, green turtle, and terrapin. These soups, which came in quart cans, were advertised as being "ready for immediate use" and would "save time and trouble of cooking."[10]

The impact of the growth of canned foods was fourfold: it introduced hitherto unknown foods to a widespread consumer market; it provided easy access to food for isolated regions; it eased the drudgery of cooking for a multitude of

T. A. Snider of Cincinnati offered consumers a variety of apparently delicious canned soups, including vegetable, julienne, mock turtle, consommé, beef, bouillon, ox-tail, mulligatawny, chicken gumbo, chicken, printanier, tomato, and mutton broth.

Home canning was greatly facilitated by the introduction of standardized jars and lids, first patented by John Landis Mason in 1858.

working- and middle-class women; and it allowed these women to serve a variety of foods once available only to the wealthy. Seafood, for example, could now be served in homes far from the sea, and exotic fruits, such as pineapple, could be available year round in northern cities. Despite the fact that many women continued to can their own produce (particularly fruits), and despite the growth of this practice with the introduction of the Mason jar in 1858, the availability of canned produce forever altered American life.[11]

Meat—beef, pork, and mutton or lamb—was one of the staple foods found every day on American tables. Pork had been the most commonly eaten meat during the first half of the nineteenth century; its early popularity was due to the ease with which pigs could be raised. They were often fed slops or table scraps, which caused concern among many people about pork as a source of disease. Eliza Leslie, in her 1857 cookbook, cautioned her readers on the problems of pork:

> No animal tastes more of its food than a pig. If allowed to eat the garbage of fish, they will not only have a fishy taste, but a smell of fish so intolerable, when cooking, that such pork cannot be endured in the house. During the two months that they are kept up to fatten, all their food must be wholesome as well as abundant, and it does them much good to have soap-suds given to them occasionally. Let them have plenty of corn, and plenty of fresh water. They will thrive better and make finer pork, if their pens are not allowed to be dirty. No animal actually likes dirt, and even pigs would be clean if they knew how. It is very beneficial to young pigs to wash them well in soap and water. We have seen this often done with great care.[12]

As Americans came to understand more about the origins of illnesses, the merits of beef came into clearer focus. Beef, the traditional food of the English, had the added enhancement of being considered more refined than pork. This fact alone helps us to understand why middle-class Americans, when given the option, chose beef over pork, as they did regularly by the 1850s. According to an article in *Harper's Weekly* in 1854, "the commonest meal in America from coast to coast is steak," and in 1861, English traveler Anthony Trollope wrote that the Americans consumed twice as much beef as the English. He described an American supper consisting of "beefsteaks and tea, and apple jam, and hotcakes, and light fixings."[13]

The application of scientific principles to the raising, transporting, slaughtering, and packing of meat—beef and pork especially—made these meats universally available to the growing number of Americans who lived in large towns and cities, far from the open countryside, where such animals were raised. This was especially true of cattle, which needed large amounts of land on which to graze. Even though some farmers still raised pigs in the city, most Americans began to buy their meat from butchers, who got their sides of meat from large-scale processors. According to *Harper's Weekly*, "During the week ending December 20, 1864, there were received in New York nearly 7,000 beeves, about 27,000 sheep, and as many swine" for the holiday season.[14] Urbanization had created a cultural dependency upon an efficient transportation network, since city dwellers no longer grew or raised much of their own food.

By the end of the Civil War, the meat industry in America was centered in Chicago. The Union Stockyards, the largest cattle market in the world, opened in 1865. From there, cattle and hogs were shipped by train to cities all over the country, to be slaughtered, dressed, and marketed. During the next twenty years,

Shopping for the Christmas game or poultry in Washington Market.

refrigerated railroad cars enabled meat packers to do their slaughtering at the beginning rather than at the end of the trip—saving the animals the hardship (and the accompanying sickness and weight loss) of the journey. The first meat shipped from Chicago to Boston in a refrigerated car made the journey in 1868, and by the mid-1880s, fresh fruit and vegetables from California were riding the rails to Eastern markets.[15] In March 1884, Mrs. Sarah Hollister, in Rochester, New York—a northern, inland city—was able to offer a menu to her dinner guests that included fresh oysters on the half shell, mock turtle soup, lobster farcis, fillet of beef with mushroom sauce, green peas, pickled peaches, French salad, oranges, grapes, and figs—none of which would have been indigenous to Rochester at that time of year.[16]

The increasing numbers of options available to consumers at the grocery store lent new meanings to certain kinds of foods. Food became a luxury item as well

Refrigerated transportation of meat and produce, which began shortly after the Civil War, greatly expanded the variety of foods available to middle-class Americans, most of whom lived in cities and towns far from the sources of supply.

as a necessity, and food producers competed to capture the growing discretionary income of middle-class families. Certain kinds of foods could effectively communicate both character and status to family and guests. Processed foods were "modern." They were scientific and efficient in an age when domestic activities were being scrutinized by analysts advocating those virtues. Purchasers using them were thus educated and up-to-date, especially if they used new products whose processing was sophisticated, such as condensed milk (patented by Gail Borden in 1856). According to Fannie Farmer in her famous *Boston Cooking-School Cook Book*: "Fresh condensed milk, a form of evaporated milk, is sold in bulk, and is preferred by many to serve with coffee. Various brands of condensed milk and cream are on the market in tin cans, hermetically sealed."[17]

The words "evaporated" and "condensed" helped to enhance the quasiscientific identity—and thus acceptability—of this product. Its popularity was strengthened by its widespread use by the Union Army during the Civil War. Many soldiers developed a taste for it and introduced it into their households after the hostilities had ended.[18] The popularity and even prestige of condensed milk is perhaps most clearly demonstrated by the mass production and marketing of its own specialized utensils. In 1891 the tableware firm of Simpson, Hall, Miller and Company offered a silver-plated "Condensed Milk Can Holder," aimed in price

COPYRIGHTED 1887 BY THE N.Y. CONDENSED MILK CO.

Condensed milk was especially recommended for children because it was thought to be safer than fresh milk.

and specificity at a middle-class consumer. The luxury status accorded condensed milk can be traced to its associations with cream, for which it was a less costly substitute. It was typically used on the tea tables of those who were unable or unwilling to pay for cream. Evidence of working-class consumption of condensed milk is evident in the food budget of a harness cleaner's family. The family of twelve spent slightly less than 10 percent a week of its $870 annual income in 1907 on food, and the weekly expenditure included $.27 for three cans of condensed milk "for tea and to spread on bread when children can have no butter."[19]

Not everyone welcomed the food and drinks in gray cylindrical tins with colorful labels. Some critics thought the new goods tasted "tinny," and with perhaps a thinly veiled concern for a life gone too soft, criticized women who relied on processed foods instead of their own cooking. Cookbook writers also stressed the nutritional and economic values of fresh meat and produce; when giving directions for outfitting a storeroom, typically the only canned or processed

With the advent of canned and bottled food came the social dilemma of deciding how best to serve them. Those who objected to the practice of placing the condensed-milk can directly on the table could pour the milk into a pressed-glass and silver-plated server or even use a special can holder.

foods mentioned were "pickles and preserves, prepared and purchased sauces and all sorts of groceries."[20]

The virtues of hard work and home cooking were so important that canned vegetables or meats were rarely listed in recipes or on menus. As early as 1829, Mrs. William Parkes discussed the virtues of homemade versus "store-bought" products: "In general, *preserves* form a part of a dessert, either West Indian or English; and when the latter are made at home, they are usually better in quality, and one half cheaper, than those purchased at the confectioner's."[21] Nonetheless, the number and variety of canned goods produced and the number of grocers, provisioners, confectioners, and other retail food suppliers listed in city directories indicate that these products were widely used in spite of advice to the contrary. Commercially prepared and processed foods were useful even to the most stringent critics. Eliza Leslie reminded her readers in 1864 that for the best homemade teacakes, "practice makes perfect," but she cautioned that one was never to serve failed cakes. In case that unfortunate circumstance should result, a woman was to "send to a shop for others," being careful, Miss Leslie maintained, to send for them in the early part of the afternoon "to allow time to return them if defrauded by the confectioner."[22]

Purchasing ready-made food outside the home united two once-separate spheres—that of domesticity and the more worldly sphere of commerce. During the early nineteenth century, as Faye Dudden has pointed out, marketing was largely done by men, who would go to the large open-air markets that existed in most cities to buy meat and produce for the family. By about 1850, a shift occurred: more and more often, women were charged with the responsibility of doing the family shopping. *The Home, A Fireside Monthly Companion and Guide* suggested that in 1856 husbands were busy enough, "without the additional burden of what properly belongs to their wives, going to market, dealing with the grocer." By the late 1880s, a husband was not expected to "understand his wife's business as well as she does herself." This change in marketing procedures paralleled a change in the structure of the marketplace itself during this period, as large wholesale markets were supplanted by smaller retail specialty outlets for meat, groceries, baked goods, and other kinds of food. In addition, as family menus and recipes became more complicated, the job of food shopping required a more sophisticated knowledge about their ingredients. A woman had to guard her home during these transactions, lest the corruption that characterized the outside sphere taint the sanctity of the inner one.[23]

Foods from distant areas were generally held in high esteem. European foods, especially French and English, were particularly impressive and would have placed an aura of refinement and "good taste" about any hostess who served

FANCY GROCERIES.

In Fancy Groceries, imported and domestic, Preserves, etc., we have the largest stock and most varied assortment of any house in New England. Our assortment includes many articles not kept in stock by any other concern in this city. The quality of these goods is, beyond question, absolutely the very finest possible to secure, and all are sold at as low prices as can consistently be made, and maintain the finest quality.

This Department is located at the extreme southerly part of our store on Washington Street, and is well worthy of a visit. Below we give a partial list of articles contained therein, but which gives only a faint idea of the immense stock and almost limitless assortment.

Weisbaden Fruits (large) . . . . . . .80 and $ .90	Crosse & Blackwell's Olives, qts. . . . . . . $ .60
" " (small). . . . . . .55 and .60	" " " pts. 35
Curtice Bros. Co.'s Preserves, 1 lb. 35	" " " ½ pts. 20
" " " 3 lb. jars . . . 1.00	Crary & Co.'s Olives, pts. 30
" " " 5 lb. " . . . 1.50	Daisy Olives 10
" " " qts. 50	French Pitted Olives 40
Teyssonneau Fruits in marasquin. 90	" Stuffed " 45
" " " juice 80	Gordon & Dilworth's Mammoth Olives 60
Gordon & Dilworth's Brandy Fruits . .90 and 1.10	Capers Capotes 15
" " Ass'd Fruits (in syrup)	" Nonpareil 25
.25, .50 and .70	" Surfines 1.00
Dunbar's Figs in Cordial 55	French Peas and Beans 35
J. H. Flickinger's California Fruits, qt. jars . . .60	" Mushrooms 40
L. & P. Worcestershire Sauce . . .25, .45 and .70	Anchovies (in oil) 65
MacUrquarht's Worcestershire Sauce .45 and .70	Moir's Soups (in glass) . . . . . . .50 and .75
Halford's Sauce . . . . .20 and .30	Pickled Lobster " 40
Walnut Catsup, C. & B. . . . . . . .20 and .40	Oysters " . . . . .35 and .60
Mushroom " " . . . . . . .20 and .35	Shrimps " 60
Ess. Anchovies " . . . . . . .35 and .60	Clams " 50
Anchovy Paste " 35	Mussels " 45
Bloater " " 30	Pickled Lamb's Tongues . . . . . . .30 and .45
Durkee's Salad Dressing . . . . . . .25 and .40	Asparagus (French) 65
Cowdrey's Salad Cream . . . . . . .25 and .40	Armour's Extract Beef (solid),2 oz. 37
Rae's Lucca Oil . . . . .25, .40 and .65	" " " 4 oz. 70
Plagniol's Olive Oil . . . . . .25, .40 and .65	" " " 8 oz. 1.35
Loubon Salad Oil . . . . . . .10, .15 and .25	" " " 16 oz. 2.40
Fontaine's Olive Oil 1.25	" " " (liquid),4 oz. 50
Crosse & Blackwell's Pickles, qts. 55	" " " 16 oz. . . . . .
" " " pts. 33	Liebig's " " (solid), 2 oz. 40
" " " ½ pts. 20	" " " 4 oz. 75
Bunker Hill Pickles, pts. 25	" " " 8 oz. 1.40
" " " ½ pts. 15	" " " 16 oz. 2.50

them. Women with some degree of discretionary income to spend on food would surely have been tempted by the imported delicacies listed in 1882 by Bray & Hayes, a Boston food importer:

> Crosse & Blackwell's English Pickles, Sauces, Condiments, Preserves; Rae & Co.'s Finest Italian Salad Oil; Keen's London Mustard; French Peas; Pâté de Foie Gras; Truffles; Italian Macaroni and Fancy Pastes; Guava Jelly; Worcestershire, Etc., Sauces; Foreign Cheese and Fancy Biscuits; Chinese Preserved Ginger; and Irish and Scotch Oatmeal.

Eliza Leslie discussed the availability and protocol for using "Store Sauces," in her 1857 *New Cookery Book*: "The celebrated English sauces for fish and game, Harvey's Sauce (which is the best), Quin's, Reading's, Kitchener's, Soyer's, & c., are all very good, and keep well, if genuine. They are imported in small sealed bottles, and are to be had of all the best grocers. To make them at home, is so troublesome and expensive, that it is better to buy them. They are, however, very nice, and are generally introduced at dinner parties, a little being mixed on your plate with the melted butter. If you have no fish castors, bring these sauces to table in their own bottles, to be carried round by a servant."[24]

Etiquette writer Eliza Leslie advised housewives to serve "store sauces" in a caster set. As today, many women probably disregarded her advice, preferring instead to bring the bottle directly to the table.

THE

BOUNTIFUL

PANTRY

1 0 7

In 1873, Elizabeth F. Ellet stated her rationale for serving imported foods: "In the dessert I generally introduce some new importation such as bananas, sugar-cane, American Lady apples, prickly pears, etc.; these also give a subject for the gentlemen to talk about when the ladies have left, as freetrade, colonial policy, etc."[25] Some of these food items were different enough and of sufficient status to induce manufacturers to produce special serving utensils. When bananas were broadly introduced in the 1880s, tableware designers and glass manufacturers quickly responded by producing special footed serving bowls, called banana bowls or banana boats, which carefully cradled a bunch of bananas. With the improvements in the transportation capabilities of the 1870s, oranges—highly perishable fruit, which had earlier been virtually unavailable in the North—became common enough that the silver tableware manufacturing company Holmes, Booth, & Haydens introduced a special "orange peeler." Patented in 1879, the tool was designed to overcome popular anxiety about the proper procedure for eating oranges. The firm's advertising literature posed this question to would-be buyers: "Who has not experienced the necessity for something of [this] kind, when compelled to peel this luscious fruit (for want of a better means) with thumb

The introduction of bananas to middle-class America in the 1880s generated a new table accessory: the banana bowl or banana boat.

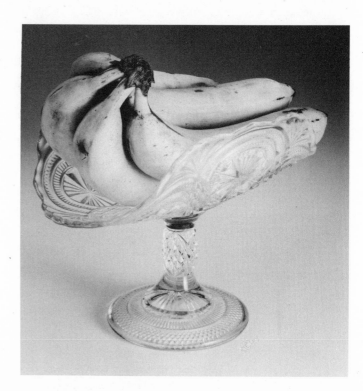

and fingers?"[26] Holmes, Booth, & Haydens was convinced that its orange peeler was a necessity for hotels, restaurants, and individual families.

Etiquette writers, as well as manufacturers, offered practical advice about the best way to eat oranges in refined society. As early as 1864, Eliza Leslie had written, "It is very ungraceful to eat an orange at table, unless having cut a bit off the top, you eat the inside with a teaspoon."[27] Within twenty years, this advice had been transformed into a specialized spoon with a small bowl and pointed tip for eating oranges. Orange spoons captured the imagination of many people. A bride in 1890 noted that she had received "a dozen sterling silver orange spoons" as a wedding gift, and in 1897 Mrs. Angus MacDonald, of Rochester, New York, noted in her diary that she had bought an "orange spoon" and had it engraved "1847–97."[28] Other orange-related tableware introduced in the 1890s included orange cups—footed dishes with corkscrew or spear devices for holding the halved orange in place—and orange knives, "in table and pocket sizes." The orange knives, distinguished by a sawtooth blade on one edge, were available with orange spoons in sets of one pair.[29]

Some foods were important not because they were imported but because of

Orange cups designed to hold half an orange in place for eating, orange knives or peelers, and orange spoons with pointed tips all enhanced the prestige of those who served fresh imported oranges.

their historical associations. Common celery was considered a high-status food by middle-class Americans in the late nineteenth century; originally native to Europe, Asia, and Africa, celery had a distinguished history traceable to Homer's *Odyssey* as *Apium graveolens*. It was first used as food in sixteenth-century France, although only as a flavoring; by the mid-seventeenth century, the stalks and leaves were sometimes dressed with oil and eaten. The plant was improved during the eighteenth century, and its use became more common among the wealthy. Growing it was labor-intensive; it had to be blanched, or surrounded by built-up piles of soil, to preserve the whiteness and sweetness of its stalks. In accord with its status, celery was given a prominent position on the table by means of special celery stands or vases. These were usually made of either decorated glass or silver—both luxury materials—and could be tall, footed, vaselike forms or low baskets. Stands were much more popular in the 1860s and 1870s and outnumbered the baskets by a ratio of 17 to 1 in silver-manufacturers' catalogues. Most popular during the 1880s, celery stands were eclipsed in the 1890s by low

Glass or silver celery vases elevated celery to a position of leafy prominence on the dinner table, in accordance with its status as a hothouse vegetable.

celery dishes: the 1888–1891 Hobbs Glass Company catalogue showed no stands, only oval-shaped celery "yachts" and "boats." By 1900, the tall celery stands were nearly completely out of fashion, as celery lost its cachet. These low stands relegated celery to a much less prominent position on the landscape of the tabletop, and their appearance was paralleled by the development in the 1880s of a new, easier-to-grow, self-blanching, commercial variety of celery, which greatly increased its availability, and made it a much more ordinary household vegetable.[30]

Sardines were another high-status food, perhaps because, as one of the first canned foods available, they remained "exotic." They were frequently listed in cookbooks as a recommended "kickshaw" (side dish or relish) during the soup course. Special sardine boxes were manufactured for serving them, often graced

Cookbooks frequently recommended sardines, a canned delicacy usually imported from Europe, as a "kickshaw" (relish) to be served during the soup course at dinner. Sardines were considered elegant enough to merit their own special serving utensils.

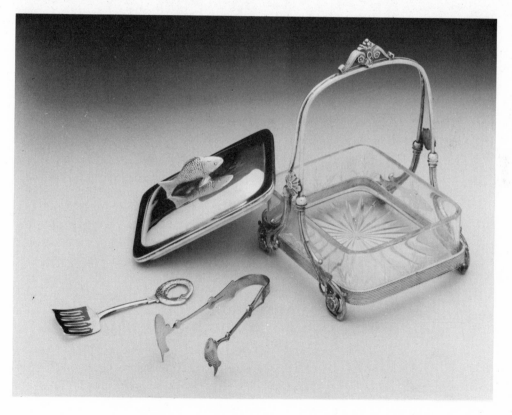

with swimming fish on the sides or as a finial on the lid. New York silver merchant J. F. Curran & Company included silver sardine boxes in its 1868 catalogue. Such boxes were also available in glass and ceramic materials—especially majolica, a brightly colored glazed ware.[31] Silver sardine boxes usually had glass inserts or boxes to prevent odors, since it was easier to clean the oily residue from glass than from metal. For those who did not own special sardine boxes, instructions for serving sardines were given in an 1891 article in the *Ladies' Home Journal*: "Open the box carefully with a can-opener, remove the lid and set the box on a china plate, providing a silver fork to serve them with."[32] Like oranges and bananas, there were special flatware implements for the consumption of sardines—sardine forks, introduced around 1880; sardine tongs, introduced about 1885; and a "sardine helper," which also appeared around 1880. Sardine utensils continued to appear in numerous other silver-manufacturers' catalogues and remained popular at least through 1895, when Caroline T. Lyon received a sardine fork as a wedding present.[33]

In addition to actual foods that came from far away, Americans were also impressed by recipes, foods, or methods of serving that had foreign associations. One American writer effusively described French food for her readers: "Such heavenly garnishes, and flowers everywhere, and the loveliest side dishes, and everything so exquisitely served! When I think of them, I abominate our great vulgar joints and stiff dinner-table."[34] Since the late eighteenth century, American cuisine had been influenced by the French, and such items as fondues, ices, salads, bonbons, sweet oils, tomatoes, and fricassees began to enter the American food vocabulary. After the Louisiana Purchase in 1803, Americans began to develop an interest in Southern dishes, like gumbo, although it is likely that some of the

dish's savory quality was lost in translation. Elizabeth Ellet's recipe for gumbo in 1873 suggests some alteration: "Two quarts fresh ochras, the same of ripe tomatoes, scalded and peeled; put them in a pan to melt with butter, pepper and salt; strain through the colander, and dish the jelly, to eat with toast."[35] As more and more European and Asian immigrants entered the United States during the last quarter of the nineteenth century, interest in other foreign cuisines flourished. A chefs' guide of 1899 listed information about German, Chinese, Oriental (Turkish), Jewish, Italian, Russian, and Scottish cookery.[36]

Salad was one of the most pervasive French influences during the early nineteenth century, and it rapidly became an integral part of any dinner. It was often preceded by the word "French," to identify it as a green, leafy salad dressed with oil and vinegar, mashed egg yolk, and a little mustard, as distinct from the chicken or lobster salads, which were also quite common. A luncheon given by Sarah Granger Hollister for fifteen friends in 1884 included bean soup, lamb chops, green peas, French salad, sherbet, cheese and crackers, fruit, olives, jelly, pickles, and punch. The author of *The American Practical Cookery-Book* outlined the protocol for serving salad for her readers in 1861, stating that it should be offered as part of the second course, "given with the roast meat; it should be placed fresh upon the table, then removed and dressed by a waiter." In the event that one encountered salad when dining at a hotel, Eliza Leslie warned her readers that salad was dressed usually by the gentlemen, not the ladies. The gentleman was to "mix up the dressing on a separate plate, and then add it to the lettuce, and offer it around, as he chose."[37]

Prior to the late nineteenth century, only wealthy people ate salad with any regularity, as Fannie Merritt Farmer noted in 1896: "Salads, which constitute a course in almost every dinner, but a few years since seldom appeared on the table." This was largely because of the perishability of lettuce. The development

THE
BOUNTIFUL
PANTRY

· —— ·

1 1 3

The elegance of salad, a fashionable dining legacy from the French, was enhanced by opulent salad servers and lettuce forks.

of glass houses for the commercial production of vegetables began in the Boston area in the 1840s, but did not really gain momentum until the 1870s. By 1900, there were two hundred acres of vegetables—mainly lettuce, radishes, tomatoes, and cucumbers—under glass around Boston, to supply American tables with fresh green salad for lunch or dinner year-round, but at a rather high price. Head lettuce from California was not commercially available prior to 1900. Although refrigerated transportation was commonly used by the 1880s, lettuce was unable to withstand the rigors of travel. In 1903, a strain we now call iceberg was developed for long-distance shipping, and has transformed the contents of the salad bowl.[38]

The publication in 1825 of Brillat-Savarin's *Physiologie du Goût (The Nature of Taste)* introduced many Americans to an unprecedented array of French foods, even if only vicariously. Within thirty years, vegetables commonly associated with France could be seen in American gardening books, such as Robert Buist's *Family Kitchen Gardener*. Buist spoke encouragingly about endive, stating that "the *French* are particularly fond of it, using it raw, pickled, fried and boiled, esteeming it exceedingly wholesome in every form...." Buist also praised cress (watercress), with the comment that "in Europe, it is daily on the tables of the wealthy."[39]

It was the elegance of French desserts, however, that most intrigued and attracted Americans. In her diary, Almira MacDonald described a "very elaborate dinner with champagne, charlotte ruche [*sic*] to complete after the gents left for the smoking room, tiny cups of coffee...."[40] Charlotte russe was one of the most impressive desserts that could have been served at the time and was mentioned frequently in accounts of dinner and dessert parties during the late nineteenth century. Catharine Beecher volunteered two different recipes for it, describing it as a combination of rich custard and tall sponge cake. One was to slice one inch from the bottom of the cake, turn it over onto its top in a mold and scoop out the insides, leaving one-inch walls. The cavity was then filled with the custard, the bottom slice replaced, and the whole chilled. It could then be turned out on a cake plate and ornamented with frosting or candy sugar flowers.[41] Eliza Leslie offered a similar recipe that she merely called Charlotte-Strawberry or Raspberry. These were both made by "arranging in glass bowls slices of cake cut in even and regular forms, and spread thickly over with fruit mashed to a jam with white sugar—the bowls being heaped with whipped cream."[42]

French cooking was admired not only for its visual effects and its gastronomic appeal, but also for its economy and careful technique. Elizabeth F. Ellet wrote:

> French cooks subject their meats to a gradual long continued action of heat, making the fibre perfectly tender. The English and Americans cook them too fast; the French would pronounce such food only fit for barbarians. Another peculiarity of French cooking is the variety of flavors imparted to meat. A great number of dishes are prepared from a few original substances, and the addition of a particular sauce gives its name to the dish. In our cooking, the flavor peculiar to each meat is preserved, and no condiment is suffered to over power it. French dishes are more sightly; light and elegant dishes, not ponderous masses, tempt the appetite. The French cooking is also more economical. Nothing is wasted; and many ingredients are brought into use which we would cast aside as useless.[43]

Mary F. Henderson, in her cookbook *Practical Cooking, and Dinner Giving* of 1878, provided the weekly menu of a typical French family "of limited means" who had recently emigrated to the United States:

Beef soup (soup bone), 10 cents
Veal blanquette and boiled potatoes (knuckle of veal), 15 cents
Salad of sliced tomatoes, 2 or 3 cents
Boiled rice, with a border of stewed small pears
(green, or of common variety), 10 cents

· ———— ·

Onion or bean soup, 5 cents
Fish (en matelote), 15 cents
Croquettes (made of the remains of the cold beef-soup meat,
and rice), with a tomato sauce
Salad of cold boiled potatoes
Fried bread-pudding

· ———— ·

Potato soup
Round steak, rolled, with baked, parboiled
onions, 25 cents
Fried bread-pudding

· ———— ·

Tomato soup
Beef à la mode, with spinach, 40 cents (enough for two
dinners)
Salad of potatoes and parsley
Rice-pudding

· ———— ·

Noodle soup
Mutton ragout, with potatoes, 25 cents
Noodles and stuffed tomatoes
Cheese omelet[44]

Not all writers were as uncritical of French food as Mrs. Ellet and Mrs. Henderson. Marion Harland wrote, "It is a substantial comfort to the Anglo-Saxon stomach for its owner to know what he is eating." She went on to describe French cooking as consisting of meals prepared, much to her evident distaste, from "Swill"—disguised by "exotic" sauces, or fish preserved in vinegar and charcoal. Indeed, one fictional upper-class inhabitant of a brownstone in Murray

Hill in New York City claimed that his French chef "could so disguise and glorify even a pair of old boot-tops with his sauces, that you would think you were eating antelope steaks, served with honey of Hymettus."[45] Americans were generally ambivalent about the French, particularly after the 1871 Paris commune, when bands of socialists and Communists seized the city. Though they greatly admired French culture—its art, fashion, manners, and cooking—France itself seemed politically corrupt, morally bankrupt, and excessive in all respects. One had to be careful: French sauces, like French culture, might be merely a veneer, concealing "swill" and decadence that had the potential to infect the American family.

Food-related terminology provided Americans with a series of cues about the nature of both food and the consumer. For example, "rich" meant more than the shortening-and-sugar connotation it has acquired in late-twentieth-century cooking. Menus and recipes frequently used this adjective for foods served at company dinners, teas, and dessert parties, where display was an important aspect of the meal. Catharine Beecher offered both "Plain" and "Rich" recipes in the categories of "Puddings and Pies" and "Articles for Dessert or Evening Parties." Typically, the ingredients that effected the transition from plain to rich were sugar, butter, cream, and eggs. "Plain Custard," for example, included four eggs, milk, flour, peach leaves for flavor, and an unspecified sweetener; "A Richer Custard" called for six eggs, milk, and sugar; and "Rich Custard" required a quart of cream, six eggs, brandy, peach water, lemon brandy, and almonds.[46] The cost of ingredients for the three varied considerably, with the price of the third increased especially by the inclusion of cream, liqueurs, and almonds. This progression of "richness" appears throughout Beecher's recipes, as well as in other cookbooks, a pattern all the more remarkable since Beecher was consciously offering her readers a nutritional respite from the harmful effects of rich foods (dyspepsia, or indigestion). Beecher's recipes constituted a "reform" of American cooking, and her proselytizing indicates just how calorie-laden, "heavy," and perhaps indigestible American cooking was. Nevertheless, her readers were ready to use her "rich" recipes when the occasion demanded it.

Butter, like sugar and cream, had traditional status as a luxury item because of its cost and perishability. Prior to 1861, when factory or "creamery" production of butter began in the United States, butter was commonly made at home by rural women, who often sold their product to city grocers. The milk was set out in the dairy in pans to raise the cream, which was then ripened and churned by hand into butter. In 1861, Alanson Slaughter, of Wallkill, New York, established the first butter factory, or creamery, using a principle that had been employed by cheese producers for about ten years—that of cooperative pooling of milk supplies by dairy farmers. Slaughter used milk from 375 cows to produce butter that, if not as good as the highest-quality farmhouse butter, had the advantage of uniformly high quality. The invention of the cream separator in 1880, which used the principle of centrifugal force to separate the heavier butterfat particles from the lighter, water portions of milk, speeded up the process considerably, with a corresponding decrease in the cost of production.[47]

Factory production did not immediately put an end to the "old way," especially on the farm. "Always to make *good butter* or cheese shows great care and excellent judgment in the farmer's wife," Elizabeth F. Ellet advised her readers in 1873. "When every department of the dairy is kept perfectly neat, there is hardly any exhibition of woman's industry more likely to make her husband proud. . . ."[48] Factory production, however, did relieve some of the burden of work for farm women, as is suggested in the diary of Julia Holmes Cook of Batavia. On 6 May 1881, she noted that she had sent "milk to factory." Two weeks later she wrote, "Have kept the milk home and packed 9 gals butter. Am glad to send the milk to the factory again." In November, she again noted: "Sen[d] off the 2nd 6 gal jar of butter made this fall." It appears that the butter she produced was mainly for resale or barter, not for family use, and was an activity she engaged in when she had time or surplus milk, because she also mentioned that in September, "I go way down to Mr. Mill's and get a firkin of butter. Have to pay 25c/pound."[49] Some city and village women also preferred

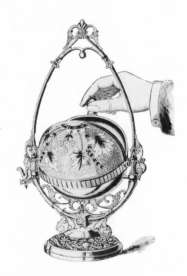

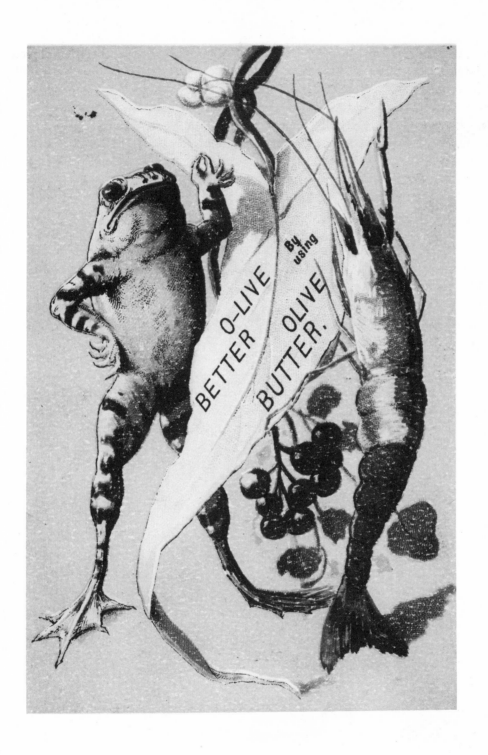

O-LIVE BETTER

By using

OLIVE BUTTER.

to make their own butter, often not trusting the quality of cream used by the new dairy firms. Butter churns remained part of many households until after 1900, especially since impure milk was linked to tuberculosis: a cautious homemaker could obtain "safe" cream from a trusted farmer, dairy, or grocery and make it into butter at home.

Farm-produced, or "dairy," butter was molded in round wooden molds, or butter prints, into one-pound cakes that were usually four inches in diameter. Often the print or molded design specified a particular maker. One of the drawbacks of dairy butter was its perishability; it had to be purchased in small quantities lest it become rancid or sour, and some housewives apparently used butter that had turned for cooking. Eliza Leslie railed against the use on the tea table of "cooking butter," which she defined as old or sour. "If the butter is not good enough to eat on the surface of cold bread or on warm cakes," she argued, "it is not good enough to eat in the inside of sweet cakes or in pastry. . . . The use of butter is to make things taste well. . . . We know, *by experience*, that it is possible to make very fine butter even in the State of New York, and to have it fresh in winter as in summer, though not so rich and yellow. Let the cows be well fed, well sheltered, and *kept fat* and clean—the dairy utensils always in perfect order—churning done twice or thrice every week—all the milk worked out and the butter will surely be good."[50]

That butter was highly regarded is apparent in the numbers of specialized butter dishes produced for its service on the table. Ceramic and, to a lesser extent, glass butter dishes had long been part of breakfast and tea services. Metal butter dishes, first of Britannia ware and shortly thereafter of silver plate, appeared as

Small, individual butter dishes or butter "pats" enabled middle-class households to apportion single servings of butter (which was expensive) to each person at the table.

early as 1855. The early metal forms employed a double-wall construction and other ingenious methods to keep the butter cool yet separate from the ice, which was usually unclean and messy. These dishes generally emulated the four-inch rounded shape of a pound of butter and had a domed lid. Other innovations in butter-dish design had to do with the lid: methods were devised to suspend the lid during service of butter, or otherwise to prevent it from having to be placed on the tablecloth during use. Hinges, hooks, and a popular "revolving" lid, among others, were introduced. By 1900, the butter dish had become reduced in form to a simple dish with removable drain and domed cover.[51]

Accompanying the butter dish, whether on the table or on the sideboard, was a special butter knife, designated to be used *only* for the serving of butter. Catharine Beecher outlined this procedure for the family breakfast or tea table: "The butter should be cooled in cold water, if not already hard, and then put into a smooth and regular form, and a butter knife be laid by the place, to be used for no other purpose but to help the butter." Individuals were never to use their own knives to take butter from the common dish. Miss Beecher also recommended that "a small plate should be placed at each place for butter, and a small salt-cup set by each breakfast or dinner plate. This saves butter and salt." This seems to be an early mention of the use of individual butter plates; late in the century there was abundant evidence of the prevalence of tiny "butter pats," as they were often called, made of glass, pottery, porcelain, and silver, as well as "bread and butter plates," introduced in the 1890s. Beecher's concern, however, reflects the dearness of both commodities, butter and salt, for middle-class householders.[52]

Although hard, sweet butter was meted out carefully from the common butter

dish, butter sauces were freely recommended for meat and fish. "Drawn butter," a combination of melted butter, flour, and water, was combined with chopped eggs and nasturtiums as a fish sauce, or mixed with oysters to pour over boiled fowl.[53] The added elements could override any old or sour butter taste. Despite the warnings of nineteenth-century cookbook writers, many cooks assuredly used rancid butter in flavored sauces.

Foods that required a great deal of time and labor to create or elaborate utensils to produce and serve carried with them the prestige of elevated purchasing power. Fancy molded desserts, for example, commonly expressed status, wealth, and, at times, manual dexterity and industriousness. Mrs. Isabella Beeton, the famous British advocate of fine cooking and author of one of the most popular cookbooks of the nineteenth century, had this to say about the role of dessert: "The dessert certainly repays, in its general effect, the expenditure upon it of much pains; and it may be said, that if there be any poetry at all in meals, or the process of feeding, there is poetry in the dessert. . . ." Such desserts satisfied the cultural sweet tooth that many Americans had inherited from their English forebears. They also, and probably more importantly, served as elaborate table decorations. Mrs. Beeton described the types of fruits, nuts, cakes, and biscuits that typically made up dessert, "together with the most costly and *recherché* [choice] wines."[54]

Beeton listed other various types of confections, including "liquid confects" (preserved fruits in syrup); "dry confects" (candied fruits, such as orange peel or citron); "marmalade, jams, or pastes"; "jellies—the juices of fruits boiled with sugar to a pretty thick consistency, so as, upon cooling, to form a trembling jelly"; "conserves" (a mixture of fresh fruits, vegetables, or flowers and dry, undissolved sugar); and "candies" (fruits boiled in sugar syrup and then dried or "candied over with sugar"). Guests were encouraged to sample freely; dental records and the thriving denture industry of the period suggest that they did so.

Even for family dinners when there were no guests to impress, some sweet dish was generally included in the menu, usually some sort of pudding, custard, or pie. Fannie Munn Field kept daily accounts of her family's meals and listed such desserts as custard, apple pie, peach shortcake, and tapioca pudding.[55] Elizabeth F. Ellet recommended for family dinner desserts bread pudding on Monday, apple pudding on Tuesday, pancakes on Wednesday, rice pudding on Thursday, baked batter pudding on Friday, and "rice in a mold with sauce" on Saturday.[56] Puddings were by far the most common dessert; they were baked, steamed, or boiled in a cloth. Pudding molds of tin or earthenware could transform this ordinary dessert into a more complicated-looking, fancy dish.

Sugar was the commodity upon which the dessert table depended first and

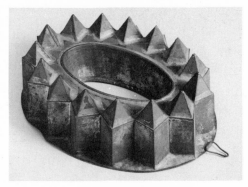

Metal or ceramic molds had the power to transform an ordinary cake, jelly, blancmange, or pudding into an elaborate and visually impressive dessert.

foremost. It was expensive throughout the nineteenth century, and most Americans ate imported West Indian sugar available in several grades. Sarah Josepha Hale explained that the most highly refined white sugar was sweetest, and that "the best has a bright and gravelly appearance." It was sold in cones or "loafs," which were to be chosen on the basis of fineness and closeness of texture. These white crystals, refined as far from their natural state as possible, were considered most desirable for all purposes except preserving, for which the "coarse, strong, open kind" was preferred. Brown sugar, a less refined but still reasonably expensive variety, was often used for cooking, and white sugar was reserved for the table. Loaf sugar, made by a costly and time-consuming process that used cone-shaped clay molds to draw off the syrup from the sugar crystals, was virtually displaced during the second half of the nineteenth century, when the invention of the vacuum pan and centrifuge revolutionized sugar-refining processes, lowering the price of white sugar to the point where most Americans could afford it. By 1898, Alice Morse Earle, popular author of a number of books about "colonial times," was writing nostalgically about loaf sugar:

> Housewives of dignity and elegance desired to have some supply of sugar, certainly to offer visitors for their dish of tea. This sugar was always loaf-sugar, and truly loaf-sugar; for it was purchased ever in great loaves or cones which averaged in weight about nine to ten pounds apiece. One cone would last thrifty folk for a year. This pure clear sugar-cone always came wrapped in a deep blue-purple paper, of such unusual and beautiful tint and so color-laden that in country homes it was carefully saved and soaked, to supply a dye for a small amount of the finest wool, which was used when spun and dyed for some specially choice

purpose. The cutting of this cone of sugar into lumps of equal size and regular shape was distinctly the work of the mistress and daughters of the house. It was too exact and too dainty a piece of work to be intrusted [sic] to clumsy and wasteful servants. Various simply shaped sugar-shears or sugar-cutters were used. . . . I can see my old cousin still in what she termed her breakfast room, dressed very handsomely, standing before a bare mahogany table on which a maid placed the considerable array of a silver salver without legs, which was set on a folded cloth and held the sugar-loaf and the sugar-cutter; and another salver with legs that bore various bowls and one beautiful silver sugar-box which was kept filled high for her husband's toddy. It seemed an interminable tedious work to me and a senseless one, as I chafingly waited for the delightful morning drive in delightful Boston.[57]

Cone or loaf sugar was the most highly refined and sweetest form of sugar. Women used sugar nippers to cut lumps from the cone for the sugar bowl, or else pounded the lumps into a fine powder to serve with fruit or sweets. As granulated sugar became available in the 1890s, sugar nippers became obsolete.

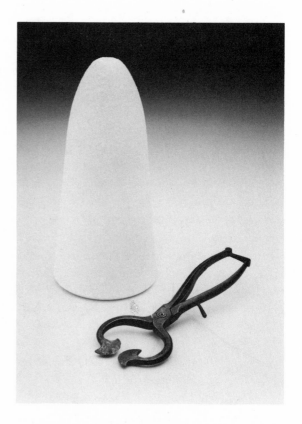

That same year, home economist Maria Parloa wrote that "the best sugar is so reasonable that there is no necessity for even poor people to seek a cheap grade." During this period, "whiteness" became a prized attribute, and brown sugar went

out of favor. According to food historians Waverley Root and Richard de Rochemont, the sugar industry conspired to accelerate this conversion from brown to white sugar by suggesting that brown sugar was contaminated with insects.[58]

For those who could not afford sugar even after its price came down, maple syrup and especially molasses were common substitutes. Molasses "cans" or pitchers with dripless metal pouring spouts were a common presence on the tea tables of the working and middle classes in the 1870s and 1880s, produced in glass, pottery, and silver. They gradually disappeared from the tableware marketplace by the early 1900s. It is possible that the increased popularity of molasses during the later nineteenth century was somehow related to the product's strong associations with colonial America; the "colonial" style in household furnishings was in fact gaining momentum during those years. Surely molasses would have been present at a "Martha Washington Tea Party," a popular costumed social event during the period of the American Centennial. It was a perfectly appropriate old-fashioned dressing for bread, biscuits, or pancakes. Some even used it as a sweetener for tea, as is suggested by the following description of life in a New

England logging camp, from William Dean Howells's *A Modern Instance*: " 'Now there's tea, for example,' he said, pointing to the great tea-pot on the stove. . . . 'And I gave it to 'em three times a day, good and strong—molasses in it, and no milk.' "[59]

Men and women did not live by bread (and meat and desserts) alone. They also drank. Tea, coffee, cocoa, water, wine, whiskey, beer, cider, mineral water, lemonade, and punch were all commonly taken in varying degrees in spite of the powerful rumblings of the temperance movement and the considerable condemnation of tea and coffee in the latter half of the century. Each of these beverages played a part in the broader rituals of dining, and each had its own specialized utensils for its service, as well as a particular set of practices that governed its consumption.

Nearly everyone, including many children, drank both tea and coffee. Tea of course commanded its own special daily meal, but it also appeared commonly at breakfast. Yet, despite its constant consumption, it was never inexpensive: in 1820, for example, a cup of tea was more expensive than a mixed drink of whiskey and water.[60] Tea and tea wares were largely imported from England or English colonies (India) and were subject to import duties throughout the century. Moreover, for some Americans of the early nineteenth century, tea had unpatriotic associations with the English crown, though this connotation was probably of little meaning by 1900.

In certain mannered situations, tea drinking also seems to have been a popular cultural metaphor for refined behavior throughout the period. The image of the

A family might want to conform to prevailing social standards but also retain some degree of individuality. This family has livened up the routine of afternoon tea by removing it from the restrictive confines of the dining room.

genteel afternoon ladies' tea party had the ability to invoke powerful upper-class associations. Cookbooks and household guides spent many paragraphs discussing the best methods for preparing tea and debating the virtues of green versus black tea. Sarah Josepha Hale recommended the use of "polished tea urns" rather than "varnished ones" because they "may be kept boiling with a much less expense of spirits of wine than such as are varnished," an important quality since boiling water was crucial to the successful brewing of tea.[61] Eliza Leslie instructed that the tea should be strong and properly made, the pot should be scalded twice and not filled with too much water, or weak tea would result. "The practice of drowning away all the flavor of the tea is strangely prevalent with servants . . . who do not, or will not, remember that the kettle should be boiling hard at the moment the water is poured on the tea—otherwise the infusion will be insipid and tasteless, no matter how liberally the Chinese plant has been afforded." Servants were to be instructed not to fill the teacups to the brim, to offer cream and sugar, and "also, send round a small pot of hot water, that those who like their tea weak may conveniently dilute it."[62]

Green tea, made from younger leaves and, according to many writers, highly esteemed for flavor, was thought by some (Catharine Beecher among them) to be excessively stimulating. Black tea, however, could have the same effect, according to Fannie Farmer: "When taken to excess, it so acts on the nervous system as to produce sleeplessness and insomnia, and finally makes a complete wreck of its victim."[63] Unless she was certain of the preferences of her guests, the obvious solution for a genteel hostess was to offer both types, since "either sort is often extremely disagreeable to persons who take the other." Green-tea drinkers think black tea tastes like "hay, herbs, etc.," Miss Leslie said, and black tea drinkers found the "enlivening qualities" of green "to affect the nerves."[64] The controversy alone must surely have enlivened many a tea party.

Coffee was the most popular American hot beverage—in 1850, Americans drank almost four times as much coffee as they did tea.[65] Breakfast coffee was served in large cups, diluted with large quantities of hot milk. Dinner-party instructions recommended that coffee be served in tiny cups, in the French manner: "After a hearty dinner, especially if the food is rich in animal oil, a small cup of strong, black coffee, drank without milk, but with a liberal allowance of sugar is found to promote digestion and a lively flow of spirits. No French dinner is complete without this *café noir*."[66] Coffeepots and cups were standard parts of tea sets, and

Rich, strong black coffee, served in demi-tasses—tiny "half" cups— with sugar but no milk, was considered the most elegant way to end a formal dinner. It was thought to improve digestion and to revive the food-and-wine-encumbered guests.

This samovar not only served but also brewed coffee. Its body has two internal chambers: in the rear chamber water is boiled to build up a head of steam, which then passes through the curved tube to condense inside the smokestack and drip through the coffee grounds into the front chamber. The locomotive even has a steam valve that whistles while the brewing takes place.

samovars were also often available to match. There were many different procedures for preparing coffee, but most commonly the roasted beans were ground and boiled, often with an egg to clarify the liquid.

If coffee and tea proved too stimulating, cocoa was recommended as an alternative. Fannie Farmer designated cocoa a "nutriment as well as stimulant," and recommended it especially for children, reflecting a growing concern among parents, educators, and nutritionists that the diets of children be carefully monitored. If children were given coffee or tea, it was only with much milk and sugar.[67] Cocoa and chocolate, its more intense (and stimulating) counterpart, were served from special chocolate pots, which became very fashionable during the 1880s and 1890s. One bride in 1895 received both a chocolate pot and a chocolate set as wedding gifts.[68] Walter Baker, who used a painting by the Swiss artist Jean-Étienne Liotard to popularize his product, was one of the major purveyors of

*Like tea and coffee, chocolate—which
had been a fashionable beverage in
Europe since the 1700s—had its
own array of specialized serving
utensils.*

chocolate in America during the nineteenth century. Porcelain figures of women carrying trays of hot chocolate, based on the painting, became popular parlor and chamber ornaments.

Men and women alike, especially those of German extraction, were fond of beer. William Dean Howells's character Bartley Hubbard of Boston had his beer "sent in by the gross—it came cheaper that way; after trying both the Cincinnati and the Milwaukee lagers, and making a cursory test of the Boston brand, he had settled down upon the American Tivoli; it was cheap, and you could drink a couple of bottles without feeling it." Bartley routinely drank a bottle for lunch and two bottles for dinner.[69] The annual consumption of beer has increased dramatically since the Civil War, from less than two gallons per capita to eighteen gallons per capita today.[70]

Prior to 1850, little beer was brewed or consumed in this country; it could not compete in popularity with cider, rum, and whiskey, probably because of the poor quality of beer produced and the high rate of spoilage. The great numbers of German immigrants who came to the United States after the economic and political dislocations of 1848 brought with them a taste for and the skills to produce the amber liquid; German brewers introduced the technique for brewing lager beer, which transformed the industry in the United States. The development of the glass industry also helped increase beer consumption. Before 1850, glass bottles were expensive and beer had to be purchased in sixteen-gallon kegs or thirty-one-gallon barrels. Most people could not afford that large an outlay of cash, and unless it was a special event, could not drink such vast quantities. But once able to purchase beer by the bottle, Americans began their still-fervent love affair with the brew. Mrs. Hale provided her readers in 1853 with instructions for keeping beer: "You should not let beer stand in a pot or jug; but, if there be any left, put it in a clean bottle, with a tea-spoonful of sugar, and cork it tightly."[71] Flat beer was unacceptable then as now.

The American love affair with beer began around 1850, when German immigrants brought the technique of brewing lager beer to this country. Widely regarded as a health food because of its malt content, it was still opposed by some because of the alcohol in it.

Wine was also highly regarded but consumed much less frequently than beer because of its high cost. Wealthy Americans, like New Yorker Martha Buell Munn, prided themselves on their knowledge of French and German wines. When she toured Europe in 1877–1878, she noted in her journal that she had visited Bordeaux, "and then visited the wine vaults of Messrs. Barton & Guestiers. These . . . underground cellars, with their narrow dark passages on either side of which were piled huge casks of precious wine, were exceedingly curious and interesting. The guide gave us some fine Château Lafitte, also some Château Margaux but the most delicious of all was the Château [d'] Yquem."[72]

Descriptions of elaborate dinners include one and usually more wines. Wealthy Americans had developed a taste for these drinks during the eighteenth century, and most favored Madeira, though champagnes were the favored drinks for dinner parties and fancy occasions throughout the period. Until about 1850, wine drinkers escaped much of the wrath of temperance advocates because, as a fermented beverage, wine was considered to be of some nutritional value, whereas whiskey and rum—distilled spirits—had none, and were vastly more intoxicating. Nearly all wine drunk in America in the nineteenth century was imported from France. Domestic production was limited to homemade concoctions and, by 1850, to the wines of vintners, such as Nicholas Longworth of Cincinnati. Imported French wines were more expensive, but the cost added to their mystique. Drinking wine was strongly associated with the dining rituals of the French and English aristocracy, and despite the fact that its cost was four times that of whiskey, it continued to be favored as an elegant social beverage.

Temperance reformers attacked rum and whiskey first, but began to make inroads against all alcoholic beverages in the 1840s. During that decade, wine consumption decreased by half, and by 1864 Eliza Leslie was advising her female readers on the protocol of dealing with temperance in social situations: "It was formerly considered ill-manners to refuse to take wine with a gentleman. Now that the fortunate increase of temperance has induced so many persons to abjure entirely the use of all liquors, it is no longer an offense to decline these invitations."[73] Throughout the rest of the century, hostesses were urged always to offer water as well as wine, and not to feel bound to serve wine if conscience advised against it.

Despite the protestations of the temperance reformers, many middle-class Americans drank to some extent during this period. The presence of wine in American households was indicated by Sarah Josepha Hale's instructions for cleaning glass "encrusted with the dregs of port wine."[74] The Edward Dickinson family of Amherst, Massachusetts, including poet daughter Emily, chose not to abstain from drinking, despite the presence of an active temperance society in

town after 1846. Edward Dickinson stored rye, sherry, port, and sweet malmsey wine (this was often served to afternoon visitors by Mrs. Dickinson), locked in his brick wine cellar in the basement. Emily herself made currant wine and often gave her homemade wine to friends as gifts.[75]

Trade catalogues and the surviving artifacts of the second half of the nineteenth century indicated that although many middle-class women did not themselves drink, they continued to serve wines and cordials as part of their public

Elaborate dinners frequently included one and often more wines and cordials, each requiring its own special glass. Champagne was served from tall, slender champagne pitchers. Drinking wine recalled the dining rituals of French and English aristocrats, and its cost—four times the price of whiskey—only enhanced its status as an elegant social beverage.

dining rituals. Increasing quantities of drinking vessels—wine, champagne, cordial, ale, and whiskey glasses, as well as a variety of decanters—were aggressively marketed to middle-class consumers during this period. Caught between the pull of temperance and the attraction of elite sophistication offered by European models of behavior, many families drank their wines and cordials secure in their belief that they were not prone to the evils of the intemperate use of liquor.

Even before the temperance movement gained momentum, there had been a variety of alternative beverages for abstainers. During the hot summer afternoons, cool drinks like lemonade, mineral water, ginger ale, root beer, iced tea, or orangeade were popular, and could either be made at home or purchased commercially bottled from grocers or druggists. The Danville Bottling Company of Danville, Pennsylvania, advertised that they could supply "lemon soda, ginger ale, champagne nectar, and all mild drinks." Iced tea was a newly popular drink in 1860, when Solon Robinson, author of *How to Live*, wrote: "Last summer we got in the habit of taking the tea iced, and really thought it better than when hot." Almira MacDonald noted in her diary that "a good drink for summer is raspberry vinegar," made by steeping red rasperries in wine vinegar for twenty-four hours, straining, adding sugar, and boiling. The ensuing syrup could be bottled and two tablespoons added to a glass of water.[76]

Root beer was first invented by a Philadelphia pharmacist, Charles E. Hires, shortly after the Civil War. Initially it was sold as a powder—when mixed with water, a twenty-five-cent package produced five gallons of root beer. Hires's first name for it was herb tea, but because it was made with yeast (which had associations with alcohol), it was condemned by the temperance reformers. Hires demonstrated that his beverage was indeed alcohol-free and changed its name to root beer. Root beer quickly became the "National Temperance Drink," and by 1894, Hires was selling more than three million packages a year.[77] In addition to being thirst-quenching, root beer, according to its promoters, had the benefit of being

unquestionably one of the best blood purifiers in the world, and for kidney disease it has no equal. Why take poisonous and disagreeable drugs when in this delicious drink you have the problem of medicine solved by its imparting strength and pure blood, which soon gives a person a clear and healthy complexion.[78]

Water was the approved alternative to wine at the dinner table, and beginning in the 1850s, ice-water pitchers appeared in silver trade catalogs. Within two decades, these pitchers had become very grand and rested in a place of honor

Root beer, invented shortly after the Civil War by Charles E. Hires, was a favored drink of the temperance reformers. It had the thirst-quenching properties of stronger alcoholic beverages— especially beer—coupled with the presumed ability to combat a wide assortment of medical afflictions.

on the sideboard. They often had ingenious patented designs for keeping the ice cool, such as special valves at the spout or ceramic insulating liners. For less grand occasions, according to the *Ladies' Home Journal,* "water bottles, or carafes, as they are commonly called, are much used and are a great convenience." As an additional gesture toward informality, the article commented that "tumblers are generally used for water; so extensively, indeed, that one rarely sees a table set with goblets. . . ."[79]

Water had not always been "the staple drink of the American dinner table," as it was called in 1894 by etiquette writer Agnes Morton.[80] Clear, potable water is a phenomenon of the twentieth century. Nineteenth-century cookbooks of the 1850s and 1860s usually included directions for purifying water, using different methods of filtration (sand and charcoal) or chemical additives such as alum. Bottled waters offered to many an appealing alternative to city water. Apollinaris—a popular mineral water—was listed on the most elegant menus as a beverage choice, often alongside the stronger beverages. Maria Parloa noted in her "Everything about the House" column in the *Ladies' Home Journal* that

mineral waters are served throughout the dinner, beginning after the meat and vegetables have been passed. They should be very cold. Have the bottles opened in the kitchen. A napkin should be folded around the bottle, which should be taken to the table immediately. In warm weather a little ice in a glass of effervescent

The problem of keeping drinking water cool was resolved by the silver industry in the 1850s with the introduction of an insulated ice-water pitcher. These pitchers used either a double-walled construction or a ceramic lining to preserve the cold. "In New York, the daily consumption of ice in the summer months amounts to upwards of 10,000 tons" (Jessup Whitehead, The Steward's Handbook, *1899).*

water is a great addition. . . . A glass dish filled with broken ice is pretty and convenient on the table. It can be used either for common water or for the mineral water glasses.

As Parloa mentioned, specialized drinking vessels were produced for mineral water; they often sat in handled silver frames that would help keep condensation off the tablecloth, as well as prevent delicate fingers from the chill of the iced beverage. "For mineral waters," Parloa wrote, "there come beautifully shaped glasses, which are almost as much of a necessity as the common water glasses."[81]

In 1891, Simpson, Hall, Miller and Company manufactured elegant silver holders that could dress up an ordinary glass of ice-cold soda water for a company dinner.

American diets, as well as the utensils with which people served and consumed their food, changed considerably during the last fifty years of the nineteenth century in response to both changing technologies as well as changing social values. Perhaps the most dramatic change that occurred was in the diversity of the menus of the middle class, a change that occurred slowly, particularly in rural areas. In the winter of 1881, Eva Rosemond, a schoolteacher in rural Cummington, Massachusetts, got her room and board from assorted families in the community. She complained in her diary about the lack of variety in the food she was given: "For four weeks there has been no variation in the menu—it is liver or pork chops, boiled cider applesauce and johnny cake, mince pie and tea— oh, for a cup of coffee!"[82] Miss Rosemond's situation was probably typical for her rural circumstances. But her counterparts in the city were feasting on out-of-season fresh fruits and vegetables, domestic and imported canned goods, meats from Midwestern stockyards, exotic seafoods, and many other culinary options that gave the table a bounty not known before. This array dovetailed with an expanded consumer power among middle-class Americans, enriching all areas of their lives with new and fancier goods to wear, to ornament their homes, to sit upon, to ride in, and, of course, to eat.

FROM SOUP TUREEN TO PUDDING DISH

5

BREAKFAST, LUNCH, DINNER, TEA, AND SUPPER

assage into the middle class for Americans was marked not only by changing manners, home environment, and food consumed but also by changes in daily schedules. The well-born Boston socialite Clara Kingsbury invited upcountry newcomers Bartley and Marcia Hubbard "to tea on Wednesday evening, at eight" in William Dean Howells's *A Modern Instance*. Because Marcia was an old family acquaintance, as well as pretty and competent, and because Bartley was a college friend of a friend, Clara wanted to welcome the couple to Boston. But because Bartley's cut was too rough and his ambition too patent, Miss Kingsbury unconsciously shuddered at the thought of embracing him as an equal. Rather than hold a nine o'clock supper in their honor, a festive event that would have indicated her complete social acceptance of the Hubbards—whom she considered visibly rural in expression and habit— Clara decided instead to have them to an informal and less significant evening meal, "literally tea, with bread and butter, and some thin, ascetic cake."

FROM

SOUP

TUREEN

TO

PUDDING

DISH

· —— ·

I 4 3

In every respect Clara's tea was an emblem of the social stakes that could be involved when two classes—and their characteristic schedules—collided in late-nineteenth-century America. As it happened, the event went off dismally; the Hubbards, who had not eaten since midday and who would normally have had a much more sustaining tea or supper at six o'clock, were famished. Bartley, ever the social climber, went home eager to "have up some cold meat and bottled beer, and talk it all over with Marcia."[1]

Meals have always been benchmarks by which people of all classes set their daily schedules. People divided the day into breakfast time, lunchtime, teatime, and dinner or supper time even before they divided it into standardized hours and minutes (which was possible only after clocks became widely available in the 1840s). Even after people commonly knew that the hour was exactly noon, "lunchtime" or "dinner time" remained the usual way to describe that time of day.

The typical daily schedule that we know today—breakfast at eight, lunch at noon, and dinner at seven—is a product of the twentieth century. In sixteenth-century Europe, the upper class ate only two daily meals: they dined (the main meal) very early in the day, at 11:00 A.M., and supped (ate lighter) at 5:00 P.M.; those of lesser economic means ate later. By the seventeenth century, the institution of breakfast had been added to daily schedules, and dinner had moved to 1:00 P.M. or 2:00 P.M.; the day still ended with a light supper. In the eighteenth century, upper-class Americans, like George Washington, were breakfasting at 7:30–8:00 A.M. and dining at 3:00 P.M. or, in the country, 2:00 P.M. Dinner was followed by tea, and then supper at 8:00 in the evening. The working class in the eighteenth century had its own schedule, shaped by the demands of their employment: breakfast was at 7:00 A.M., dinner at noon, and supper between 6:00 and 7:00 P.M.[2]

Meal names were as varied as their times. "Breakfast" was the only generally consistently held term—it was always a morning meal. Almira MacDonald noted in her diary that she "got up at five to get breakfast" and that Florence, her house guest, came down at six. When Charles Dickens visited America in the 1840s and rode on a canal boat, he noted that breakfast took place at seven o'clock; in 1886, Fanny Munn Field of Rochester, who was meticulous about recording meals in her diary, noted that breakfast on September 19 of that year took place at 8:20.[3] In 1864, travelers staying in hotels were exhorted by Eliza Leslie to arrive at the breakfast table before 9:00 A.M. A level of informality was encouraged at the breakfast table, and individual preferences were to be accommodated if at all possible. In 1883, John Ruth, the author of *Decorum*, described the practice in homes of the wealthy, who with sufficient servants allowed members

FROM
SOUP
TUREEN
TO
PUDDING
DISH

· ——— ·

1 4 4

of the household to eat whenever they wished. He recommended, however, that in "smaller households"—those without a large corps of hired help—breakfast should be served punctually, but "at a reasonable hour."[4]

The class-linked implications of preferring to dine at one particular time of day are elucidated in Webster's 1860 definition of the verb "to dine":

> To eat the chief meal of the day. This meal seems originally to have been taken about the middle of the day, at least in northern climates, as it still is by laboring people. Among people in the higher walks of life, and in commercial towns, the time of dining is from two to five or six o'clock in the afternoon.

Noah Webster in 1860 defined lunch as "a slight repast between breakfast and dinner, eaten in company," and dinner as "the meal taken about the middle of the day; or the principal meal of the day, eaten between noon and evening."[5]

Around 1840, Philip Hone, a former mayor of New York, described in the *Herald Tribune* a new French dining custom, *déjeuner à la fourchette*, where "the company assembles at about one o'clock and partakes of coffee and chocolate, light dishes of meat, ice-cream and confectionary, with lemonade and French and German wines." Hone called this custom breakfast-dinner, and it sounds re-

Breakfast, as pictured by Charles Dana Gibson: "Oatmeal and the Morning Paper" (1898).

FROM
SOUP
TUREEN
TO
PUDDING
DISH

· —— ·

1 4 5

markably similar to that which today we call brunch.[6] It is probably, however, the fashionable forerunner of the idea of lunch—an informal meal that quickly became a practical necessity as the growth of urban industries and bureaucracies meant more and more men worked away from home, and therefore could not be present for a lengthy family dinner at noon.

For those families whose circumstances permitted the husband to take off an hour or two at midday and come home, the tradition of taking the main meal of the day at noon continued. When the Hubbards moved out of their humble Clover Street house in Boston, they selected a townhouse in the Back Bay to be convenient to Bartley's office at the newspaper, because Marcia "wanted Bartley at home for their one o'clock dinners."[7] The family of lawyer Angus MacDonald always referred to the noon meal as dinner; in 1879, Almira MacDonald mentioned that Henry—possibly either a relative or a boarder—was "taking his dinner with us the last time before [his] marriage. . . . We all went to wedding at 2½ P.M." On 9 September 1883, she noted that "Angus came home to dinner and escorted Anne and I to depot 2:40 train. . . ." The following year Mrs. MacDonald's daughter, Lollie, bore a son and "dinner had to wait until after one as Lollie needed attention." The term "dinner" seems to have been used whether Mr. MacDonald was present or not. He often was not—as on Election Day in 1884, when "Angus [was] not home to dinner or tea." The rest of the household, which included Mrs. MacDonald's mother, aunt, nephew, and three children, generally all dined together, with one servant, a "hired girl," assisting.[8]

The terms "lunch" and "luncheon," although more time specific than dinner, could have several different connotations depending upon the level of formality, the gender of people present, and the type of food served. One writer described it as an informal, midday family meal, much less formal than dinner since the husband was not present:

> Luncheon is a recognized institution in our large cities, where business forbids the heads of families returning to dinner until a late hour.
> There is much less formality in the serving of lunch than of dinner. Whether it consists of one or more courses, it is all set upon the table at once. When only one or two are to lunch, the repast is ordinarily served up on a tray.[9]

The *Oxford English Dictionary* traces the word "lunch" to the word "lump"— "as of bread or cheese."[10] The easily transportable nature of a crust of bread and a chunk of cheese has traditionally made it ideal fare for workers or travelers who have to be away from home during the day. This practice has entered the vocabulary as a "ploughman's lunch" in England. Nineteenth-century industrial

FROM
SOUP
TUREEN
TO
PUDDING
DISH

· ——— ·

1 4 6

Lunch pails or lunch boxes, traditionally filled with a crust of bread and a hunk of cheese, were a ubiquitous presence among industrial workers, who could not afford to break for a large midday meal.

workers typically left home in the morning carrying a "lunch" pail, and lunch is most frequently the meal partaken of by picnickers. In 1859, a French traveler in Knight's Ferry, California, described a "luncheon" served on a "grubby" tablecloth in which all food was served on the same plate, a less formal practice more characteristic of lunch than of dinner.[11]

By the late nineteenth century, with men at home less at noon and with women finding themselves increasingly at leisure, "luncheon" took on a new meaning: it had become a women's social event and a male business function. An 1894 etiquette book defined it as a midday meal, taking place between eleven

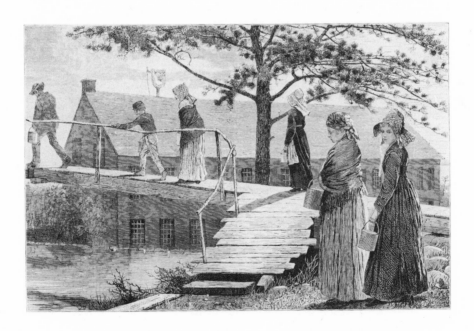

FROM

SOUP

TUREEN

TO

PUDDING

DISH

· —— ·

1 4 7

and three o'clock, varying in form from casual to formal. The atmosphere, this author said, should be that of an "open house," with an irregular number of guests, who would go to table singly rather than in a formal procession; dress was not defined, nor was the hour rigidly fixed.[12] More typical was a luncheon that was a lesser version of dinner in formality of service and number of courses. The ability of women to have luncheons, an activity that required an outlay of both time and capital, was an indication of the family's status and position in the community.

There seem to have been two types of tea—afternoon tea and evening tea. The eighteenth-century upper-class tradition of taking tea around four o'clock was adopted by middle-class women in the 1840s. Afternoon tea was specifically a female event, generally lasting about two hours, although men might have joined the party at the end of their workday. Many families expanded afternoon tea into a full meal, usually referred to as high tea or six o'clock supper, while for a few tea merely filled the void between lunch or dinner at noon, and supper much later in the evening—at eight or nine o'clock.

The Angus MacDonalds, for example, had tea every day, a meal that probably included a fairly substantial amount of food, since Almira MacDonald generally mentioned only two meals a day—dinner and tea, in that order—in her diaries. When she referred to "supper," it was either an early evening meal for guests, which presumably involved more extensive preparations than tea, or an evening meal taken outside the home, usually at church. She mentioned, for example, that on 10 March 1885, "Angus . . . returned at five in time to be with invited company to supper," and on several occasions, she made references to suppers at the church.[13]

Evening teas such as that to which Clara Kingsbury invited the Hubbards were also very popular during the late nineteenth century. The practice had originated a century earlier, when fashionable members of the wealthy classes had dinner in the middle of the afternoon and supper late in the evening. Dinner usually began at three o'clock, and by the time it was finished, it might have been six or seven o'clock. Tea was served shortly thereafter and was usually followed by supper at nine o'clock. Many fashionable Victorians emulated this eighteenth-century tradition in the forming of evening tea parties, which sometimes included supper as part of the affair.[14]

"Suppertime" is another term that is laden with ambiguity—although its meaning in any given context was probably clear to individual nineteenth-century families. For some, supper was a six o'clock meal; for others, it took place at

FROM
SOUP
TUREEN
TO
PUDDING
DISH

· —— ·

1 4 8

nine. Six o'clock supper was considered unfashionable in the mid-nineteenth century as more and more middle-class people ate their dinner at that hour; it tended to be more common among the working classes, rural people, or those who wished to keep traditional ways intact. Webster in 1860 defined supper as "the evening meal," but only for certain classes: "People who dine late eat no supper. The dinner of fashionable people would be the supper of rustics."[15] For those who had to work away from home during the afternoon or for servants, supper at the workday's end was essential and commonplace. As American middle-class household schedules became more and more subject to the schedules of industry, the main meal of the day was moved from noon to early evening. That meal, however, was more formal and substantial than supper—which had always been characterized by the service of relatively light, hot foods—and was more commonly called dinner by the end of the century.

These ladies were of sufficient means (and had sufficient leisure) to enjoy their meal out-of-doors, picnicking.

How—and how much—food was served changed considerably, along with changing notions of symmetry, social display, and nutrition. Setting the table was a ritual whose procedures were probably more rigidly prescribed than any other associated with dining. In 1885, *Godey's Lady's Book* set them out clearly:

> Lay a plate, right side up, for each person. If the table be long, place one plate at each end, and those at the sides opposite each other. Place the napkin at the right of the plate, and at dinner, place a piece of bread between the folds of the napkin. Place the knives, butter-plate, and tumbler at the right of the plate, the forks at the left, and the soup-spoon in front, the handle towards the right end, the number of each depending upon the number of courses, the fruit dish or flowers should occupy the centre of the table; the salt and pepper, butter, jelly, pickles, etc., at the corners. Place the various dishes on the table in regular order, straight with the table, or, if at an angle, let there be some uniformity, never helter-skelter.[16]

There were many versions of the proper way to lay out napkin, fork, knife, and spoon around the plate. The napkin was placed here to the left of the plate; the knife, customarily placed at the right of the plate just inside the spoon, is shown here at the top of the plate. Each individual's place was enclosed in a sort of corral by the napkin and flatware—a clue to concerns about privacy and personal space.

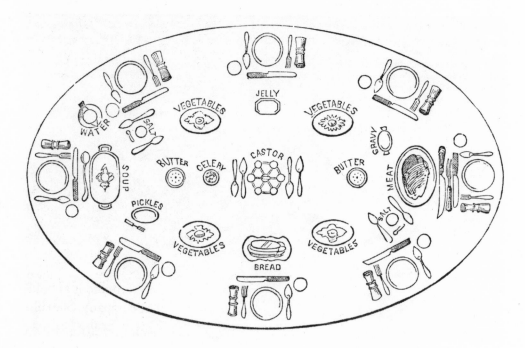

FROM
SOUP
TUREEN
TO
PUDDING
DISH

· —— ·

150

A horticultural extravaganza in a dinner table set for a party of twelve.

Until the last third of the nineteenth century, the main method for arranging a table and serving food was that which was referred to by some etiquette writers as the Old English plan. All of the food was on the table at once, at the beginning of each of several courses. The term "course" was thoughtfully defined by an anonymous mid-century cookbook writer as "the number of dishes which are served on the table at one time. A repast of *one course* comprises all that is served between the soup (if there is any) and the dessert. . . . In a meal of *two courses*, the head and side dishes are served at the same time—this is the favorite style in the country—and the empty plates and dishes are replaced, at various times, by hot plates and refilled dishes. The second service is dessert." Depending on the number of people present, the social importance of the meal, and the amount of food required, the number and size of the courses could be increased accordingly. Family dinners were usually limited to two or three courses; company dinners generally had five or often more.[17]

This opulent and cumbersome style of service, with its roots in the labor-intensive and mannered rituals of courtly feasts, was beginning to go out of style by the mid-nineteenth century. In 1853, Sarah Josepha Hale referred to it as "old-fashioned" but recommended it as proper for either family or company. She, like her colleagues, stressed the importance of good form for family meals (lest they

FROM
SOUP
TUREEN
TO
PUDDING
DISH

· —— ·

1 5 1

be unsuitable for unexpected company). "Should there be only a joint [a roast leg of beef or mutton] and pudding," a refined housekeeper would serve them up separately, "and the dishes, however small the party, should always form two courses." She offered her own guidelines for this type of meal structure, both for a small and large dinner: "the soup and fish are placed at the top and bottom of the table, removed by the joint with vegetables and pastry; or, should the company consist of eight or ten, a couple or more of side-dishes in the first course, with game and a pudding in the second, accompanied by confectionary, are quite sufficient."[18] For family dinners, which were conducted on a much less grand scale, essentially the same format prevailed, except that family members did all or much of the serving and helping.

American travelers to Paris in the 1830s reported about a new style, "service à la russe," which would slowly make its way into the dining rooms of middle-class Americans, at first only for "company meals," but later for family dining as well.[19] *Our Deportment*, an etiquette book published first in 1879, provided an explanation of the new service:

> The latest and most satisfactory plan for serving dinner is dinner à la Russe (the Russian style)—all the food being placed on a side table, and servants do the carving and waiting. This style gives an opportunity for more profuse ornamentation of the table, which as the meal progresses, does not become encumbered with partially empty dishes and platters.[20]

The idea of removing the food from the table to the sideboard or serving table had several appealing aspects, in addition to its fashionability. Without the usual array of platters, serving bowls, and dishes, the table surface was available for artistic ornamentation. Where previously food had been the primary display, flowers, vases, decorative figures, and ornamental lights could now prevail. Decoration of the entire home was on the rise, as women strove to create environments for their families that would be morally uplifting, civilized, and reflective of their husbands' success as breadwinners.

> In the country, a table may be superbly decorated, at a trifling expense, in the following way: Let the carpenter make a foundation of wood, proportioned to the size and shape of the table, and the space you wish to fill. This wood, arched at the ends, should be supported on little feet, like those of the pedestal of a clock. Cover this about three inches deep with clay or potter's earth, covered again with moss and gravel, laid out in walks. Plant in this boughs of green, bushes, and all the flowers that can be filled in. Nothing is prettier, in the centre

FROM
SOUP
TUREEN
TO
PUDDING
DISH

· ——— ·

1 5 2

of a table, than this little parterre. . . . Variety may be made by adding rocks, vases, and columns to the parterre; vases of flowers, at the corners of the table, may also be added.[21]

The success of any elaborate Victorian meal, whether Old English or *à la russe*, depended upon the presence of well-trained domestic help to assist the hostess with cooking and serving. Although cooks, kitchen helpers, and waiters could be hired for special occasions, one or two (or more) servants were commonplace in most homes of the wealthy and the middle class—almost 25 percent of *all* urban and suburban households in 1880 employed at least one servant.[22] The increasing numbers of servants in middle-class homes were both a result of and a factor in the elaboration of domestic rituals—particularly those related to food. Servants provided most of the labor that enabled such events to take place, and women were able to embrace more freely the intricate behaviors of the wealthy knowing that they had adequate support from their domestic help.

In 1858, Catharine Beecher commented on the necessity of servants for the execution of even a simple dinner party for ten persons. "Such a dinner party . . . may be got up and carried through comfortably by a housekeeper, if she is provided with an experienced cook and well-trained waiter," she commented. "But without these, it is absolute cruelty for a husband to urge, or even allow

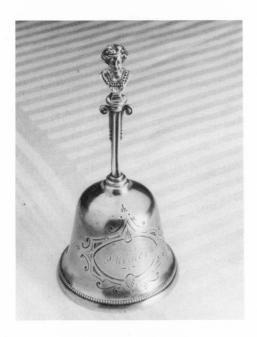

Well-trained domestic help was crucial to the successful execution of an elaborate Victorian dinner party. The service bell, a popular affectation, allowed the hostess to get around the rule that she must never speak to the help during the meal: all instructions were given in advance and carried out wordlessly at the genteel tone of the bell.

FROM

SOUP

TUREEN

TO

PUDDING

DISH

• —— •

his wife to go on through all the toil, anxiety, and effort needful for such an affair."[23] The quantity of food provided and large numbers of serving dishes and clean plates required would have resulted in a logistical nightmare for a hostess without serving help.

The Old English system assumed that servants would clear between courses and bring on the next course. Household manuals such as *The American Practical Cookery-Book* delineated this practice for inexperienced servants and hostesses alike: at the completion of each course, the maid, waiter, or butler was to remove all "dishes, plates, silver knives, and salad; leave the pitchers of water, clean wineglasses, and tumblers." They were then to brush the crumbs from the table with a crumb brush, a silver "crumber," or a rolled napkin onto a waiter or tray, and then set on the dessert wares—"a plate, saucer, knife, fork, and spoon before each person."[24] Even in service *à la russe* servants had to be available to bring each successive course from the kitchen, carve and serve the food from the sideboard, and distribute the plates to the guests, serving with the left hand while clearing with the right.

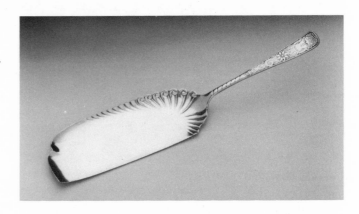

Crumbers for cleaning the tablecloth between courses came into widespread use in the 1890s. By that time, most Americans had abandoned the practice of laying two or three cloths on a dinner table, each to be removed after a given course.

FROM

SOUP

TUREEN

TO

PUDDING

DISH

· —— ·

1 5 4

"The servant problem," as it was generally termed, was no twentieth-century phenomenon; the difficulty of hiring "good" servants in the last half of the nineteenth century was a common complaint. Julia Holmes Cook, a farmwife from Batavia, New York, who did most of her own cooking, cleaning, cheesemaking, fruit processing, and also helped on the farm, was constantly on the lookout for someone to relieve her of some of the demands of her difficult life. In February, 1881, she noted in her diary: "Irving finds a girl who is looking for a place and we hire her for $2 a week. Now that Ella [her daughter] has left for school, I would rather do alone for a month or so, but must hire when I can find a girl."[25]

The ideal servant was more than thirty years old—presumably more stable and less likely to quit. Other desirable qualities included cleanliness, "good character," and the ability to perform household tasks efficiently and unobtrusively—ideally, invisibly. During a meal, servants were supposed to be able to perform all necessary functions without speaking at all, following explicit instructions given prior to the meal. Women were encouraged to draw up detailed table and course plans, outlining for the servant exactly where each dish was to be placed, or when and how each course was to be carved, placed on the dish, and served. As social demands became more elaborate, women looked not just for "help" to ease the burdens of housework, but also for much more specialized and professional "domestics," who would be able to satisfy the rising expectations of his or her employer. The interdependent nature of that relationship led to frequent conflicts between employer and employee. According to historian Faye Dudden, "the peculiar rancor of complaints in the mid-nineteenth century stemmed in part from the status functions of domestics. Their employers hoped to buy not just labor but that rare commodity, the admiration of others."[26] The expectation of professionalism set high standards, rarely met. American servants—usually Irish immigrants—were universally characterized as unreliable, conniving, and unintelligent. An exchange from a play entitled *The Dining-Room*, which appeared in an 1885 issue of *Godey's Lady's Book*, illustrates the commonly held social stereotypes about Irish-born servants. In the play, Mrs. Browne, a fashionable hostess, is addressing Mrs. Smythe, a "much-dressed elderly guest." The soup course is in progress and Talbot, the "stylish man-servant" (who is actually her daughter Julia's lover in disguise), has just been asked to remove the tureen: a dishcloth has been discovered in the soup.

> *Mrs. Browne*   Talbot, remove this soup! Oh, my dear friends, this is a great mortification to me, and shocking carelessness in my cook, who is a raw Irish girl, perfectly untrained, and I fear, untrainable. But even this, I feel, is not sufficient apology *for this contretemps!*

> *Mrs. Smythe*   Say no more, we beg, my dear Mrs. Browne. Such accidents will happen, even in the best regulated families like your own! I assure you I can understand the matter, and can sympathize for we are all at the mercy of stupid help.[27]

With the exception of the Irish, European servants were thought to have generations of training bred into them, making them "contented and happy in their condition without aspirations after change."[28]

FROM

SOUP

TUREEN

TO

PUDDING

DISH

· —— ·

155

Yet nineteenth-century America, with its promise of social mobility to a degree unknown in Europe, made domestic service one of the least appealing options for immigrant laborers. It was a necessary entryway into the workplace for many, but it was usually viewed as a transitional stage rather than as a lifetime occupation. From the perspective of the employers, the transient quality of the domestic force was a serious and constant problem. In 1873, Elizabeth Ellet wrote that

> the greatest trouble in housekeeping is the difficulty of procuring and retaining good servants. . . . Too often, men and women look upon service as degrading to them, and will prefer any hardship or privation to engaging in it as a business. Those who do so for a time, are usually tormented with jealous fears that their dignity will be infringed on, or are found neither qualified nor trustworthy. Housekeepers are mainly dependent on the Irish and German emigrants, who as a rule are utterly ignorant of household service, and have to be taught everything.[29]

Ellet was expressing a common belief, generations in the making; Catharine Beecher had complained of the same problem in her *Domestic Receipt Book* in 1858.

The problem of finding and retaining satisfactory servants, coupled with a growing reformist interest in simplifying America's eating habits, made the "servantless household," as it came to be called, a widespread architectural and social reality by the first decades of the twentieth century. By World War I, the number of servants in the United States dropped from 80 per thousand families in 1900 to 39, and those families that had servants tended to have day workers rather than live-in workers.[30] Middle-class houses were designed to be smaller, more efficient, and easier to maintain; the kitchen in particular was scientifically organized to be run by the woman of the house. As the number of servants declined and women increasingly wanted to spend more time outside of the home, either working for pay or for charity, the home and household rituals—including those related to dining—were streamlined.

Food reformers, concerned with the nation's health, were increasingly vocal by the end of the century, responding in part to growing ethnic and racial paranoia. Reformist rhetoric was evident in the etiquette and cookbooks of the late 1880s

FROM
SOUP
TUREEN
TO
PUDDING
DISH

· —— ·

1 5 6

Political cartoonists had a field day with the often contentious relations between mistress and servant (opposite). Employers were quick to blame the inadequacies of household workers (slanderously linked to their ethnic origins) for their own unrealized social aspirations. Servants could take their own turn at mocking the pretenses of the lady or gentleman of the house.

Mistress: *"Bridget, I told you to Boil the Eggs soft—and they're quite Hard!"*

Bridget: *"Soft is it, Mem? Why I've been Bilin' 'em this hour, and the Water won't get 'em Soft anyhow!"*

"Studies in Expression"

FROM
SOUP
TUREEN
TO
PUDDING
DISH

· —— ·

1 5 7

and 1890s, which often employed scientific justifications for their advice. Maria Parloa warned her readers in 1898 about the health dangers of overlong meals because of poor ventilation: "The dinner is usually given at night, and it must be remembered that the lights, guests, and attendants soon exhaust the oxygen of the air, therefore the ventilation of the dining-room must be carefully attended to, and it must be seen that no one is exposed to a draft." She also praised the simplified modern dinner party, with its diminished emphasis on abundance of food and elaborate ritual: "Fashion changes in the manner of dinner giving, as in everything else," Parloa wrote. "Formerly, the company dinner was, with its numerous choices and long hours at table, a thing to be dreaded as much by the guests as by the hostess. Today the dinner is much simpler, and generally much more successful as a gastronomic and social affair."[31] By getting the dishes of food removed from the table, service *à la russe* changed the emphasis from quantity of food that had dominated the "groaning board" to quality. In addition, once the "laden table" mentality of the first half of the nineteenth century had begun to disappear, it was an easy transition from servants' dishing food onto individual plates from the sideboard to the housewife's serving family meals in the kitchen and bringing the plates to the table.

BREAKFAST

The American breakfast should be a pleasing medium between the heavy cold beef and game pie of the English and the . . . too light morning refeshment of the French.[32]

FROM
SOUP
TUREEN
TO
PUDDING
DISH

· —— ·

1 5 8

Aside from being the ideal "pleasing medium," the American breakfast was probably also the least structured of all meals, European and American. "At this first meal of the day a certain amount of freedom is allowed which would be unjustifiable at any other time," John Ruth wrote in 1882. "The head of the house may read his morning paper and the other members of the family may look over their correspondence if they choose. And each may rise and leave the table when business or pleasure dictates, without waiting for a general signal."[33]

Because breakfast for most people took place shortly after they rose from bed, Ruth and other menu planners agreed, that "people bring less keenness of hunger to this than any other [meal]." Marion Harland, whose cookbook *Breakfast,*

Luncheon and Tea attempted to cater to potentially finicky morning appetites, recommended variety in breakfast foods, a cheerful demeanor on the part of the hostess, flowers on the table (which itself should be situated in an east window to catch the morning light), and perhaps a pot of trailing ivy or a singing canary to further brighten the scene.[34]

Breakfast typically included whatever fruit was in season; some type of cereal; coffee, tea, or cocoa; eggs; meat or fish; potatoes; and toast, muffins, bread, waffles, pancakes, or biscuits. If cold meat was going to be served, as it was "in some families," according to Mrs. Hale, every attempt was to be made to make it appealing. It should be "laid out neatly on clean and rather small-sized dishes [platters], with breakfast plates and small clean knives and forks."[35] Both hot and cold cereal increased in popularity throughout the post-Civil War era, and by 1895 the Montgomery Ward catalogue offered three-piece oatmeal or mush-and-milk sets, which included a cereal bowl, cream pitcher, and plate.[36]

Marion Harland called eggs, "the cheapest food for the breakfast or lunch-table of a private family." They were served boiled, fried, "dropped" or poached,

FROM
SOUP
TUREEN
TO
PUDDING
DISH

· —— ·

1 5 9

Cooked cereal or bread and milk—often served in special deep bread-and-milk bowls—was thought to be an especially nourishing and healthy breakfast food for children.

FROM

SOUP

TUREEN

TO

PUDDING

DISH

· ——— ·

1 6 0

scrambled, and baked. Eggs were to be boiled "never by guess"—according to Sarah Josepha Hale's 1853 instructions to the cookmaid for preparing breakfast—but by the clock or sandglass.[37] They were often boiled in tin, Britannia, or silver-plated egg boilers, which could be brought right to the table. The etiquette for dealing with eggs in the shell was carefully spelled out:

> If boiled eggs are brought on in the shell, egg cups should be provided, the small end of the egg should be placed in the cup, and an opening made at the top of the egg large enough to admit a teaspoon. If egg cups are not supplied, the egg should be cut open with a knife and the contents removed with a spoon.[38]

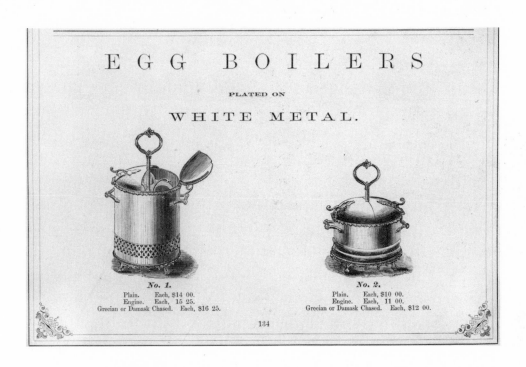

EGG BOILERS

PLATED ON

WHITE METAL.

No. 1.

Plain.   Each, $14 00.
Engine.   Each, 15 25.
Grecian or Damask Chased.   Each, $16 25.

No. 2.

Plain.   Each, $10 00.
Engine.   Each, 11 00.
Grecian or Damask Chased.   Each, $12 00.

134

*Eggs could be coddled or boiled right on the
breakfast table in silver-plated egg boilers (above),
or served already cooked from a silver egg stand,
complete with detachable cups, gold-lined spoons,
and flower-enameled salt and pepper shakers (left).*

FROM

SOUP

TUREEN

TO

PUDDING

DISH

· —— ·

1 6 1

In 1878, Mary F. Henderson, author of *Practical Cooking, and Dinner Giving*, introduced the idea of breakfast parties to her readers, claiming that such parties were "very fashionable, being less expensive than dinners, and just as satisfactory to guests." She added, "They are served generally about ten o'clock, although any time from ten to twelve o'clock may be chosen." Mrs. Henderson preferred that the hour remain closer to ten or even nine o'clock, fearing that guests "might prefer to retain their strength by a repast at home if the breakfast-hour were at twelve o'clock." These breakfast parties were carried out in a manner very similar to dinner parties—"the dishes are served in courses precisely as for dinner," Mrs. Henderson noted—except that at a breakfast party, tea and coffee were served throughout the meal. This type of social event, she said, was especially esteemed in English literary circles, where, because of the intimacy engendered by the morning hour, the sentiment prevailed that "dinner parties are mere formalities; but you invite a man to breakfast because you want to see him."[39]

BREAKFAST MENUS

February Breakfast

Oranges

Oatmeal   Cocoa or Chocolate

Eggs *à la Dauphine*

Baked Potatoes

Soda Biscuit

July Fourth Breakfast

Strawberries   Wheat-Germs   Coffee

Dropped Eggs on Toast

French Fried Potatoes

Rusks

October Breakfast

Pears   Wheat-Germs   Coffee

Corn Beef Hash

Tomatoes Broiled

Waffles

FROM
SOUP
TUREEN
TO
PUDDING
DISH

. ———— .

1 6 2

December Breakfast

Oranges
Cracked Wheat
Coffee, Chocolate
Fish Balls
Brown Bread Brewis

•

—*1095 Menus, Breakfast, Dinner, and Tea,* ca. *1891*

Early Spring Breakfast Party

1st Course.—An Havana orange for each person, dressed on a fork.

2nd Course.—Larded sweet-breads, garnished with French pease. Cold French rolls or petis pains. Sauterne.

3rd Course.—Small fillets or the tender cuts from porter-house-steaks, served on little square slices of toast, with mushrooms.

4th Course.—Fried oysters; breakfast puffs.

5th Course.—Fillets of grouse (each fillet cut in two), on little thin slices of fried mush, garnished with potatoes *à la Parisienne.*

6th Course.—Sliced oranges, with sugar.

7th Course.—Waffles, with maple sirup.

Summer Breakfast Party

1st Course.—Melons.

2nd Course.—Little fried perch, smelts, or trout, with a sauce Tartare, the dish garnished with shrimps and olives. Coffee, tea, or chocolate.

3rd Course.—Young chickens, sauted, with cream-gravy, surrounded with potatoes *à la neige.* Claret.

4th Course.—Poached eggs on anchovy-toast.

5th Course.—Little fillets of porter-house-steaks, with tomatoes à la Mayonnaise.

6th Course.—Peaches, quartered, sweetened, and half-frozen.

—Mary F. Henderson, *Practical Cooking, and Dinner Giving,* 1878

FROM
SOUP
TUREEN
TO
PUDDING
DISH

• —— •

1 6 3

LUNCH

Lunch, in both the quantity of food served and in the degree of elaboration of the service and table arrangements, was less complicated than dinner. It was often only for the women and children of a family, but could also be expanded to a fashionable meal to which a woman would invite her friends. Mary F. Henderson described this practice at length in her book *Practical Cooking, and Dinner Giving*: "This is more especially a ladies' meal," she wrote. "If one gives a lunch party, ladies alone are generally invited. It is an informal meal on ordinary occasions, when everything is placed upon the table at once. A servant remains in the room only long enough to serve the first round of dishes, then leaves, supposing that confidential conversations may be desired." These ladies' luncheons did not always require advance planning, she said; "familiar friends often 'happen in' to lunch, and are always to be expected."[40] The seeming ease with which these spontaneous events were to be managed would obviously have been offset by the constant anxiety of their anticipation.

Sarah Granger Hollister, a well-to-do woman from Rochester, New York, was fond of giving luncheons and described several elaborate ones in her journals. In February of 1884, she invited fifteen married women friends for bean soup, lamb chops, green peas, French salad, sherbet, cheese and crackers, fruit, olives, jelly, pickles, and punch. Her luncheon began at 1:30 P.M. and ended at 4:30 P.M.

Lunch casters were introduced to Victorian America along with the practice of eating lunch. Paralleling the informality of that meal and the lesser amount of food served, these casters were usually smaller than dinner casters and contained only salt and pepper, although sometimes mustard, and less often oil and vinegar cruets, were included.

Later the same month she invited twelve married women for a meal of clams with lemon and crackers, black bean soup, salmon with mayonnaise dressing, breaded lamb chops with green peas, coffee, pickled peaches, oyster "patees" (probably patties), chicken salad, ice cream and sponge cake, crackers and cheese, and finally a fruit course of bananas, oranges, and candy.[41]

Almira Virginia MacDonald, a woman of more rural circumstances living in Iowa in the 1880s, also noted with enthusiasm in her diary that she had attended a luncheon: "in afternoon went to Mrs. Ragan's to the luncheon given her mother, met about 30 ladies." Almira appeared duly impressed when "Mrs. Ragan ordered her carriage to bring some of us home." Several years later, in New York State, Mrs. MacDonald wrote that she had given a lunch herself, to celebrate the return of her daughter and son-in-law from a trip to South America. Those present included family and five guests; lunch was at noon and featured were beef tongue, stuffed tomatoes, bread sandwiches, grapes, peaches, and lemonade.[42]

In "In Society Here and There" (a social column in a Rochester, New York, newspaper), the benefits of the "standing luncheon"—a social practice introduced from Washington—were discussed in 1890. At this affair "large numbers of ladies and gentlemen were invited to drop in at any time between the hours of one and three. A large supply table set with cold game, salad, and bread and butter, and followed by some light confection was all the refreshment offered, and it was simple." Because it was essentially an informal meal, it "established no burdensome tax upon either hostess or guests."[43]

Everyday lunches for people of ordinary means most often consisted of warmed-up leftovers, cold meat and bread, soup, or stew. *The Successful Housekeeper*, a household manual "especially adapted to the everyday wants of American House-

FROM
SOUP
TUREEN
TO
PUDDING
DISH

· —— ·

1 6 5

wives," provided four menus for "Cold Lunches for Washing Days, or Other Days of Extra Labor." Simple dishes such as cold sliced corned beef or veal, chicken pie, or fish casserole were suggested as entrees; these were accompanied by bread and butter or potatoes, and dessert. Working-class families followed much the same structure, to the extent that they could afford to do so. Cold meat and tea served as lunch for the family of a policeman around the turn of the twentieth century, and the thrifty wife of a glassworker made a tasty soup out of inexpensive ingredients at hand—onions, salt pork, and macaroni—for herself and her children.[44]

LUNCHEON MENUS

Woman's Favorite Sandwich

Restaurant-keepers unanimously agree that the favorite woman's lunch is a cup of bouillon, with a sandwich so thin that it can be rolled up and tied with ribbon.

—Jessup Whitehead, *The Steward's Handbook*, 1899

FROM
SOUP
TUREEN
TO
PUDDING
DISH

· ——— ·

1 6 6

The Successful Housekeeper's
Cold Lunch for Washing Days, or Other Days of Extra Labor

Cold Corned Beef, nicely sliced
Baked Potatoes
Bread, Butter, and Pickle
Dessert—Mince Pie and Cheese

Lenten Lunch Meal

Sardines   Egg Sandwiches
Lemon Pudding   Hard Sauce   Fruit

—The Ladies' Home Journal, 1891

Fannie Munn Field's Boardinghouse Lunch, 15 September 1886

Lamb warmed over with toast
Sweet Potatoes   Bread   Tea

—Fannie Munn Field Diary

Mrs. Collier's Lunch (February 2d.)

Bouillon; sherry
Roast oysters on half-shell; Sauterne
Little vols-au-vent of oysters
Thin scollops, or cuts of fillet of beef, braised;
French pease; Champagne.
Chicken croquettes, garnished with fried parsley;
potato croquettes
Cups of chocolate, with whipped cream
Salad—lettuce dressed with tarragon
Biscuits glaces; fruit-ices
Fruit   Bonbons

—Mary F. Henderson, *Practical Cooking, and Dinner Giving,* 1878

FROM
SOUP
TUREEN
TO
PUDDING
DISH

.———.

DINNER

The hour of dinner has been pronounced by Dr. Johnson to be, in civilized life, the most important hour of the twenty four.[45]

Dr. Johnson's point of view was certainly shared by nineteenth-century Americans; in the United States, the menu, course structure, and manner of presentation of dinner always made it the most elaborate meal of the day. Whether they were for family or company, nineteenth-century dinners had a fairly predictable structure, with complexity increasing according to the level of formality the occasion demanded. They began with either soup or fish and appetizers. A roast or some other form of meat or poultry accompanied by assorted vegetables followed, and the meal ended with something sweet.

The origins of this progression can be found in the Middle Ages and its bountiful feasts, which typically began with the plainer foods and moved through a succession of courses toward the delicacies. A medieval banquet might have begun with "pork (or boar) served with mustard or pepper sauce and either bacon with pease pottage [stew] or venison with frumenty [cracked wheat in broth]," as well as other roasted or boiled meats and probably a meat pie or "pastry." Two subsequent courses included more roasts—probably game birds, meat and poultry pottages, and fishes in different sauces. The richest foods were served at the end of the meal, including pastries, fritters or other fried dishes, jellies, and other sweets. The feast concluded with fruit, nuts, and wafers.[46] Though much less grand, Fannie Munn Field's 1886 schoolgirl dinner of lamb, mashed potatoes, string beans, raw tomatoes, and apple pie follows the same line as its medieval precursor.[47]

Family dinners were usually three separate courses—soup, meat and vegetables or occasionally salad, and dessert; sometimes further simplified by eliminating the soup course. Concerns about economy and nutrition interacted with a desire for novelty and variety in the process of menu planning. Once or twice a week, the focus of a menu might have been roast of beef, lamb, mutton, turkey, or chicken. Roast beef was often provided for Sunday dinner or some other special meal, with its traditional companion, Yorkshire pudding. Lamb was roasted until well done and was accompanied by a sauce made either of mint, sugar, and vinegar or of chopped pickles, butter, and vinegar. Boiled meats were also often

FROM
SOUP
TUREEN
TO
PUDDING
DISH

· —— ·

1 6 8

mentioned, including pork, corned beef, and turkey, the latter stuffed with a mixture of bread, butter, cream, oysters, and egg yolks, and served with a sauce of drawn butter and oysters. These might, in turn, have provided the makings of other dinners—hashes, ragouts, curries, scalloped dishes, fricassees, or stews. Steaks and chops were a favorite form of meat because of the ease of preparing them— they were usually fried or broiled.

Organ meats, such as liver, kidneys, or sweetbreads, further diversified the weekly dinner menu, as did fish and shellfish when it was available at a reasonable price. Dishes like broiled halibut with egg sauce, boiled cod with *sauce hollandaise*, baked blue fish, or some form of oysters (either stewed, roasted, pickled, scalloped, or creamed) appeared at least once a week on family dinner tables, and for many families, fish or clam chowder was traditional fare on Friday. If fresh fish was unavailable or too expensive, canned fish was readily accessible. A can of Cape Breton salmon was often mixed with chopped boiled potatoes, formed into cakes, breaded, and fried in butter to produce salmon crumpets, a tasty and perfectly acceptable alternative to fresh fish. A housewife or cook could prepare mackerel *à la mode*, Scotch stew, clam pie, oyster fritters, or lobster fricassee with equal ease merely by following the directions printed on the can's label.

All of these main dishes were accompanied by some form of white or sweet potato—baked, boiled, mashed, riced, or made into croquettes or puffs—and usually one, maybe two vegetables, either fresh or canned. Frank Hanford, a student

FROM
SOUP
TUREEN
TO
PUDDING
DISH

· —— ·

169

at the U.S. Naval Academy in 1884, wrote home about the prevalence of mashed potatoes in his cadet diet: "You mention mashed potatoes among the good things of your dinner—we have mashed potatoes every day—but such mashed potatoes—oh, ye gods!—I often eat them when I can't get boiled ones—but they're horrid."[48]

At dinner, the vegetables might on occasion have been eliminated in favor of a salad of some sort. Lettuce or dandelion greens with French dressing, coleslaw, or cucumber dressed with oil and vinegar all appeared with some regularity when the ingredients were in season. Out-of-season produce was reserved for special occasions, when hothouse lettuce or celery could be obtained (at a dear price) in city markets.

A well-planned dinner was not complete without its final course—dessert. A multitude of pies, puddings, cakes, and ice cream paraded before the imaginations of menu planners, all of them appealing choices for concluding the meal. Pudding—which the English had traditionally eaten early in the meal in an effort to stave off hearty appetites before the meat was brought on—had become one of the most popular American desserts by the nineteenth century. There were hundreds of varieties, both savory and sweet, some boiled in a cloth, some baked. Jessup Whitehead, author of *The Steward's Handbook* (1899), described pudding as being "English by its name and English by its nature," although in his pudding recipes he still felt compelled to elevate it to the status of French cooking by referring to it as "le pouding."[49]

Mrs. Isabella Beeton listed 108 different pudding recipes in the *Book of Household Management*, a cookbook that was gospel to generations of American women, and she offered her readers a historical overview that traced pudding back to biblical times.[50] Pudding was a frequent dessert in the MacDonald household, as recorded in Mrs. MacDonald's diary:

31 December 1883:   "Busy making pudding for dinner . . ."

17 June 1885:   "I made bread pudding . . ."

27 February 1886:   "I made graham pudding."

20 March 1886:   "I made cake and plum pudding . . ."[51]

FROM
SOUP
TUREEN
TO
PUDDING
DISH

· —— ·

170

Pies may have been even more common than puddings in American diets; mincemeat pie certainly was for the fictional loggers whom William Dean Howells described in *A Modern Instance*: " 'Today's pie-baking day,' the logging camp cook Kinney said. 'But you needn't be troubled on that account. So's tomorrow and so was yesterday. Pie twenty-one times a week, is the word; . . . They say

Rolling out the dough for a perfect piecrust.

FROM

SOUP

TUREEN

TO

PUDDING

DISH

· —— ·

1 7 1

old Agassiz recommended fish as the best food for the brain. Well, I don't suppose but what it is. But I *never* saw anything like meat pie to make ye dream'."[52] Mincemeat—a mixture of chopped boiled beef and suet, sugar, apples, raisins, brandy, cider, and spices—was especially popular at Thanksgiving and Christmas. The strong preference that Kinney and (by inference) many of his fellow countrymen felt for pie was lamented by one of the growing numbers of food reformers in America during the second half of the nineteenth century, people who felt that reform of the nation began with reform of the nation's stomach. Pie, at least for C. W. Gesner, was emblematic of all that was wrong with America's eating habits:

> We are fond of pies and tarts. We cry for pie when we are infants. Pie in countless varieties waits upon us through life. Pie kills us finally. We have apple-pie, peach-pie, rhubarb-pie, cherry-pie, pumpkin-pie, plum-pie, custard-pie, oyster-pie, lemon-pie, and hosts of other pies. Potatoes are diverted from their proper place as boiled or baked, and made into a nice heavy crust to these pies, rendering them as incapable of being acted upon by the gastric juice as if they were sulphate of baryta, a chemical which boiling vitriol will hardly dissolve. . . . How can a person with a pound of green apples and fat dough in his stomach feel at ease?[53]

FAMILY DINNER MENUS

Economical Dinners

FROM
SOUP
TUREEN
TO
PUDDING
DISH

. ⸺ .

Sunday.—Roast Beef, potatoes, and greens. Dessert—pudding or pie, cheese.
Monday.—Hashed Beef, potatoes, and bread pudding.
Tuesday.—Broiled Beef, vegetables, apple pudding.
Wednesday.—Boiled Pork, beans, potatoes, greens, and pie or rice pudding.
Thursday.—Roast or broiled fowl, cabbage, potatoes, lemon pie, cheese.
Friday.—Fish, potato croquettes, escalloped tomatoes, pudding.
Saturday.—*À la mode* beef, potatoes, vegetables, suet pudding and mince pie, cheese.

—*The Successful Housekeeper*, 1883

A Simple Menu for Four Persons

Soup, with fried bread (*aux croutons*)
Chicken, with rice
Macaroni, with tomato sauce
Lettuce, with Mayonnaise Dressing
Corn-starch Pudding,
with a circle of peach marmalade around

·

—Mary F. Henderson, *Practical Cooking, and Dinner Giving*, 1878

Boardinghouse Dinner

Veal

Boiled Potatoes   Gravy and Dressing
Stewed Tomatoes   Corn
Custard

·

—Fannie Munn Field Diary, 16 September 1886

A Family Dinner for Thursday, June 18

Mullagatawny Soup
Veal Cutlets, Brown Sauce
Riced Potatoes   String Beans
Dessert
Tipsy Pudding

·

—*1095 Menus, Breakfast, Dinner, and Tea*, ca. 1891

Lollie Osborne's Birthday Dinner for Codie

"Lollie gave Codie a birthday dinner today."

Roast Chicken
Mashed Potato   Boiled Parsnips   Peas
Lemon Pie   Bread Pudding
Cheese—Oranges cut up—bananas

·

—Almira Virginia MacDonald Diary, 20 April 1891

FROM
SOUP
TUREEN
TO
PUDDING
DISH

· —— ·

1 7 3

While dining at home with the family was, of course, preferable, the alternatives when traveling were not necessarily financially hazardous.

Inexpensive Dinner in a New York Restaurant, 1866

An economical person may procure a small dinner at the best restaurants for $2, or may get one quite as good down town for 65 cents. For example:

Union Square

Plate of beef	65 cents
Fried potatoes	25 cents
Bread	20 cents
Spinach	40 cents
Bottle of Scotch ale	50 cents
	2 dollars

William Street

Plate of beef	15 cents
Fried potatoes	5 cents
Bread (gratis)	00 cents
Spinach	10 cents
Bottle of Scotch ale	30 cents
	60 cents

The William Street beef will be better cooked than the other. There is a steamy sodden flavor about the up-town dishes.

—C. W. Gesner, *Harper's New Monthly Magazine*, 1866

FROM
SOUP
TUREEN
TO
PUDDING
DISH

· —— ·

1 7 4

COMPANY DINNERS

In 1879, Almira MacDonald described an "elaborate dinner party" to which they had been invited by a neighbor, which commenced at 6:30 P.M.[54] Company dinners, as these state occasions were called, were more elaborate than family dinners in every way. The table was dressier, the food fancier and more plentiful, and etiquette and service rituals more complicated.

The American Practical Cookery-Book; or, House-Keeping Made Easy described for its readers in 1861 the prevailing organizational scheme for a dinner party. For a three-course meal, according to this scheme, the first course would consist of soup, meat from the soup, and "kickshaws" (another word for appetizers, derived from the French *quelque chose*, and used to denote a delicacy, fancy dish, or relish, possibly oysters, anchovies, shrimp, sardines, celery, olives, or pickles). For a

FROM
SOUP
TUREEN
TO
PUDDING
DISH

· —— ·

175

dinner of eight to twelve people, this course might also have featured several entrees—"a dish of minced meat, trimmed with leaves of parsley," stewed hare, game hash, stewed veal, trimmed with sorrel leaves, fricassee of chicken, or sole cooked with tomato sauce. These dishes were also called the sides, because they lined the sides of the table, as opposed to the ends and the center. Two sides and four kickshaws were considered adequate for four to six people. Tables were set according to an ordered and symmetrical plan, with the center occupied either by a fancy decoration or the most prominent dish. Next in prominence were the ends, then the sides, and any space in between was filled with the kickshaws. For the second course, a roast of beef or mutton would occupy the center or the ends, with sides of roast poultry or game, one or two vegetables, perhaps a lobster or chicken salad, and a green salad. The third, or dessert, course was equally elaborate and laden with food, namely "dainty sweets and delicate wines, with fruit in season."[55]

The third course might have included a pudding, a pie, or "Chantilly cheese" as center, surrounded by dishes or preserved fruits "richly trimmed with flowers,"

Exotic fruits and flowers, carefully arranged for balance, symmetry, and visual surprise, helped transform a dinner-party table (below) and dessert table (right) from mere furniture into spectacularly landscaped formal gardens.

FROM
SOUP
TUREEN
TO
PUDDING
DISH

·——·

1 7 6

fresh fruit or nuts, frozen creams, and pastry, stewed or brandied fruits and a plate of "little sweetcakes, candies, or crackers."[56] Cream and finely powdered sugar filled in the empty spaces on the table. Desserts were to be served in elegant, usually footed glass or china bowls or compotes, called tazzas in 1851, which were to line the center of the table. These were to be flanked on the sides by lower dishes and plates of dried fruits, nuts, candies, and chocolates, all ornately garnished with flowers, leaves, and vines. Artificial foliage was also widely used; Isabella Beeton recommended it for those who live "in town, [where] the expense and difficulty of obtaining natural foliage is great, but paper and composite leaves are to be purchased at almost nominal price."[57] Sugar flowers, leaves, and figures were also popular adornments and were available from confectioners like H. J. Seiler, of Boston, who advertised in 1882 the availability of "Table Ornaments, Such as Plain and Fancy Maccaroons and Candied Fruit, Pyramids, Marangue and Fruit Baskets, Spun Sugar . . ."[58]

To accommodate this luxurious display on the dessert table, brides like Lucy

FROM

SOUP

TUREEN

TO

PUDDING

DISH

. ——— .

I 7 7

Vincent Rice, of Grand Haven, Michigan, or Frances Emily Munn, of Rochester, New York, were given as wedding presents an array of special dessert wares. Ethel Rafter wrote to her beau about the pleasures of buying such a gift for her friend:

> Here I am once again in Roch. Just came home this morning and then went right back down street to get Nellie B—— a wedding present. I got a pudding dish something like the one you gave Ada. I looked at alot of things and had a great time deciding.[59]

Manufacturers' catalogues confirm that Ethel Rafter had a great deal to choose from: silver, glass, or porcelain fruit bowls, cake baskets, ice-cream sets, sugar

The Victorian sense of whimsy was often apparent in the design of serving implements. This nut bowl and set of nut picks interpret in a very literal and somewhat humorous way the connection between form and function.

FROM

SOUP

TUREEN

TO

PUDDING

DISH

· —— ·

1 7 8

sifters, ivory-handled fruit knives, nut bowls and nutpicks, pie servers, jelly glasses, and sweetmeat dishes. The term "sweetmeat" referred to any of a variety of dessert delicacies, including sugared, preserved, or candied cakes, pastries, fruits, nuts, or even flowers.

In 1867, R. H. Tucker of Wiscasset, Maine, purchased a French porcelain gold-band dinner set that included among the plates and tureens a three-tiered custard stand, with a dozen custard cups—an item that surely was the crowning glory of an elegant dinner table. Two years later, he added a gilt-band china fruit dish and another half dozen custard cups, as well as "1 Doz Plated nut picks in case" and a pair of nutcrackers. At the same time, Tucker also purchased a dozen after-dinner coffee cups and saucers, to support the fashion for French *café noir*.[60]

The centerpiece was the high point, literally and figuratively, of a fancy table. This example of "saccharine architecture" was made of molded sugar and was perhaps intended for a Centennial or Fourth of July celebration.

FROM

SOUP

TUREEN

TO

PUDDING

DISH

· —— ·

179

As a finale, and probably as a welcome relief to the overburdened dinner guests, the Tuckers might have had a servant pass small glasses of *eau sucre*—water sweetened with sugar—one hour after coffee.

DINNER PARTY MENUS

Six O'Clock Dinner for Eight

1st Course	Oysters in Half Shells
2nd Course	Mock Turtle Soup
3rd Course	Lobster Farcis
4th Course	Fillet of Beef (Mushroom Sauce)

Croquettes	Green Peas
Jelly Pickles	Pickled Peaches

5th Course	French Salad	Lemon Pie		
6th Course	Ice Cream	Nut Cake		
7th Course	Oranges	Grapes	Figs	Candy
8th Course	Coffee			

—Sarah Granger Hollister Diary, 6 March 1884

A Simple Company Dinner

Oysters on the half shell

Soup à la Reine

Sherry   Salmon with green pease or cucumbers sliced

Filet de Boeuf and Mushrooms

White Wine   Fried Potatoes

Champagne   Salad of lettuce or tomatoes

Cold Chicken

Madeira   Olives

Ices and Jellies, Cheese

Sherry   Fruits

Coffee

Cordials

FROM
SOUP
TUREEN
TO
PUDDING
DISH

· —— ·

—*The Successful Housekeeper*, 1883

City.

7.15 o'clock.

D.M.

Tuesday January 26th 1892.
Dinner 16 Covers.
Mrs. Munn.
18. W. 58th

Menu.

Caviar, on toast. Oysters Anchovies, on toast,
Soups.
Consommé, Sovereign
Green turtle, clear. (small pieces)
Side dish
Timbales, Imperial fashion
Fish
Fried Oyster crabs. Cucumbers.
Remove
Saddle of lamb, Salvandé
Entrées
Breast of chicken, Lucullus
Peas with lettuce,
Artichokes, Hollandaise lioinade

Terrapin, Newberg style (in the turtles) (désossées.)
Fresh mushrooms, Sous cloche

Awning if raining.
Sherbet, Paradise

One girl.

Roast,
Canvas back ducks.
Cold.
Border of foies gras, Maréchale
Escarolle salad.
Sweets.
Pears, Richelieu
Orange Jelly. Bavarian cream, Vanilla
Fancy ice creams
Fruits. Cakes. Bonbonnières
Mottoes Bonbons
Coffee.

New York dinner party for sixteen. Dr. and Mrs. John Pixley Munn, 1892.

FROM
SOUP
TUREEN
TO
PUDDING
DISH

• —— •

1 8 1

MENU

Soup.

Bouillon.

Fish.

Boiled Salmon with Green Peas.

Cucumbers.   Radishes.   Sliced Tomatoes.

Roast.

Spring Chicken.   Spring Lamb.

Sirloin Beef.   Green Goose.

Vegetables.

Mashed Potatoes.   Green Peas.

Asparagus.   String Beans.

Olives.   Pickles.

Entrees.

Chicken Salad.   Lobster Salad.

Fillet of Beef with Mushrooms.   Chicken Croquettes.

Game.

Potted Pigeons.   Brant.

Dressed Lettuce.

Dessert.

Frozen Pudding.   Charlotte Russe.   Bisquet Tortoui.

Cafe Parfait.   Vanilla Ice Cream.

Strawberry Ice Cream.   Orange Sherbet.

Raspberry Sherbet.   Roman Punch.

Fruit.

Oranges.   Bananas.   Pineapples.

Nuts.   Raisins.

Strawberries and Cream.

CHEESE.

French Coffee.

DOOLING, CATERER.

FROM
SOUP
TUREEN
TO
PUDDING
DISH

· —— ·

1 8 2

Dinner for the 249th Anniversary of the Ancient and Honorable Artillery Company, Faneuil Hall, Boston, 1887.

Mr. and Mrs. William Osborne's
Dinner Party for the Supervisors

The dinner served at one & two tables set for 29—the menu each one a photo of new jail residence tied to the menu card—1st raw oysters (blue points) on ice & lemon, soup (mulligatawny), roast turkey, oyster sauce, turnip, boiled ham, cranberry sauce, potatoes, pickled peaches, chicken salad, ice cream, cake, fruit, coffee.

—Almira Virginia MacDonald Diary, 15 October 1895

SUNDAY DINNERS

We dined on salt pork, vegetables, pies; corned beef also, and always, on Sunday, a boiled Indian pudding.[61]

Sunday dinner often had its own set of rituals, attributable to the traditional importance for Christians of the Sabbath as a day of rest. Although by the nineteenth century few Americans kept the Sabbath as strictly as had their ances-

FROM
SOUP
TUREEN
TO
PUDDING
DISH

·———·

1 8 3

tors, many still went to church in the morning, and it remained difficult to prepare a large dinner by midday. They traditionally resolved that dilemma by preparing a pot of baked beans and brown bread on Saturday; these could then be placed in the oven to warm while the family attended the Sunday-morning service. The Indian pudding of the Beecher family served the same purpose: it could boil away unattended all morning and would be ready to eat by dinner time.

During the second half of the nineteenth century, Sunday dinner took on an added importance that corresponded to the increasingly moral context of the American home. As the domestic sphere more and more functioned as a sanctuary for the family from the outside world, a place where Christian values could be reinforced, Sunday dinner, of all dinners, should have emblemized those values. A successful home was one that reflected not only adherence to Christian virtue, but also, indirectly, success in the world of business and society.[62] A properly designed Sunday dinner had the power to communicate both values: it brought the family together in appreciation of God's grace and confirmed a celebration that conformed in all respects—form, etiquette, food, and environment—to the exacting standards of the competitive outer world.

SUNDAY DINNER MENUS

Economical Sunday Dinner, 1857

Roast Beef

Potatoes   Greens

Yorkshire Pudding

.

—Alexis Soyer, *The Modern Housewife, or Ménagère,* 1857

FROM

SOUP

TUREEN

TO

PUDDING

DISH

· ⸻ ·

1 8 4

A Sunday Dinner for March

Oyster Stew

Baked Chicken with Dressing

Mashed Potatoes

Cabbage Salad   Lima Beans

Cranberry Tarts   Oranges   Cheese

Wafers   Nuts   Coffee

.

—Grace Townsend, *Dining Room and Kitchen,* 1891

TEA

I was almost grown before I was introduced to . . . "a real old New England tea-table." During one delicious vacation I learned, and reveled in knowing, what this meant. Black tea with cream (I have never relished it without, since that idyllic summer), round of brown bread, light, sweet, and fresh; hot short-cake in piles that were very high when we sat down, and very low when we arose; a big glass bowl of raspberries and currants that were growing in the garden under the back windows an hour before; a basket of frosted cake; a plate of pink ham, balanced by one of shaved, *not* chipped beef—and *sage cheese*! I had never eaten it before. I have never tasted it anywhere else than in that wide, cool tea-room, the level sun-rays flickering through the grape-vines shading the west side of the house, and through the open casements opposite, a view of Boston bay— all purple and rose and gold, dotted with hundreds of white sails. This was what

Teatime.

FROM
SOUP
TUREEN
TO
PUDDING
DISH

. ——— .

1 8 5

we had, when, in that Old New England farm-house, Polly, the faithful—who had startled me, for a time, by saying, "proper glad," and "sweet pretty"; who "hadn't ought" to do this, and "should admire" to do that—Polly, whom nobody thought of calling a servant, but was a "help" in every conceivable sense of the word—had "put the kettle on and we all had tea!"[63]

Tea was still the final meal of the day for many families in 1875, when cookbook author Marion Harland published this stirring recollection of an old-fashioned tea. Maria Parloa described it to her readers in 1898: "This meal usually consists of tea, bread and butter, cold meat or some hot relish, cake and some form of cooked or preserved fruit. . . . When the usual tea is replaced by a hot supper, it is necessary to have warm plates, and to change plates when the sweets are served."[64]

Cold meat might have been sliced from a leftover roast or perhaps from something specially prepared. Almira MacDonald noted in her diary that she "made pressed veal for tea."[65] In 1891, *1095 Menus, Breakfast, Dinner, and Tea* suggested a wide variety of cold dishes for tea, including roast beef, ham, mutton, smoked tongue, Bologna sausage, corned beef, spiced beef, potato and beef salad, sweetbreads mayonnaise, or potted fish. As "hot relish," it proffered lobster cutlets,

FROM
SOUP
TUREEN
TO
PUDDING
DISH

· —— ·

1 8 6

A well-supplied family tea table would have included, in addition to tea, milk, and sugar, a choice of cold meat, tea cakes or muffins, and some form of fresh or preserved fruit.

baked eggs, fancy roast oysters, broiled smoked salmon, coquilles of grouse, boiled sausages, or omelet. Cakes, biscuits, toast, rolls, griddle cakes, rusks, cookies, crumpets, and wafers, along with fruit, completed its recommendations. The meal was usually a simple homey one that could be easily expanded to accommodate friends who might drop in unexpectedly. Eliza Leslie remarked that "in a well-provided house, there can be no difficulty in adding something to the family tea-table, which, in genteel life, should never be discreditably parsimonious."[66] Tea usually took place in the dining room, and Catharine Beecher's directions for setting the table provide further indication that this was to be a comparatively simple meal (in contrast to dinner):

> In setting a tea table, small-sized plates are set around, with a knife, napkin and butter-plate laid by each in a regular manner; while the articles of food are to be set, also, in regular order. On the waiter are placed tea cups and saucers, sugar-bowl, slop-bowl, cream cup, and two or three articles for tea, coffee, and hot water, as the case may be.[67]

In addition to family tea, Victorian women frequently conducted or attended afternoon tea parties. These could be simple gatherings of a few friends or elaborate social events for many people. Mrs. Burton Kingsland, in "A Talk about Teas" in the *Ladies' Home Journal*, characterized the "modern 'tea'" as a "lineal descendant of the 'salon' which, for years in England, and especially in France, played so conspicuous a part, and where woman first attained that social pre-eminence that has been since conceded as her special prerogative.[68]

The American Centennial celebration of 1875–1877 had an invigorating effect on American tea-drinking habits. Americans loved to re-enact "Old Fashioned Tea Parties," as they imagined their eighteenth-century predecessors (Mayflower descendants all, no doubt) must have done. Lollie (not yet married to William Osborne) and her brother Arthur MacDonald attended such a party in November of 1876, and their mother recorded the details in her diary: "Arthur and Lollie at old fashioned tea party this eve at Ruth Siddon's—Lollie dressed in my green striped silk with a high ruche at neck and hair dressed high on the head—Arthur wore ruffled and puffed shirt bosom & white silk neck tie of his G'fathers—coat turned back, etc."[69]

A story describing an old-fashioned tea party, given by a young New York socialite in honor of her grandmother, was read eagerly by subscribers to the *Ladies' Home Journal* in 1892 for details about food, table, costume, and customs:

> The guests came in old-fashioned costumes, with hair well powdered, carried old-fashioned reticules, wore tiny black patches upon their faces, and, of course,

FROM
SOUP
TUREEN
TO
PUDDING
DISH

. ——— .

1 8 7

their choicest pieces of lace. Tea was served in the dining-room; a snowy damask tablecloth covered the table, at the head of which was placed a large silver tray, upon which were arranged, in perfect symmetry, the dainty white and gold dinner teacups and saucers. Upon either side was placed the quaint silver tea service of Queen Anne pattern, with its gracefully-curved, fluted handles. Old-fashioned candelabra, with plain white wax candles, and no new-fangled paper shades, stood upon lace mats on either side of a china bowl filled with crimson dahlias. The guests were in number ten. At each place was laid a plate of white and gold, a large damask table napkin folded perfectly square, a knife and two-pronged fork, both with white ivory handles, and a heavy silver dessert spoon. At the foot of the table was a large white and gold platter filled with slices of cold chicken garnished with nasturtium leaves, and upon either side similar dishes, containing daintily-cut slices of ham and tongue. The bread was cut in thin slices and buttered,

FROM
SOUP
TUREEN
TO
PUDDING
DISH

· ——— ·

1 8 8

"Old-fashioned tea parties," costumed re-enactments of eighteenth-century teas, were popularized by the American Centennial in 1876.

so that neither butter plates nor butter dishes were needed. At certain equal distances stood little white pots of preserved strawberries and gooseberries, a jar of orange marmalade, and a pretty china dish of honey in the comb. Tiny little dishes in which these dainties were to be served and silver spoons of dessert-size stood near. Low baskets of silver covered with lace held golden sponge and rich, dark fruit-cake, and upon two silver trays, covered with lace, stood little Dresden china cups filled with custard, upon which a generous supply of nutmeg had been grated. The tea was hot and fragrant. There was no ice-water, nor, indeed, ice visible anywhere, yet everything looked cool, attractive and beautiful. . . .[70]

A WEEK OF FAMILY TEAS FOR JANUARY

Sunday

Tea, Cocoa
Scrambled Eggs
Water Toast
Spice Cake, Stewed Apples

Monday

Tea, Cocoa
Lobster Cutlets
Graham Biscuit
One-Egg Cake, Orange Jelly

Tuesday

Tea, Cocoa
Meat Cakes
Dutch Apple Cake
Wafers

Wednesday

Tea, Cocoa
Potato and Beef Salad
Muffins, Toasted
Cream Cakes, Preserved Pineapple

Thursday

Tea, Coffee
Cold Roast Beef
Crumpets
Orange and Cocoanut Cream Cake

Friday

Tea, Cocoa
Bologna Sausage
Tea Cakes
Wafers
Crab-Apple Jelly

FROM
SOUP
TUREEN
TO
PUDDING
DISH

· —— ·

190

Saturday

Tea, Cocoa
Potato Salad
Parker House Rolls
White Mountain Cake, Preserved Strawberries

—1095 Menus, Breakfast, Dinner, and Tea, ca. 1891

SUPPER

In 1811, Timothy Dwight, Yale College president and clergyman, offered an analysis of the structural make-up of supper:

> Supper in most parts of the country is like the breakfast, except that it is made up partially of preserved fruits, different kinds of cakes, pies, tarts, etc. The meats used at breakfast and supper are generally intended to be dainties.[71]

The format Dwight described changed very little during the course of the nineteenth century. Supper remained a relatively light meal and was usually marked by a high degree of informality. The presence of some hot delicacy on the table—Welsh rarebit, fried oysters, or Saratoga potatoes—usually distinguished it from family tea. Often these hot dishes were additional preparations made for company, as in the MacDonald household. Mrs. MacDonald noted on Saturday, 12 March 1887, that her family was having supper with company and that her daughter Anne "fried Saratoga potatoes, had beef tongue, currants, etc." Again on Saturday, 26 March, she wrote, "Anne cooking potatoes and fried oysters etc. for supper—asked Dudley to supper." Dudley, Anne's beau, was the recipient of many evenings of Anne's Saratoga potatoes before they eventually, and secretly, married.[72]

Sunday-night super was an important social occasion for the Hookers, a well-to-do family from Rochester, New York. Fan Bissell, a family cousin, reminisced about these gatherings at Bienvenue, the Hookers' home: "In summer on the south veranda. In winter in the back parlor. Plain supper, white or graham bread and butter, cheese, pickles and plain cake. Tea and coffee. Plenty of people and good talk. Something to look forward to."[73]

"Gentlemen's suppers" were all-male evening social events analogous to ladies' luncheons. They were held in both private homes and public establishments. Mary F. Henderson commented on the utility involved for the woman who decided to act as hostess at these stag parties: "If one has not a reliable cook, it is very convenient to give these entertainments, as the hostess has a chance to station herself in the *cuisine* (of course, out of earshot of the men) to personally superintend the supper." Mrs. Henderson's ready relegation of a wife to the role of servant to her husband and his friends may be for some women a

FROM
SOUP
TUREEN
TO
PUDDING
DISH

· —— ·

1 9 1

far from ideal assignment.[74] Private caterers, hotels, and restaurants offered men another option, one that was frequently adopted by a number of fraternal and military organizations in the late nineteenth century. Such a supper, given in honor of General George H. Chapman by the members of the late eighth New York Cavalry, was held on Thursday evening, 9 June 1881, at the Clinton Hotel in Rochester. The bill of fare began with clams on the half shell, and continued with soup, entrees, salad, vegetables, dessert, and coffee.[75]

Supper could also be a late evening meal, often held in conjunction with a social event—such as the Napier Ball, held at the Willard Hotel in Washington, D.C., to introduce Lord and Lady Willard to the fashionable elite of that city. Supper was presented at 11:30 P.M. and was described in great detail in *Harper's Weekly*, so that those who were not invited could vicariously absorb the elegance:

> It was a banquet which would have gladdened Lucullus, and Soyer could not have prepared a more elaborate repast *à la Francaise*, while there were also terrapin from the Potamac, oysters from the fundum of James's River, canvas-back ducks from the Delaware, reed birds from the Savannah, wild turkeys from Kentucky, prairie hens from Iowa, mutton from the Cumberland mountains, venison from

FROM
SOUP
TUREEN
TO
PUDDING
DISH

· ——— ·

1 9 2

The Napier Ball Supper, 1859.

North Carolina, and other "native American" dishes. The saccharine architecture was wonderful, especially two temples, crowned with statues of Britannia and America, ornamented with the arms of the United Kingdom and of the States, and decorated with the British and American flags. Fierce was the attack made upon luxuries and delicacies, but a corps of waiters behind the tables kept reinforcing empty dishes, and meanwhile there was a running fire of champagne corks, many of the fair ones eating most heartily. . . .[76]

S U P P E R   M E N U S

S a t u r d a y   N i g h t   S u p p e r   a t   H o m e

Lima Beans
Canned Peaches
Fresh Peaches
Grapes
Bread and Butter
Cookies and Muffins

·

—Fannie Munn Field Diary, 18 September 1886

A   G e n t l e m e n ' s   F i s h   S u p p e r ,   1 8 7 7

1st Course.—Raw oysters served in a block of ice. [The ice has a pretty effect in the gas-light.]
2nd Course.—Shad, maitre d'hotel sauce, garnished with smelts.
3rd Course.—Sweet-breads and tomato sauce.
4th Course.—Boiled sardines, on toast.
5th Course.—Deviled chicken, Cunard sauce.
6th Course.—Fillets of duck, with salad of lettuce.
7th Course.—Mayonnaise of salmon, garnished with shrimps.
8th Course.—Welsh rare-bit.
9th Course.—Charlotte Russe.
10th Course.—Ice-cream and cake.

—Mary F. Henderson, *Practical Cooking, and Dinner Giving*, 1878

FROM
SOUP
TUREEN
TO
PUDDING
DISH

· —— ·

Supper table, 1883.

Church Supper

"Lollie prepared egg sandwiches & eggs of cream & gelatine e.c. We all took our supper at church."

—Almira Virginia MacDonald Diary, 19 April 1892

Boston Restaurant Supper, 1880s

I went into the Parker House one night about midnight, and I saw four doctors there eating lobster salad, and deviled crab, and washing it down with champagne; and I made up my mind that the doctors needn't talk to me any more about what was wholesome. I was going in for what was *good*. And there ain't anything better for supper than Welsh rabbit in *this* world.

—William Dean Howells, *A Modern Instance*, 1882

FROM
SOUP
TUREEN
TO
PUDDING
DISH

. ——— .

1 9 5

HOLIDAYS AND SPECIAL OCCASIONS

We have our customary chicken and are *thankful* it is as well with us as it is![77]

Beginning with New Year's Day, traditionally a time for open houses, parties, and receptions, Americans eagerly celebrated a succession of holidays during the Victorian period. Twelfth Night, St. Valentine's Day, Easter, the Fourth of July, Thanksgiving, and Christmas all provided opportunities for special meals for family and company, much as they do today. Despite the religious orientation of many of these holidays, their meals—breakfast, dinner, and supper—actually often served as the central focus of the day. As one social commentator in *Harper's Weekly* explained it, "In connection with the Birth-feast of Him . . . there can be nothing inappropriate in the emphasis which is laid by all good Christians upon the Christmas Dinner and the elements of its composition."[78]

Thanksgiving and Christmas dinners were probably the most carefully planned meals of the year for most families. Women typically began to finalize preparations days in advance. Almira Virginia MacDonald, in anticipation of Thanksgiving 1870, noted in her diary on November 22 that she had "prepared mincemeat for pies and made gold and silver cake." The next day she "made 4 mince pies & prepared stuffing for turkey." The following day was Thanksgiving; the family went to church and dined at three o'clock, despite the absence of Mr. MacDonald, a lawyer, who was busy on a murder case all day. The hour was an eighteenth-century custom and probably also observed for Christmas and for New Year's dinner.[79]

Maria Parloa recommended to her readers that they begin making their mince pies somewhat earlier than Mrs. MacDonald had. "Mincemeat improves with age," she advised. "Make it as early in the month as possible. When making the Thanksgiving pies, add to every two quarts of the prepared mince-meat one

The American flag is an unusual addition to the decor of this Groton, New York dining room.

Thanksgiving dinner, 1867.

pound of candied fruit—cherries, apricots, and pineapple, all cut fine: also a tumbler of crab-apple or quince jelly. Bake the pies five or six days before Thanksgiving and warm them before using, reserving one for such guests as may prefer it cold."[80]

With the increased work load, women often collaborated on the cooking, cleaning, and baking, especially if they had no servants or, as was customary, had given the servants a day off. In 1882, Mrs. MacDonald found herself in that predicament: "Thanksgiving Day—12 to dinner & no hired girl, but was able with mother & Anne's help to get a good dinner of roast turkey, chicken salad, onions, potatoes, cranberry sauce, lemon pie, mince pie, & cider. . . ."[81]

The MacDonalds' Thanksgiving meal, although simpler, was not far from the formulaic Thanksgiving menu that was published in Fannie Farmer's *Boston Cooking-School Cook Book* in 1896. That menu combined the symbolic foods that connoted "Pilgrim" and "America" with the elegance and complicated course structure of the European aristocracy—a statement in microcosm of late-nineteenth-century America's desire to be itself, and yet not be itself at the same time![82]

Turkey was the traditional roast for Christmas dinner, too, although some families followed the English custom of serving roast beef or roast goose. *Godey's*

FROM
SOUP
TUREEN
TO
PUDDING
DISH

· —— ·

1 9 8

Lady's Book in 1885 led novice cooks through the intricacies of roasting a Christmas bird, as well as instructions for boiled turkey, with oyster sauce or purée of celery, and a galantine of turkey—boned and rolled around with pounded veal and chopped tongue, then boiled and, when cold, glazed with jelly. Other foods *Godey's* recommended for a Christmas dinner included plum pudding with brandy butter, mince pies, and apple cheesecake.[83] Sarah Tyson Rorer, writing for the *Ladies' Home Journal* in 1897, offered a Christmas menu that began with oysters on the half shell and included such oddities as "devilled spaghetti"—macaroni and cheese with bread crumbs on top—and ginger sherbet. For the turkey, she recommended chestnut stuffing, which, unlike bread, will not "draw the juices from the meat, leaving it dry and lifeless." Rorer's menu featured a salad course of lettuce, toasted crackers, and cheese balls. "The salad course is no small part of a dinner," she said. "If you cannot get lettuce or celery, do not object to the inner white portion of a hard head of cabbage. Serve it with French dressing, delicate crackers toasted in the oven, and hot cheese balls."[84] Since lettuce and celery were such popular items on holiday menus, many nineteenth-century growers raised special glasshouse crops, timed for the Christmas market.[85]

Even after all of the midafternoon festivities, many families, like that of May Bragdon, gathered again in the evening for supper. She described her family's Christmas supper in 1893, with several tables—a large one for the adults and smaller tables for the young people. The supper included coffee, bread and butter, chicken salad, ice cream, macaroons, and "Frank's birthday cake with 7 candles."[86] Mrs. Rorer, as well, referred to the evening meal on Christmas Day with the following advice: "While man seems to be endowed with extraordinary capacity, and almost superhuman power of digestion at this festive season of the year, it is not well to have a heavy supper following the Christmas dinner." She suggested a light meal at 7:30, consisting of clam bouillon, broiled oysters on toast, jelly cubes, and sponge cake.[87]

New Year's Day was another traditional occasion for feasting in the Bragdon and in many other American families. May Bragdon described the meal: ". . . I took the turkey & his surroundings—poor turkey! He was being splattered over the table in all directions by a couple of amateur carvers. We had a jolly meal tho'—and a long one ending with 'apple snow' and nuts, oranges (they later, in the parlor)." Still later, they ate "chocolate, cold turkey, then bread and butter, cake, and oranges."[88]

For the hot-weather holiday of the Fourth of July, fried chicken and strawberry shortcake have been standard fare at least since 1861, when Katherine Bragdon wrote that she "went to Pulaski and tired ourselves out looking round, then came home to chicken and strawberry shortcake and had a nice ride on the water."[89]

FROM

SOUP

TUREEN

TO

PUDDING

DISH

· —— ·

199

On the Fourth in 1870, the MacDonald family sailed across Seneca Lake to Johnson's Cove for a "pic-nic." Mrs. MacDonald did not mention what her packaged fare was, but it might have included cold roast chicken, sardines, hard-boiled eggs, Boston brown bread, buttered rolls, sweet pickles, plum jelly, Saratoga chips ("carried in fancy papers which can be thrown away"), jelly, watermelon, chocolate loaf cake, fruit, cookies, lemonade, iced tea, and, of course, ice cream. To carry ice cream to a picnic without having it melt, one was to pack ice well around the freezer and then wrap the whole in a heavy carpet.[90]

Although they were not holidays in the formal sense, birthdays, especially children's birthdays, were often given the status of a family celebration. Sarah Granger Hollister wrote in her diary in 1885 about a party she gave for twenty-four people, which may have been a birthday celebration: the menu included creamed oysters, fillet of beef, lobster salad, ice cream and cake.[91] Almira Virginia MacDonald described a very different sort of party that she gave for her daughter, Anne, in 1873:

> Anne's fifth birthday party—20 little ones were here; had biscuit buttered, little cakes iced with a spot of red sugar sand on top, lemon cake, grapes—beef tongue, oranges—candy & mottoes—but the best fun after tea was —— which look like paper mottoes but snap when pulled & a fancy paper bonnet is found rolled in the middle which each put on and marched in—we also had the magic lantern. . . . All seemed happy, very. . . .[92]

In 1894, Mrs. MacDonald, by then a grandmother, was helping to put on a birthday party for her two grandsons, Bush and Henry: "Busy all day—helping get house ready for boy's party for 5:30 to 8:30. 40 boys & girls here . . . sandwiches, potato balls, nuts—cheese straws, ice cream & cake."[93]

FROM
SOUP
TUREEN
TO
PUDDING
DISH

· —— ·

2 0 0

MENUS FOR SPECIAL OCCASIONS

Almira Virginia MacDonald's
Thanksgiving Dinner, 1882

Roast Turkey
Onions and Potatoes   Cranberry Sauce
Chicken Salad
Lemon Pie   Mince Pie   Cider

Fannie Farmer's Menu for Thanksgiving Dinner

Oyster Soup   Crisp Crackers
Celery   Salted Almonds
Roast Turkey   Cranberry Jelly
Mashed Potatoes   Onions in Cream   Squash
Chicken Pie
Fruit Pudding   Sterling Sauce
Mince, Apple, and Squash Pie
Neapolitan Ice Cream   Fancy Cakes
Fruit   Nuts and Raisins   Bonbons
Crackers   Cheese   Cafe Noir

·

—*Boston Cooking-School Cook Book*, 1896

Christmas Supper, 1890

Stewed Terrapin   Saratoga Chips
Parker House Rolls
Preserved Pears   Waffles
Coffee

·

—*1095 Menus, Breakfast, Dinner, and Tea*, ca. 1891

Christmas Dinner

Oysters on the Half Shell
Clear Soup   Custard and Spinach Blocks
Olives   Celery
Deviled Spaghetti
Roasted Turkey, Chestnut Stuffing   Cranberry Jelly
Sweet Potato Croquettes
Peas Served in Turnip Cups
Ginger Sherbet   Lettuce Salad   Cheese Balls
Toasted Crackers
Plum Pudding, Hard Sauce
Coffee   Bonbons   Almonds

·

—*The Ladies' Home Journal*, December 1897

FROM
SOUP
TUREEN
TO
PUDDING
DISH

· —— ·

Bill of Fare for a Picnic for Forty Persons

A joint of cold roast beef, a joint of cold boiled beef, 2 ribs of lamb, 2 shoulders of lamb, 4 roast fowls, 2 roast ducks, 1 ham, 1 tongue, 2 veal-and-ham pies, 2 pigeon pies, 6 medium-sized lobsters, 1 piece of collared calf's head, 18 lettuces, 6 baskets of salad, 6 cucumbers.

Stewed fruit well sweetened, and put into glass bottles well corked; 3 or 4 dozen plain pastry biscuits to eat with the stewed fruit, 2 dozen fruit turnovers, 4 dozen cheesecakes, 2 cold cabinet puddings in moulds, 2 blanc-manges in moulds, a few jam puffs, 1 large cold plum-pudding (this must be good), a few baskets of fresh fruit, 3 dozen plain biscuits, a piece of cheese, 6 lbs. of butter (this, of course, includes the butter for tea), 4 quartern loaves of household bread, 3 dozen rolls, 6 loaves of tin bread (for tea), 2 plain plum cakes, 2 pound cakes, 2 sponge cakes, a tin of mixed biscuits, ½ lb. of tea. Coffee is not suitable for a picnic, being difficult to make.

Things not to be forgotten at a Picnic

A stick of horseradish, a bottle of mint-sauce well corked, a bottle of salad dressing, a bottle of vinegar, made mustard, pepper, salt, good oil, and pounded sugar. If it can be managed, take a little ice. It is scarcely necessary to say that plates, tumblers, wine-glasses, knives, forks, and spoons, must not be forgotten; as also teacups and saucers, 3 or 4 teapots, some lump sugar, and milk, if this last-named article cannot be obtained in the neighbourhood. Take 3 corkscrews.

Beverages.—3 dozen quart bottles of ale, packed in hampers; ginger-beer, soda-water, and lemonade, of each 2 dozen bottles; 6 bottles of sherry, 6 bottles of claret, champagne à discrétion, and any other light wine that may be preferred, and 2 bottles of brandy. Water can usually be obtained; so it is useless to take it.

—Isabella Beeton, *Mrs. Beeton's Book of Household Management*, 1859–1861

FROM
SOUP
TUREEN
TO
PUDDING
DISH

· —— ·

2 0 2

RECIPES & INSTRUCTIONS

TABLE OF WEIGHTS AND MEASURES*

4 teaspoonfuls of liquid	=	1 tablespoonful
4 tablespoonfuls of liquid	=	½ gill, ¼ cup, or 1 wineglassful
1 tablespoonful of liquid	=	½ ounce
1 pint of liquid	=	1 pound
2 gills of liquid	=	1 cup or ½ pint
1 kitchen cup	=	½ pint
1 heaping quart of sifted flour	=	1 pound
4 cups of flour	=	1 quart or 1 pound
1 rounded tablespoonful of flour	=	½ ounce
3 cups of corn meal	=	1 pound
1½ pints of corn meal	=	1 pound
1 cup of butter	=	½ pound
1 pint of butter	=	1 pound
1 tablespoonful of butter	=	1 ounce
Butter the size of an egg	=	2 ounces
Butter the size of a walnut	=	1 ounce
1 solid pint of chopped meat	=	1 pound
10 eggs	=	1 pound
A dash of pepper	=	⅛ teaspoonful, or 3 good shakes
2 cups of granulated sugar	=	1 pound
1 pint of granulated sugar	=	1 pound
1 pint of brown sugar	=	13 ounces
2½ cups of powdered sugar	=	1 pound

* An important result of the application of scientific principles to the art of cookery was the standardization of weighing and measuring ingredients, replacing casual instructions like "butter the size of an egg." This typical late-nineteenth-century table contains two errors that should be noted in adapting recipes. One tablespoon of butter equals one half-ounce, not one ounce. The size of a modern teaspoon has increased to five milliliters, so that three—not four—teaspoons equal one tablespoon.—Ed.

BEVERAGES

The infusion or decoction of the roasted seeds of the coffee-berry, when not too strong, is a wholesome, exhilarating, and strengthening beverage; and when mixed with a large proportion of milk, is a proper article of diet for literary and sedentary people.

Sarah Josepha Hale, *The New Household Receipt-Book*, 1853

Instructions for Roasting and Brewing Coffee

Mocha and Old Java are the best, and time improves all kinds. Dry it a long time before roasting. Roast it quick, stirring constantly, or it will taste raw and bitter. When roasted, put in a bit of butter the size of a chestnut. Keep it shut up close, or it loses its strength and flavor. Never grind it till you want to use it, as it loses flavor by standing.

To prepare it, put two great spoonfuls to each pint of water, mix it with the white, yolk, and shell of an egg, pour on hot, but not boiling water, and boil it not over ten minutes. Take it off, pour in half a tea-cup of cold water, and in five minutes pour it off without shaking. When eggs are scarce, clear with fish skin, as below. Boiled milk improves both tea and coffee, but must be boiled separately. Much coffee is spoiled by being burned black instead of brown, and by being burned unequally, some too much and some too little. Constant care and stirring are indispensable.

Catharine E. Beecher, *Miss Beecher's Domestic Receipt Book*, 1858

French Method of Preparing Coffee

Divide the quantity to be roasted into two parts; roast one part in a coffee roaster, turn it constantly, till the coffee is the color of dried almonds, and has lost one eighth of its weight. Roast the other part, till the color of chestnuts, and it has lost one-fifth of its weight. Roast and grind your coffee the day it is to be used; mix the two parts, and grind them in a coffee mill. To two ounces of ground coffee put four cups of cold water; draw this off, and set it one side. Put to the same coffee, three cups of boiling water; draw this off and add it to the cold infusion. When wanted, heat it quickly, in a silver coffee pot. Do not let it boil, the perfume will be lost by evaporation. Do not make the coffee in a tin vessel. Make it in China, delft-ware, or in silver.

Mrs. A. L. Webster, *The Improved Housewife*, 1853

Turkish Coffee

The coffee must be slowly roasted, not burnt, and brought only to an amber brown: it must be roasted day by day. The flavor dissipates in a few hours; it must be reduced by pounding to an impalpable powder. In making it, two opposite and, apparently, incompatible ends are to be secured—strength and flavor. To obtain the first, it must be boiled; by boiling, the second is lost. The difficulty is surmounted by a double process—one thorough cooking, one slight one; by the first a strong infusion is obtained; by the second, that infusion is flavored. Thus a large pot with coffee-lees stands simmering by the fire; this is the sherbet. When a cup is wanted, the pounded coffee is put in the little tin or copper pan, and placed on the embers; it fumes for a moment, then the sherbet is poured on; in a few seconds the froth (*caïmah*) rises; presently an indication that it is about to boil is made manifest, when the coffee is instantly taken from the fire, carried into the apartment, turned into the cup, and drank.

Sarah Josepha Hale, *The New Household Receipt-Book*, 1853

Tea

The Chinese have a tea-kettle boiling on the table, and put the tea into an ordinary tea-pot, upon which they pour the boiling water, and allow it to stand only a few seconds before it is used. If a second cup is wanted a fresh infusion is made.

The most approved method in this country for black tea, is to pour a small quantity of boiling water on the tea; let it stand on a hot stove (not to boil) for twenty minutes, then put it into the tea-pot intended for the table, and fill it up with boiling water. In pouring out black tea into the cup always put in the sugar first, then the cream, and the tea last. It alters the flavor entirely to add the sugar or cream afterward.

RECIPES

Sarah E. Scott, *Every-Day Cookery for Every Family*, 1868

Tea à la russe

Make tea in the usual way; let it get cold on the leaves; then strain off into a pitcher, and slice two or three *peeled* lemons into each quart. The slices should be thin. Put sugar and ice into tumblers and fill up with the tea.

Great bowls of this, ice-cold and well-sweetened, are popular at fairs, church-receptions, and picnics, and have become a fashion at evening-parties where wines and punch are not served.

Marion Harland, *The Cottage Kitchen*, 1883

Chocolate

A nice preparation of chocolate is to grate half a cake of the best chocolate, and pour over it a pint of boiling water to dissolve the chocolate; then add a pint of fresh milk; let this all boil for five minutes, then beat up the yolk of two eggs very smoothly, and stir in; sweeten to the taste, and serve hot, with hot, dry toast.

Cocoa shells are also very nutritious and palatable; they must be roasted with the same care as coffee, turned slowly during the operation, but constantly and in a tightly covered cylinder. After being carefully roasted a deep brown, when cool it must be triturated smoothly in a mortar, as much as may be required; when reduced to a paste, and all the little husks removed, then pour over a spoonful of the paste a cupful of boiling water, thus proportioned to the quantity required; then boil it for twenty minutes, stirring, but kept covered; then serve as coffee, diluting with boiling milk or cream, and sugar to the taste; this forms a very agreeable beverage.

Sarah E. Scott, *Every-Day Cookery for Every Family*, 1868

Currant Wine

Pick and mash the currants, either with your hands or a clean block, in a tub; strain them, and to one gallon of juice, put two gallons of water; and to each gallon of the mixture, put three pounds of sugar; stir it until the sugar is dissolved, then put it in a clean cask that has never been used for beer or cider; put it in a cellar or cool place, and let it work out at the bung for several weeks; have a gallon of it saved in a jug to fill up with, as it works out. When it is done working, bung it up.

You may rack it off towards spring, or it will not hurt it to stand a year.

If you want a barrel of wine, you must have eight gallons of currant juice, sixteen of water, and seventy-two pounds of sugar; put in a quart of brandy after it has done working; if you can get a clean brandy barrel to put it in, it is better than a new one.

•

Elizabeth F. Lea, *Domestic Cookery, Useful Receipts, and Hints to Young Housekeepers*, 1865

Eau Sucre

Sweeten boiling water with sugar to your taste. This beverage is considered soporific; is good for weak nerves; and is much used by French ladies.

•

Mrs. A. L. Webster, *The Improved Housewife*, 1853

Roman Punch

Roman punch is generally served as a course just after the beef. It is a refreshing arrangement, preparing one for the game which comes after. In England, punch is served with soup, especially with turtle or mock-turtle. One often sees Roman punch served as a first course just before the soup.

•

Mary F. Henderson, *Practical Cooking, and Dinner Giving*, 1878

•

1 quart of lemon water-ice
½ pint of champagne
½ pint of Jamaica rum
1 gill of maraschino
1 teaspoonful of vanilla.

Have the lemon water-ice frozen very hard, thin it slowly with the liquors, beat well. Pack and cover the freezer well, stand it away four or five hours to ripen. It must not be frozen hard, as it is better when served rather liquid and frothy. Serve in glasses.

•

Sarah Tyson Rorer, *Mrs. Rorer's Philadelphia Cook Book*, 1886

A Cheap and Easy Method of Brewing Beer

One bushel of malt and three-quarters of a pound of hops will, on an average, brew twenty gallons of good beer.

For this quantity of malt, boil twenty-four gallons of water; and, having dashed it in the copper with cold water to stop the boiling, steep the malt (properly covered up) for three hours; then tie up the hops in a hair-cloth, and boil malt, hops, and wort, altogether, for three-quarters of an hour, which will reduce it to about twenty gallons. Strain it off, and set it to work when lukewarm.

In large brewings, this process perhaps would not answer, but in small ones, where the waste is not so great, and where the malt can be boiled, the essence is sure to be extracted.

Sarah Josepha Hale, *The New Household Receipt-Book*, 1853

Ginger Beer

Pour four quarts of boiling water, upon an ounce and a half of ginger, an ounce of cream of tartar, a pound of clean brown sugar, and two fresh lemons, sliced thin. It should be wrought twenty-four hours, with two gills of good yeast, and then bottled. It improves by keeping several weeks, unless the weather is hot, and it is an excellent beverage. If made with loaf instead of brown sugar, the appearance and flavor are still finer.

Mary Hooker Cornelius, *The Young Housekeeper's Friend*, 1864

Ginger Beer Powders, and Soda Powders

Put into blue papers, thirty grains to each paper, of bicarbonate of soda, five grains of powdered ginger, and a drachm of white powdered sugar. Put into white papers, twenty-five grains to each, of powdered tartaric acid.

Put one paper of each kind to half a pint of water. The common soda powders of the shops are like the above, when the sugar and ginger are omitted.

Soda powders can be kept on hand, and the water in which they are used can be flavored with any kind of syrup or tincture, and thus make a fine drink for hot weather.

Sarsaparilla Mead

One pound of Spanish sarsaparilla. Boil it in four gallons of water five hours, and add enough water to have two gallons. Add sixteen pounds of sugar, and ten ounces of tartaric acid.

To make a tumbler of it, take half a wine-glass of the above, and then fill with water, and put in half a teaspoonful of soda.

Catharine E. Beecher, *Miss Beecher's Domestic Receipt Book*, 1858

Spruce Beer

For *white* spruce [beer], pour ten gallons of boiling water upon six pounds of good raw or lump sugar, and four ounces of essence of spruce; ferment with half a pint of good yeast, put into stone bottles, cork and tie them over. For *brown* spruce use treacle instead of sugar.

Essence of spruce is a remedy for colds, rheumatisms, &c., if drunk warm at bedtime.

Sarah Josepha Hale, *The New Household Receipt-Book*, 1853

BREAKFAST CAKES, MUFFINS, TEA CAKES, AND BREAD

However improbable it may seem, the health of many a professional man is undermined, and his usefullness curtailed, if not sacrificed, because he habitually eats *bad bread*.

Mary Hooker Cornelius, *The Young Housekeeper's Friend*, 1864

Directions for Griddle and Other Breakfast Cakes

The best method of greasing a griddle is, to take a bit of salt pork, and rub over with a fork. This prevents adhesion, and yet does not allow the fat to soak into what is to be cooked.

In putting cakes on to griddles, be careful to form them [into] a regular round shape, and put on only one at each dip, and so as not to spill between the cakes.

In frying mush, cold rice slices, and hominy cakes, cut them half an inch thick, and fry in fresh lard, with enough to brown them handsomely. Make the slices smooth and regular.

Buckwheat Cakes

Take a quart of buckwheat flour, and nearly an even tablespoonful of salt. Stir in warm water, till it is the consistency of thin batter. Beat it thoroughly. Add two tablespoonfuls of yeast, if distillery, or twice as much if home-brewed.

Set the batter where it will be a little warm through the night. Some persons never stir them after they have risen, but take them out carefully with a large spoon.

Add a teaspoonful of pearlash in the morning, if they are sour. Sift it over the surface, and stir it well.

Some persons like to add one or two tablespoonfuls of molasses, to give them a brown color, and more sweetness of taste.

Catharine E. Beecher, *Miss Beecher's Domestic Receipt Book*, 1858

Breakfast Rice Cakes

Put half a pound of rice to soak over night; boil it very soft in the morning, drain off the water, mix it with four ounces of melted butter, and set it away to cool. When cold, stir it into a quart of milk, adding a little salt; then stir in, alternately six eggs and half a pint of sifted flour. Beat all well together, and bake on the griddle in cakes about the size of a small dessert plate. Butter and send them to the table, hot.

Instead of preparing the rice, cold boiled rice makes very nice cakes, mixed and cooked as the prepared.

Mrs. A. L. Webster, *The Improved Housewife*, 1853

Sour Milk Cakes

1 quart sour, or "loppered" milk	About 4 cups sifted flour
2 teaspoonfuls soda, dissolved in boiling water	3 table-spoonfuls molasses
	Salt to taste

Mix the molasses with the milk. Put the flour into a deep bowl, mix the salt through it; make a hole in the middle, and pour in the milk, gradually stirring the flour down into it with a wooden spoon. The batter should not be too thick. When all the milk is in, beat until the mixture is free from lumps and very smooth. Add the soda-water, stir up fast and well, and bake immediately.

These cakes are simple, economical, wholesome, and extremely nice. "Loppered" milk, or "clabber," is better than buttermilk. Try them!

Susie's Flannel Cakes (Without Eggs)

2 cups white Indian meal	Flour for good batter
2 quarts milk	Boiling water
½ cup yeast	A little salt

Scald the meal with a pint or so of boiling water. While still warm stir in the milk, and strain through a cullender; then, add the flour, lastly the yeast. Cover and let the batter stand until morning. Salt, and if at all sour stir in a little soda.

These cakes will make a pleasant variety with "buckwheats," in the long winter season. They will be found very good—so good that one will hardly believe that they contain neither "shortening" nor eggs.

"You can put in an egg or two, if you wish," says "Susie," modestly, "but to my notion they are quite as nice without."

And we, who have tested the "flannel" of her making, are content to "let well enough alone."

Marion Harland, *Breakfast, Luncheon and Tea*, 1875

Johnny Cakes

Take one quart of sour milk, or buttermilk; stir in as much corn meal as will make a pancake batter; take one teacupful of flour, and one teaspoonful of saleratus; beat well together; then add three eggs well beaten, and one half a teaspoonful of salt; thoroughly mix all together; pour into well buttered pans, and bake quickly in a hot oven. Small-sized pans should be used for this kind of bread. Eat hot, with good butter.

Sarah E. Scott, *Every-Day Cookery for Every Family*, 1868

Raised Waffles

One quart of flour	Three tablespoonfuls of yeast
Teaspoonful of salt	Two ounces of butter
One and a half pints of milk	Three eggs
Half a teaspoonful of soda	

Put the yeast with the warm milk, butter that has been creamed, and salt to rise overnight. When required in the morning, add three eggs well beaten, and the soda dissolved in warm water. Heat the waffle iron, butter it well, and fill nearly three-quarters full; take care not to scorch them.

Godey's Lady's Book, September 1885

Tea Crumpets

Put two well beaten eggs in a quart of milk, and as much flour as will make them rather thicker than batter pudding. Then make your bake stone very hot, and grease it well; pour a large spoonful of batter, so that it may run the size of a saucer. When ready to use, toast them crisp, and butter them.

Soda Biscuit

Stir into one quart of flour two teaspoonsful of cream of tartar, and one teaspoonful of salt; dissolve in three gills of new milk one teaspoonful of soda; stir it into the flour quickly; pour all on the board, and roll out and cut into little cakes. Bake them in a quick oven.

Sarah E. Scott, *Every-Day Cookery for Every Family*, 1868

Ginger Biscuits

Work into quite small crumbs three ounces of good butter, with two pounds of flour; then add three ounces of pounded sugar and two of ginger, in fine powder, and knead them into a stiff paste, with new milk. Roll it thin, cut out the biscuits with a cutter, and bake them in a slow oven until they are crisp quite through, but keep them of a pale color. A couple of eggs are some-times mixed with the milk for them, but are no material improvement; an additional ounce of sugar may be used when a sweeter biscuit is liked. To make good ginger *cakes*, increase the butter to six ounces, and the sugar to eight, for each pound of flour, and wet the ingredients into a paste with eggs; a little lemon-grate will give it an agreeable flavor.

Sarah Josepha Hale, *The New Household Receipt-Book*, 1853

Delicate Graham Muffins

1 pint sweet milk	2 cups Graham flour
1 egg	1 cup wheat flour
½ cup brown sugar	2 teaspoons cream t[artar]
2 tablespoons butter	1 [tsp] soda or 3 teaspoons baking powder

Stir butter and sugar together and then add the well-beaten egg; next milk, saving a little to dissolve the soda in. Mix well the two kinds of flour & cream t. or baking powder if preferred & stir into other ingredients with dissolved soda. Bake in tins or muffin rings from 20 to 30 minutes in a quick oven. Very nice for breakfast or tea.

Mary Parmenter recorded this recipe for Graham muffins (named for food reformer Sylvester Graham) in her handwritten cookbook in 1867.

Bread

It requires experience to make good bread. One must know, first, how long to let the bread rise, as it takes a longer time in cold than in warm weather; second, when the oven is just of proper temperature to bake it. Bread should be put in a rather hot oven. It is nearly light enough to bake when put in; so the rule for baking bread differs from that of baking cake, which should be put into a moderate oven at first, to become equally heated through before rising. As bread requires a brisk heat, it is well to have the loaves small, the French-bread loaves being well adapted to a hot oven. After the bread is baked, the loaves should be placed on end (covered) at the back of the table until they become cool.

To Make Yeast

Ingredients: A cupful of baker's yeast; four cupfuls of flour; two large potatoes, boiled; one cupful of sugar, and six cupfuls of boiling water.

Mix the warm mashed potatoes and sugar together; then add the flour; next, add the six cupfuls of boiling water, poured on slowly: this cooks the flour a little. It will be of the consistency of batter. Let the mixture get almost cold, stirring it well, that the bottom may become cool also. It will spoil the yeast if the batter be too hot. When lukewarm, add the teacupful of yeast. Leave this mixture in the kitchen, or in some warm place, perhaps on the kitchen-table (do not put it too near the stove), for five or six hours, until it gets perfectly light. Do not touch it until it gets somewhat light; then stir it down two or three times during the six hours. This process makes it stronger. Keep it in a cool place until needed.

This yeast will last perpetually, if a teacupful of it be always kept, when making bread, to make new yeast at the next baking. Keep it in a stone jar, scalding the jar every time fresh yeast is made.

In summer, it is well to mix corn-meal with the yeast, and dry it in cakes, in some shady, dry place, turning the cakes often, that they may become thoroughly dry. It requires about one and a half cakes (biscuit-cutter) to make four medium-sized loaves of bread. Crumb them, and let them soak in lukewarm water about a quarter or half an hour before using.

To Make the Bread

Ingredients: Flour, one and a half cupfuls of yeast, lukewarm water, a table-spoonful of lard, a little salt.

Put two quarts of flour into the bread-bowl; sprinkle a little salt over it; add one and a half cupfuls of yeast, and enough lukewarm water to make it a rather soft dough. Set it one side to rise. In winter, it will take overnight; in summer, about three hours. After it has risen, mix well into it one table-spoonful of lard; then add flour (not too much), and knead it half an hour. The more it is kneaded, the whiter and finer it becomes. Leave this in the bread-bowl for a short time to rise; then make it into loaves. Let it rise again for the third time. Bake.

Mary F. Henderson, *Practical Cooking, and Dinner Giving*, 1878

Yorkshire Muffins

Sift two pounds of wheat flour into a pan, warm one pint and a half of new milk, and cut up in it two large spoonsful of butter, and stir it into the flour; beat three eggs very lightly; add half a small teaspoonful of salt; beat these all well together until thoroughly mixed; then add three spoonsful of good yeast; set it to rise, and when risen bake in muffin rings in an oven.

A Practical Housekeeper, *Cookery As It Should Be*, 1856

Rusk

Take a quart of milk, a tea-cup of cream, half a pound of lard, quarter of a pound of butter, a spoonful of salt, and boil them together; beat well two eggs with a pound of sugar, and pour the boiling milk on them gradually, stirring all the time; when nearly cold, add a tea-cup of yeast, and flour sufficient to make a stiff batter; when quite light, knead it up as bread, and let it lighten again before moulding out; when they are moulded out, wet them over with sugar and cream, and let them rise a few minutes and bake them; grate a little sugar over when they come out of the oven.

Elizabeth F. Lea, *Domestic Cookery, Useful Receipts, and Hints to Young Housekeepers*, 1865

Water Toast

Cut stale bread into slices half an inch thick and pare off all the crust. Nobody likes toast-crusts. . . . Have a clear, smokeless fire, and close by on the range a pan of boiling water, in which put a tablespoonful of butter to a pint of the liquid and half a teaspoonful of salt. As each slice is toasted, scrape off every symptom of a scorch or burn and dip quickly in the boiling water and butter. Pile neatly in a hot, deep dish; pour the little water that remains when all is done on the top, and cover closely to keep hot.

Marion Harland, *The Cottage Kitchen*, 1883

Real New England Brown Bread

Take equal proportions of sifted rye and Indian meal, mix them well together; add half a teaspoonful of molasses, and two gills of good yeast, to about three quarts of the mixed meal. Wet this with good new milk, sufficient to make a dough that can be easily worked, even with one hand. For economy's sake, milk that has stood for twelve hours, and from which the cream has been taken, may be a substitute for the new milk; or water which has been pressed from boiled squash, or in which squash has been boiled, is a much better substitute than pure water. But warm water is more commonly used. The ingredients should be thoroughly mixed, and stand, in cold weather, for twelve hours; in warm weather, two hours may be sufficient before baking. If baked in a brick oven, a three quart loaf should stand in the oven all night. The same quantity in three baking-pans will bake in about three hours. Serve this warm from the oven, with good, sweet-butter, and we could fast upon it every morning for breakfast from January to December.

A Practical Housekeeper, *The American Practical Cookery-Book*, 1861

BREAKFAST CEREALS AND PORRIDGES

I advocate the general use of oatmeal porridge for breakfast. Nothing is more wholesome, and nothing more relished after a little use. If not natural, the taste should be acquired. It is invaluable for children, and of no less benefit for persons of mature years. Nearly all the little Scotch and Irish children are brought up on it. When Queen Victoria first visited Scotland, she noticed the particularly ruddy and healthy appearance of the children, and, after inquiry about their diet and habits, became at once a great advocate for the use of porridge. She used it for her own children, and it was at once introduced very generally into England. Another of its advantages is that serving it as a first course enables the cook to prepare many dishes, such as steaks, omelets, etc., just as the family sit down to breakfast; and when the porridge is eaten, she is ready with the other dishes "smoking hot."

Marion Harland, *Breakfast, Luncheon and Tea,* 1875

Hominy

Hominy is white indian corn, shelled from the cob, divested of the outer skin by scalding in hot lye, and then winnowed and dried. It is perfectly white. Having washed it through two or three waters, pour boiling water on it; cover it, and let it soak all night, or for several hours. Then put it into a pot or sauce-pan, allow two quarts of water to each quart of hominy, and boil it till perfectly soft. Then drain it, put it into a deep dish, add some butter to it, and send it to table hot, (and *uncovered*) to eat with any sort of meat; but particularly with corned beef or pork. What is left may be made next day into thick cakes, and fried in butter. To be *very good*, hominy should boil four or five hours.

Eliza Leslie, *Miss Leslie's New Cookery Book,* 1857

| 1 quart of boiling water | 2 cups Indian meal |
| 2 tablespoonfuls of flour | 1 teaspoonful of salt—heaping |

Wet up meal and flour in cold water enough to make a thick paste, salting them while dry. Be sure the water on the fire is boiling when you put in the paste. Boil one hour—not less, and more will not hurt—stirring often down to the bottom, and beating with a wooden spoon to get out lumps. Empty into a deep, uncovered dish, and eat in saucers with milk poured over it. Some sprinkle each saucerful with sugar.

Marion Harland, *The Cottage Kitchen*, 1883

EGGS
AND EGG DISHES

This is the most simple of all things to cook, and yet it is the least attended to; and I am never surprised, when I am traveling, to find the eggs either too much or too little done. They will not take the trouble to distinguish a large one from a small one. Whilst some weigh only an ounce and a half, others weigh two and a half; but as that is a whim of nature, and the servants are so fond of attending to other frolics, they will not see the difference in this; but as all cookery books say three minutes, and the mistress has told them the same, they are right and she is wrong. From two and a half to four minutes, according to size, is the time they will take. Ten minutes is sufficient to set an egg hard, not thirty, or more, as some persons do by neglect.

A Practical Housekeeper, *The American Practical Cookery-Book*, 1861

Boiled Eggs

Put eggs into boiling water; if you like the white just set, boil about two minutes; if you like the yolk set, boil three; if for a salad, boil ten minutes. Boil a new-laid egg half a minute longer than a stale one. Another mode, which is very nice for fish, is to break the shells, and drop the eggs into a pan of scalding water; let the pan stand till the white has set; then place it on a moderate fire; when the water boils up the eggs are done. Eggs look very pretty done in this way, the yolk being just visible through the white. Serve them up with burnt butter, if not wanted for a garnish.

Mrs. A. L. Webster, *The Improved Housewife*, 1853

Pickled Eggs

Boil the eggs until very hard; when cold, shell them, and cut them in halves lengthways. Lay them carefully in large mouthed jars, and pour over them scalding vinegar, well seasoned with whole pepper, allspice, a few pieces of ginger, and a few cloves of garlic. When cold, tie up closely, and let them stand a month. They are then fit for use. With cold meat, they are a most delicious and delicate pickle.

To Preserve Eggs

Nearly fill a deep earthen vessel with fresh-laid eggs, closely and regularly packed in with the small ends downwards. In another vessel put as much quicklime as you think will turn enough water to fill up the egg vessel into the consistency of thick cream. Let the lime and water stand two or three days, stirring it frequently, and then, if thick enough, pour it over the eggs, filling the vessel quite up. Take care to place the egg vessel in some corner where it will not be likely to be disturbed, and the eggs will keep good any length of time. The experience of many years proves this to be the simplest, but most effective.

A Practical Housekeeper, *The American Practical Cookery-Book*, 1861

Scotch Woodcock

Toast and butter three or four slices of bread on both sides; take nine or ten anchovies washed, scraped, and chopped fine, and put them between the slices of bread. Beat the yolks of four eggs in half a pint of cream, and set it on the fire to thicken, *but not to boil*. Then pour it over the toast, and send it to table as hot as possible.

Elizabeth F. Ellet, *The New Cyclopaedia of Domestic Economy, and Practical Housekeeper*, 1873

Eggs and Minced Meat

Chop *one pint* of *cold chicken, ham*, or *veal* fine, and rub it to a smooth paste; add *one tablespoonful* of *melted butter, one tablespoonful* of *chopped parsley, salt* and *pepper* to taste, and *two beaten eggs*. If too dry, moisten with a little *cream* or *stock* or *gravy*, but do not have it too soft to shape. Heat it in a frying-pan just enough to warm through, letting it dry off if too moist. Form it on a hot platter into a flat mound; hollow the centre, leaving a ridge of the mixture round the edge. Keep it hot, and put *three* or *four poached eggs* in the centre. Garnish with triangles of *toast* laid round the base of the meat. Or, if you have a larger quantity of meat, prepare as above, and make a mound one inch deep on a round dish and a smaller mound above that, and place eggs baked in cups, or hard-boiled eggs cut in halves, or egg baskets on the space between the mounds. Garnish with *parsley*.

Mrs. D. A. Lincoln, *Mrs. Lincoln's Boston Cook Book*, 1889

Nothing is more simple than to make an omelet, yet very few can make one. The eggs stick to the pan, or they are overdone, and tough.

Senator Riddle, of Delaware, a decided epicure, took much pleasure in his superior knowledge on this important subject. Once when breakfasting with Mrs. Crittenden, of Kentucky, a piece of omelet of doubtful appearance was presented to him. "Before we proceed with our breakfast," said he, "let me teach you a valuable accomplishment." They repaired at once to the kitchen range, where the senator demonstrated at once his qualifications as a first-class cook. My own first lesson was from Mr. Riddle, so of course I have the correct *modus operandi*; afterward in London, however, I heard a lecture upon omelets from a cooking professor, and was astonished at the multiplicity of dishes which could be made from this simple preparation; not only breakfast dishes, but also the variety of sweet omelets for dessert.

The fire should be quite hot. All cookery-books especially expatiate on the necessity of a pan to be used for omelets alone. Any clean, smooth iron spider, or *sauté* pan, is a good enough omelet-pan. Put the pan on the fire to become heated; break the eggs into a kitchen basin; sprinkle over them pepper and salt, and give them twelve vigorous beats with a spoon. This is enough to break all the yolks, and twelve beats was Mr. Riddle's rule. Now put butter the size of an egg (for five eggs) in the heated pan; turn it around so that it will moisten all the bottom of the pan. When it is well melted, and *begins to boil*, pour in the eggs. Holding the handle of the omelet-pan in the left hand, carefully and lightly with a spoon draw up the whitened egg from the bottom, so that all the eggs may be equally cooked, or whitened to a soft, creamy substance. Now, still with the left hand, shake the pan forward and backward, which will disengage the eggs from the bottom; then shaking again the omelet a little one side, turn with a spoon half of one side over the other; and allowing it to remain a moment to harden a little at the bottom, gently shaking it all the time, toss it over on to a warm platter held in the right hand. A little practice makes one quite dexterous in placing the omelet in the centre of the platter, and turning it over as it is tossed from the omelet-pan.

However, if one is unsuccessful in the tossing operation, which is the correct thing, according to the cooking professor, the omelet can be lifted to the platter with a pancake-turner. It should be creamy and light in the centre, and more firm on the ouside.

I will specify several different omelets. A variety of others may be made in the same way, by adding boiled tongue cut into dice, sliced truffles, cooked and sliced kidneys with the gravy poured around.

Omelet with Tomatoes

Make the plain omelet; and just before turning one half over to the other, place in the centre three or four whole tomatoes which have been boiled a few minutes previously and seasoned. When the omelet is turned, of course the tomatoes will be quite enveloped. Serve with tomato-sauce poured around it.

Omelet with Rum

This is a most delicious omelet. Add a little sugar to the eggs, say a sherry-glassful to six eggs, and make the omelet as a plain omelet. When turned on to the dish, sprinkle a little handful of sugar over the top, and pour over five or six table-spoonfuls of rum. Set it on fire, and serve it at the table burning.

Mary F. Henderson, *Practical Cooking, and Dinner Giving*, 1878

Eggs à la crème

Boil *three eggs* twenty minutes. Cut off a slice at each end, and cut the eggs in halves crosswise. Remove the yolks, and cut them in thin slices. Mix with them an equal amount of small thin pieces of *cold chicken, ham, salmon,* or *lobster,* and season to taste. Fill the white cups with the mixture. Place them on a shallow dish and pour *one cup* of *thick cream sauce* around them. The sauce should come nearly to the top of the cups. Or cut the eggs in halves, and place them with the cut side down and serve in the sauce.

Mrs. D. A. Lincoln, *Mrs. Lincoln's Boston Cook Book*, 1889

Baked Eggs

6 eggs

4 tablespoonfuls good gravy—veal, beef or poultry (The latter is particularly nice.)

1 handful bread-crumbs
6 rounds buttered toast or fried bread

Put the gravy into a shallow baking dish. Break the eggs into this, pepper and salt them, and strew the bread-crumbs over them. Bake for five minutes in a quick oven. Take up the eggs carefully, one by one, and lay upon the toast which must be arranged on a hot, flat dish. Add a little cream, and, if you like, some very finely-chopped parsley and onion, to the gravy left in the baking-dish, and turn it into a saucepan. Boil up once quickly, and pour over the eggs.

Marion Harland, *Breakfast, Luncheon and Tea*, 1875

SOUPS

It is usual to commence with soup, which never refuse. . . . When all are seated, send a plate of soup to every one. Do not ask anyone if they will be helped, as everyone takes it, of course.

An American Lady, *True Politeness*, 1853

On Serving Soup

Soup is generally served alone; however, pickles and crackers are a pleasant accompaniment for oyster-soup, and many serve grated cheese with macaroni and vermicelli soups. A pea or bean soup (without bread *croutons*) at one end of the table, with a neat square piece of boiled pork on a platter at the other end, is sometimes seen. When a ladleful of the soup is put in the soup-plate by the hostess, the butler passes it to the host, who cuts off a thin wafer-slice of the pork, and places it in the soup. The thin pork can be cut with the spoon. Hot boiled rice is served with gumbo soup. Well-boiled rice, with each grain distinct, is served in a dish by the side of the soup-tureen. The hostess first puts a ladleful of soup into the soup-plate, then a spoonful of the rice in the centre. This is much better than cooking the rice with the soup.

Sometimes little squares (two inches square) of thin slices of brown bread (buttered) are served with soup at handsome dinners. It is a French custom. Cold slaw may be served at the same time with soup, and eaten with the soup or just after the soup-plates are removed.

Mary F. Henderson, *Practical Cooking, and Dinner Giving*, 1878

Bouillon

4 pounds beef, from the middle of the round	1 tablespoonful salt
2 pounds bone	4 peppercorns
2 quarts cold water	4 cloves
1 tablespoonful mixed herbs	

Wipe and cut the meat and bones into small pieces; add the water, and heat slowly; add the seasoning, and simmer five hours. Boil down to three pints; strain, remove the fat, and season with salt and pepper. Serve in cups at luncheons, evening companies, etc. Boil one onion, half a carrot, and half a turnip with it if you like.

Mrs. D. A. Lincoln, *Mrs. Lincoln's Boston Cook Book*, 1889

Oriental Mulligatawny

This is the true Oriental recipe for making this delicious soup. Boil a pair of fowls with care, skimming continually whilst boiling, and keeping them covered with water. When tender, take out the chicken and remove every bone from the meat; put a large lump of butter in a frying pan, and dredge the chicken meat well with flour; lay it in the hot pan and fry it a nice brown, and keep it hot and dry. Take a pint of the chicken water, and stir in two large spoonsful of curry powder, two spoonsful of butter and one of flour, one teaspoonful of salt and a very little cayenne. Stir this until smooth; then mix it with the broth in the pot; when well mixed, simmer five minutes; then put in the browned chicken. Boil a pint of rice very dry to serve with it.

A Practical Housekeeper, *Cookery As It Should Be*, 1856

Mock Turtle Soup

Boil together a knuckle of veal (cut up) and a set of calves' feet, to it. Also the hock of a cold boiled ham. Season it with cayenne pepper; but the ham will render it salt enough. You may add a smoked tongue. Allow, to each pound of meat, a small quart of water. After the meat has come to a boil and been well skimmed, add half a dozen sliced parsnips, three sliced onions, and a head of celery cut small, with a large bunch of sweet marjoram, and two large carrots sliced. Boil all together till the vegetables are nearly dissolved and the meat falls from the bone. Then strain the whole through a cullender, and transfer the liquid to a clean pot. Have ready some fine large sweetbreads that have been soaked in warm water for an hour till all the blood was disgorged; then transferred to boiling water for ten minutes, and then taken out and laid in very cold water. This will blanch them, and all sweetbreads should look white. Take them out; and remove carefully all the pipe or gristle. Cut the sweetbreads in pieces or mouthfuls, and put them into the pot of strained soup. Have ready about two or three dozen (or more) of force-meat balls, made of cold minced veal and ham seasoned with nutmeg and mace, enriched with butter, and mixed with grated lemon-peel, breadcrumbs, chopped marjoram and beaten eggs, to make the whole into smooth balls about the size of a hickory nut. Throw the balls into the soup, and add a fresh lemon, sliced thin, and a pint of Madeira wine. Give it one more boil up; then put it into a tureen and send it to table.

This ought to be a rich soup, and is seldom made except for dinner company.

If the above method is *exactly* followed, there will be found no necessity for taking the trouble and enduring the disgust and tediousness of cleaning and preparing a calf's head for mock turtle soup—a very unpleasant process, which too much resembles the horrors of a dissecting room. And when all is done a calf's head is a very insipid article.

It will be found that the above is superior to any mock turtle. Made of shin beef, with all these ingredients, it is very rich and fine.

Eliza Leslie, *Miss Leslie's New Cookery Book*, 1857

Split Pea Soup

Save the water in which corned beef or pork has been boiled. If too salty, only use one half, and the other half plain water. Into this put either some beef bones or mutton bones, to give it a relish. Take some of this broth—only a little—and after having washed them, put in a quart of split peas; simmer them for three hours slowly, and then pass them through a cullender to remove the skin; mash them finely, and on them pour two quarts of the broth in which the bones have been boiling; grate two carrots and two turnips, and stir in; cut finely two heads of well cleaned celery and add an onion finely chopped; stew this very slowly for an hour. When ready, fry two slices of stale bread a nice brown; cut them into small squares, lay them in the tureen and dust on a little cayenne over them; then pour on your hot soup. Serve very hot.

A Practical Housekeeper, *Cookery As It Should Be*, 1856

Black Bean Soup

1 pint of turtle beans	2 hard-boiled eggs
1½ quarts of boiling water	1 lemon
1 quart of stock	Salt and pepper to taste
If you use wine, 1 gill	

Wash the beans well in cold water and soak them over night. In the morning, drain the water off and cover them again with one quart of the boiling water. Boil until tender, about two hours. Now add the stock and the pint of boiling water. Press the whole through a sieve; wash the kettle, return the soup and bring it to a boil; add salt and pepper. Cut the eggs and lemon into slices and put into the tureen, pour the boiling soup over, and serve.

If wine is used, put it in the tureen with the lemon and egg.

Sarah Tyson Rorer, *Mrs. Rorer's Philadelphia Cook Book*, 1886

Potage à la reine
(Queen Victoria's favorite soup)

Remove the fat from *one quart* of the water in which *a chicken* has been boiled. Season highly with *salt, pepper,* and *celery salt,* and a little *onion* if desired, and put on to boil. Mash the yolks of *three hard-boiled eggs* fine, and mix them with *half a cup* of *bread* or *cracker crumbs,* soaked until soft in a little *milk.* Chop the white meat of the chicken until fine like meal, and stir it into the egg and bread paste. Add *one pint* of *hot cream* slowly, and then rub all into the hot chicken liquor. Boil five minutes; add more salt if needed, and if too thick add more cream, or if not thick enough add more fine cracker dust. It should be like a purée.

Mrs. D. A. Lincoln, *Mrs. Lincoln's Boston Cook Book*, 1889

Pepper Pot

To four quarts of water put one pound of corned pork, two pounds of the neck or scrag of mutton, and a small knuckle of veal. Let this simmer slowly three hours, skimming all the while, and then take out the mutton (as that will serve for a dish for table, with drawn butter and celery.) Into this broth put four sliced white turnips—if in season, six or eight tomatoes—if not, a tablespoonful of the tomato catsup, an onion sliced thinly, a small piece of the garden pepper, and half a teaspoonful of salt. Have ready boiled a quarter of a pound of nice white tripe; cut this into strips of an inch in length; add six potatoes thinly sliced, about a dozen whole cloves, and a pint bowl full of nice little light dumplings, the size of a walnut; let this simmer slowly for an hour. Serve hot; but take out the pork and veal bones before serving.

Sarah E. Scott, *Every-Day Cookery for Every Family*, 1868

Chowder, An Old Recipe, 1834

To make a good chowder and have it quite nice,
Dispense with sweet marjoram parsley and spice;
Mace, pepper and salt are now wanted alone.
To make the stew eat well and stick to the bone,
Some pork is sliced thin and put into the pot;
Some say you must turn it, some say you must not;
And when it is brown, take it out of the fat,
And add it again when you add this and that.
A layer of potatoes, sliced quarter inch thick,
Should be placed in the bottom to make it eat slick;
A layer of onions now over this place,
Then season with pepper and salt and some mace.
Split open your crackers and give them a soak.
In eating you'll find this the cream of the joke.
On top of all this, now comply with my wish,
And put, in large chunks, all your pieces of fish;
Then put on the pieces of pork you have fried—
I mean those from which all the fat has been tried.
In seasoning I pray you, don't spare the cayenne;
'Tis this makes it fit to be eaten by men.
After adding these things in their reg'lar rotation,
You'll have a dish fit for the best of the nation.

Jessup Whitehead, *The Steward's Handbook*, 1899

New England Chowder

Have a good haddock, cod, or any other solid fish, cut it in pieces three inches square, put a pound of fat salt pork in strips into the pot, set it on hot coals, and fry out the oil. Take out the pork, and put in a layer of fish, over that a layer of onions in slices, then a layer of fish with slips of fat salt pork, then another layer of onions, and so on alternately, until your fish is consumed. Mix some flour with as much water as will fill the pot; season with black pepper and salt to your taste, and boil it for half an hour. Have ready some crackers soaked in water till they are a little softened; throw them into your chowder five minutes before you take it up. Serve in a tureen.

Sarah Josepha Hale, *The New Household Receipt-Book*, 1853

Clam Soup

Wash fifty of the small sand clams very clean. Put them into an iron pot, set it in a hot place and cover it up. When they become heated, the clams open; then take them from the shells. Put the clams aside in a pan, and pour the juice into a stew-pan; let it simmer for five minutes, strain it and rub two tablespoonfuls of butter and one of flour smoothly together; put the juice on to cook, and slowly add the flour and butter, stir it well together, add half a teaspoonful of salt, half of a nutmeg grated, and a pint of good cream; stir this well, let it simmer for ten minutes, chop up some parsley and throw in; then pour in the clams. One boil-up finishes, as the clams, like oysters, require very little cooking. If you use the large clams, they must be chopped.

A Practical Housekeeper, *Cookery As It Should Be*, 1856

Stewed Oysters

Boil up the oysters in their own liquor, with a piece of butter the size of a walnut, and pepper and salt to taste. Have ready a pint or more of rich boiled milk, the quantity acccording to the number of oysters. Pour it hot into the soup tureen, and as the oysters come to a boil, skim them, let them boil up once, and then pour them into the milk.

Jane Warren, *The Economical Cook Book*, ca. 1882

FISH

Steel imparts a disagreeable flavor to cooked fish; never use a steel knife or fork in serving it.

Maria Parloa, *Home Economics,* 1898

Broiled Shad

Soak a salt shad a day or night previous to cooking; it is best to drain an hour before you put it to the fire; if it hangs long exposed to the air, it loses its flavor: grease the gridiron to keep it from sticking; have good coals, and put the inside down first. Fresh shad is better to be sprinkled with salt, an hour before it is put to broil; put a plate over the top to keep the heat in. In broiling shad or other fresh fish you should dust them with corn meal before you put them down.

Elizabeth F. Lea, *Domestic Cookery, Useful Receipts, and Hints to Young Housekeepers,* 1865

Maître d'Hôtel Sauce

2 tablespoonfuls of butter
1 tablespoonful of chopped parsley

1 tablespoonful of lemon juice
¼ teaspoonful of salt

Mix all the ingredients and knead well together in a bowl. It should be perfectly smooth. Served with salt fish, broiled or fried. This is also called Maître d'Hôtel Butter.

Sarah Tyson Rorer, *Mrs. Rorer's Philadelphia Cook Book,* 1886

Mackerel, salmon, blue-fish, and all oily fish should never be fried. Smelts, perch, and other small pan-fish may be fried whole. When fried smelts are used as a garnish, fry them in the shape of rings by pinning the tail in the mouth. Cod, halibut, etc., should be skinned and boned, and cut into slices one inch thick, and two or three inches square. Flounder and bass may be cut in fillets . . . each fillet seasoned with salt and pepper, and fastened with a small wooden skewer. Small fish may be boned without parting in the middle, and rolled from tail to head. Fish for frying should be thoroughly cleaned and dried, seasoned with salt and pepper, and covered first with flour or fine bread crumbs, then dipped in beaten egg, then in crumbs again. If this does not cover them completely, repeat the process.

When the fish has been kept on ice, let it become slightly warm before frying, as otherwise it will chill the fat and become greasy. Fry in deep, smoking hot fat . . . testing the fat first with bread; and after the first plunge into the hot fat set the kettle back to keep from burning; then reheat before frying any more. Fry from two to five minutes. Drain and serve with tomato, or Tartare, or any acid sauce. Garnish with slices of pickle or lemon, and parsley.

Arrange small fish with heads and tails alternating; or two or three on a skewer, one skewer for each person; or in a circle round a silver cup, placed in the centre of the platter and holding the sauce. Slices or rolled fillets may be arranged in a circle, with the sauce in the centre.

•

Mrs. D. A. Lincoln, *Mrs. Lincoln's Boston Cook Book*, 1889

Codfish Tongues

Wash four codfish-tongues thoroughly in cold water; put them on the range in hot water slightly salted, and boil thirty minutes; drain; arrange neatly on a folded napkin placed upon a hot dish; garnish with parsley and slices of lemon, and send to table with *a white sauce*. Fried like oysters and served with *sauce tartare* they are very good.

•

Thomas J. Murray, *The Book of Entrees*, 1889

Potted Fish

Three shad or *six small mackerel,* uncooked; *one third* of *a cup* of *salt* with *half a saltspoonful* of *cayenne pepper* mixed with it, and *half a cup* of *whole spices,*—cloves, peppercorns, and *allspice* mixed in about equal proportions. *Vinegar* to cover. Clean, remove the skin, split in halves, cut each half into three pieces, and remove all the larger bones. Pack the fish in layers in a small stone jar. (Earthenware must not be used on account of the vinegar.) Sprinkle the salt and spices over each layer. Add *one onion* sliced thin, if you do not dislike the flavor. Add vinegar enough to completely cover the fish. Tie a thick paper over the top, or tie a cloth over and cover with a crust of dough to keep in all the steam. Bake in a very moderate oven five or six hours. Remove the dough-crust, and when cooled cover, and keep in a cool place.

This will keep some time, if the fish be kept under the vinegar; the bones will be dissolved, and it makes an excellent relish for lunch or tea.

Mrs. D. A. Lincoln, *Mrs. Lincoln's Boston Cook Book,* 1889

Scotch Stew

Thicken a pint of hot water with two tablespoonfuls of flour, adding one hard-boiled egg chopped and a piece of butter the size of an egg, add one pound of Salmon and three split crackers or same quantity of bread. Cook the whole in a stewpan ten minutes.

Cape Breton salmon can label, Portland Packing Company, ca. 1875

Salmon Croquettes

Take a one-pound can of salmon, open it neatly, take out the fish and mince it fine; add salt and pepper and a tablespoonful of chopped parsley or celery tops; moisten it with very little water, add a raw egg and a little walnut ketchup, mix thoroughly, put it in a small saucepan, and place the saucepan in another containing hot water. When quite hot, turn it out upon a dish to become cold; then roll it into cones, dip these in beaten egg seasoned with salt and pepper, roll them in bread-crumbs, drop them into boiling fat, and fry a delicate brown; drain them a moment, arrange neatly on a hot dish, and serve with or without sauce.

Thomas J. Murray, *The Book of Entrees,* 1889

Fish Balls

1 cup raw salt fish	1 egg, well beaten
1 pint potatoes	¼ saltspoonful pepper
1 teaspoonful butter	More salt, if needed

Wash the fish, pick in half-inch pieces, and free from bones. Pare the potatoes, and cut in quarters. Put the potatoes and fish in a stewpan, and cover with boiling water. Boil twenty-five minutes, or till the potatoes are soft. Be careful not to let them boil long enough to become soggy. Drain off all the water; mash and beat the fish and potatoes till very light. Add the butter and pepper, and when slightly cooled add the egg and more salt, if needed. Shape in a tablespoon without smoothing much, slip them off into a basket, and fry in *smoking hot lard* one minute. Fry only five at a time, as more will cool the fat. The lard should be hot enough to brown a piece of bread while you count forty. Or, first dipping the spoon in the fat, take up a spoonful of the fish and plunge it into the hot fat. Drain on soft paper.

These fish balls should be mixed while the potatoes and fish are hot. If you wish to prepare them the night before, omit the egg, and in the morning warm the fish and potato in a double boiler, then add the egg. Keep the fish in a bowl of cold water while picking it apart, and it will need no further soaking.

Contrary to all old theories, boiling the fish with the potato does *not* harden it. When well mashed and beaten with a strong fork, the fish will only be recognized in the potato by the taste, and not by the presence of hard, lumpy pieces. Never chop salt fish. If picked apart into small pieces and then rubbed with a potato masher till it is reduced to fine threads, it will blend with any mixture better than it will when chopped. These are the most quickly prepared and the most delicious fish balls ever made, and are worthy the superlative adjectives which have been given them by enthusiastic pupils.*

Mrs. D. A. Lincoln, *Mrs. Lincoln's Boston Cook Book*, 1889

* Fish balls were a common breakfast food, especially in New England where fish were plentiful and cheap. William Dean Howells wrote in 1882 that breakfast in a New England logging camp in 1882 consisted of fish balls three times a week, on Sundays, Tuesdays, and Thursdays.—Ed.

Mackerel à la Mode

Open the Can and set it in boiling water until hot; drain off the liquor and serve with drawn butter; garnish with hard boiled eggs and sliced lemon.

Seguin mackerel can label, Portland Packing Company, ca. 1875

Clam Pie

Make Pastry in the usual way, cover the plate and fill with clams, adding a little pepper, butter and salt; shake over the clams one finely powdered cracker, put on the crust and bake in a quick oven.

Old Orchard Beach clams can label, Portland Packing Company, ca. 1875

Lobster Farci

2 cups of boiled lobster
Yolks of three hard-boiled eggs
1 tablespoonful of chopped parsley
1 tablespoonful of butter
2 tablespoonfuls of bread crumbs
½ pint of milk
1 even tablespoonful of flour
¼ nutmeg, grated
Salt and cayenne to taste

Cut the lobster into small pieces. Put the milk on to boil. Rub the butter and flour together and stir into the milk when boiling; stir until smooth, take from the fire, add the bread crumbs, parsley, lobster, hard-boiled eggs mashed fine, salt and cayenne; mix all well together. Be careful when opening the lobster not to break the body or tail shells. Wash the shells and wipe them dry, and with a sharp knife or scissors cut off the under part of the shell. Now join the large ends of the two tail shells to the body, forming a boat. Put the farce into these shells, brush it over the top with beaten egg, sprinkle lightly with bread crumbs and place in a quick oven for fifteen minutes to brown. Serve hot in the shells garnished with parsley.

Sarah Tyson Rorer, *Mrs. Rorer's Philadelphia Cook Book*, 1886

These are crabs that, having cast their old shells, have not yet assumed the new ones. In this, the transition state, they are considered delicacies. Put them into fast-boiling water, and boil them for ten minutes. Then take them out, drain them, wipe them very clean, and prepare them for frying by removing the spongy part inside and the sand-bag. Put plenty of fresh lard into a pan; and when it boils fast, lay in the crabs, and fry them well, seasoning them with cayenne. As soon as they are done of a nice golden color, take them out, drain off the lard back into the pan, and lay them on a large *hot* dish. Cover them to keep warm while you fry, in the same lard, all the best part of a fresh lettuce, chopped small. Let it fry only long enough to become hot throughout. When you serve up the crabs cover them with the fried lettuce. Stir into the gravy some cream, or a piece of nice fresh butter rolled in flour; and send it to table in a sauce-boat, seasoned with a little cayenne.

Soft crabs require no other flavoring. They make a nice breakfast-dish for company. Only the large claws are eaten, therefore break off as useless the small ones.

Instead of lettuce, you may fry the crabs with parsley—removed from the pan before it becomes brown. Pepper-grass is still better.

Eliza Leslie, *Miss Leslie's New Cookery Book*, 1857

Raw Oysters Served in Block of Ice

The man had sure a palate covered o'er
With brass or steel, that on the rocky shore
First broke the oozy oyster's pearly coat,
And risked the living morsel down his throat.

Jessup Whitehead, *The Steward's Handbook*, 1899

Put a rectangular block of *clear ice*, having smooth, regular surfaces, in a large pan. With a hot brick or flat-iron melt a cavity large enough to hold the desired number of oysters. Pour the water from the cavity, and fill with oysters, which should first be drained, and seasoned with *salt* and *pepper*. Place a thick napkin on a platter, put the ice upon this, cover the dish with *parsley* or *smilax*, and garnish with *lemon*. The ice is sometimes roughly chipped to resemble a rock. If the dinner be served from the sideboard, individual plates of ice are made.

Mrs. D. A. Lincoln, *Mrs. Lincoln's Boston Cook Book*, 1889

To Pickle 100 Oysters

Drain off the liquor from the oysters, wash them and put to them a table-spoonful of salt, and a tea-cup of vinegar; let them simmer over the fire about ten minutes, taking off the scum as it rises; then take out the oysters, and put to their own liquor a table-spoonful of whole black pepper, and a tea-spoonful of mace and cloves; let it boil five minutes, skim, and pour it over the oysters in a jar.

Elizabeth F. Lea, *Domestic Cookery, Useful Receipts, and Hints to Young Housekeepers*, 1865

Oyster Pie

Make a nice paste and lay into a deep dish, turn a teacup down in the centre. This will draw the liquor under it, and prevent it from boiling over; it also keeps the upper crust from falling in and becoming clammy. Lay in the oysters, add a little pepper, butter, and flour; make a wide incision in the upper crust, so that when the pie is nearly done, you can pour in half a teacup of cream or milk. Secure the edges of the crust according to the directions for making Pastry, and bake it an hour. It should be put into the oven immediately, else the under crust will be clammy. Use but little of the liquor.

Mary Hooker Cornelius, *The Young Housekeeper's Friend*, 1864

Oyster Fritters

Oysters fried in oil were introduced by the late noted Philadelphia *restaurateur* Minico Finelli, an Italian by birth. People who visited Philadelphia always made it a point to go to his restaurant to enjoy this specialty. They were delicious and delicate, beautifully brown, and without a suspicion of grease.

Have ready at hand a strong batter, consisting of flour, water, and three fresh eggs well beaten up with it. Take one dozen of oysters, open them over a clean basin, so as to save the briny juice that pertains to the fish. Add to them a saltspoonful of Cayenne, a whole nutmeg grated, and little salt; throw them into the batter, stirring it well round, until they are fully intermixed with the latter. Be provided with a pan over a moderate fire, and fry the batter with the fish in it, in three distinct proportions, with a good share of sweet butter. When both sides of the fritters present to the eye a rich brown complexion, remove them, and serve them up with mashed potatoes, in hot plates.

Godey's Lady's Book, March 1866

REMOVES: MEAT, GAME, AND POULTRY

These are dishes which remove the fish and soup, served upon large dishes, and placed at the top and bottom of the table; great care should be evinced in cooking them, as they are the "pièce de résistance" of the dinner.

Alexis Soyer, *The Modern Housewife*, 1857

MUTTON DITTY

But a plain leg of mutton, my Lucy,
I Pr'ythee get ready at three:
Have it smoking, and tender, and juicy,
And what better meat can there be?

Jessup Whitehead, *The Steward's Handbook*, 1899

Roast Mutton

The saddle, shoulder, and leg are used for roasting.

Rub the mutton with butter, and then with salt and pepper, and some add pounded allspice, or cloves. Put butter, or lard, in the dripping-pan, with a quart of water, or a pint for a small piece, and baste it often. Set the bony side toward the fire, at some distance, that it may heat through before roasting. Allow about a quarter of an hour for every pound. Mutton should be cooked rare.

Make a brown gravy, and serve it with currant jelly.

Catharine E. Beecher, *Miss Beecher's Domestic Receipt Book*, 1858

Roasting Beef

The cook must have her roaster clean and bright; a clear, brisk fire. It is impossible to give a specific rule as for time, but slow roasting is important. The season of the year—the length of time which the meat has been kept—all has an influence. As a general rule, a quarter of an hour to the pound is the best. The young and tender should be roasted; the strong and full grown animal boiled or stewed. Basting is a most important operation in roasting, as the more meat is basted, the sooner and better it is roasted. Never pour gravy over either roasted or boiled joints, as many prefer the juices of the meat to gravy which is made.

A well selected roasting piece of beef—the noble sirloin of about fifteen pounds—will require about three hours and a half. The beef should be kept for several days after it is killed, if the weather will allow; in winter a week.

Have ready the spit and roaster before putting it down. Rub the beef all over with white ground ginger—nothing else; never salt roasted meat, it draws out the juice; do not place it too near at first, but allow it to gradually warm; baste it well at first with a little cold water. When it begins to cook, pin a thick piece of paper on it, to preserve the fat. Keep the fire clear and brisk. Continue every quarter of an hour to baste it. The last half hour remove the paper; then sprinkle over it a little salt, baste it with a little melted butter, and dredge it with flour; then let it remain until the froth rises; then serve on a hot dish. Take the drippings, skim off all the fat, (which must be saved for the dressing of made dishes;) thicken the gravy with a very little browned flour, which is done by sifting flour on to a tin plate and browning it in an oven. This is nice for all kinds of brown gravies.

A Practical Housekeeper, *Cookery As It Should Be*, 1856

Yorkshire Pudding

Beat three eggs very light. Add *one scant teaspoonful* of *salt* and *one pint* of *milk*. Pour *half a cup* of this mixture on *two thirds* of *a cup* of *flour*, and stir to a smooth paste. Add the remainder of the mixture and beat well. Bake in hot gem pans forty-five minutes. Baste with the drippings from the beef. This is a more convenient way than to bake in the pan under the beef, and gives more crust. Serve as a garnish for roast beef.

Mrs. D. A. Lincoln, *Mrs. Lincoln's Boston Cook Book*, 1889

Beefsteak

The best steaks are those from the tender-loin. Those from the round or rump require beating with a rolling-pin. A steak-mallet tears them and destroys the juices of the meat. Without beating they will generally be found too tough or hard for an American taste, though much liked in Europe, where tender-loin steaks are considered too expensive. But they are here so much preferred, that, on good tables, any others are seldom seen. Have all the steaks nearly of a size and shape, and about half an inch thick. Trim off the fat, and cut short the bone, or remove it altogether. Season them with black pepper, but sprinkle on no salt till they have done cooking; as salt, if put on at first, hardens them. Set your gridiron over a bed of bright clear coals, having first rubbed the bars with a little beef suet, or dripping. Not mutton fat, as it will give the taste of tallow.

A beef steak cannot be cooked in perfection unless over wood coals. To cook them before an anthracite fire, on an upright gridiron, is more like toasting than broiling, and much impairs the true flavor. A gridiron of the usual shape, with grooved or hollow bars to catch the gravy, is best of all. Broil the steaks well; and when done on one side, turn each steak with steak tongs; or a knife and fork, and an inverted plate.

Roast Lamb

The roasting pieces for lamb are the forequarter, and hind-quarter; and the saddle, or both hind-quarters together, not having been cut apart. If the saddle is cooked whole, it should be of a small delicate lamb, nice and fat, and is then a fashionable dish at company dinners. Like all other young meat lamb should always be thoroughly done, not the least redness being left perceptible any where about it. A hind-quarter of eight pounds will require at least two hours—a fore-quarter, rather longer. It should be placed before a clear brisk fire, but not very near at first. Put a little water in the dripping-pan, and baste it with that till it begins to cook, adding a little nice fresh butter. Then place it nearer the fire, and when the gravy begins to fall, baste it with that, and repeat the basting very frequently. When the lamb drops white gravy it is nearly done, and you may prepare for taking it up. Skim the gravy that is in the dripping-pan till all the fat is taken off. Then dredge over it a little flour, and send it to table in a gravy boat, having stirred in one or two tablespoonfuls of currant jelly. Lettuce is always an accompaniment to cold lamb.

Rare Meat

Underdone meat (foolishly called *rare*) is getting quite out of fashion, being unwholesome and indigestible, and to most Americans its savour is disgusting. To ladies and children it is always so, and even the English have ceased to like it. It is now seldom seen but at those public tables, where they consider it an object to have as little meat as possible eaten on the first day, that more may be left for the second day, to be made into indescribable messes, with ridiculous French names, and passed off as French dishes, by the so-called French cook, who is frequently an Irishman.

Eliza Leslie, *Miss Leslie's New Cookery Book*, 1857

How To Cook a Christmas Turkey

A plump young turkey
Half a pound of bread crumbs
Half a pound of suet
A small bunch of parsley
Three small onions
One pint and a half of cream

Two tablespoonfuls of flour
Seasoning
A little nutmeg
One teacupful of milk
Six whole tomatoes, and the juice of six
Half a pound of butter

After the turkey has been cleaned, wash it well inside and out, thoroughly dry, and dust lightly with flour. Take the bread crumbs, suet, parsley and onions, chop finely together. Mix with one pint of the cream some salt, pepper and a little nutmeg. Make this up into balls, about two inches in circumference. Take tomatoes that have been canned whole and then place inside the turkey, alternately, one ball and tomato, until full. Take the juice of the other six tomatoes, half a pound of butter, seasoning, and a teaspoonful of flour. Allow this to simmer in a saucepan slowly until thick. When the turkey is first basted, throw the whole of the sauce well over it. Continue to baste until thoroughly well browned and crisp. The gravy is made by pouring the balance of the cream and milk into the dripping-pan, which put back into the oven and stir until it boils well. Place in a sauce-tureen and serve both as hot as possible. A more delicious way of cooking a turkey it is impossible to imagine.

Godey's Lady's Book, December 1885

To Boil a Turkey

Make a stuffing for the craw, of chopped bread and butter, cream, oysters, and the yolks of eggs. Sew it in, and dredge flour over the turkey, and put it to boil in cold water, with a spoonful of salt in it, and enough water to cover it well. Let it simmer for two hours and a half, or if small, less time. Skim it while boiling. It looks nicer if wrapped in a cloth dredged with flour.

Serve it with drawn butter, in which are put some oysters.

Catharine E. Beecher, *Miss Beecher's Domestic Receipt Book*, 1858

Drawn Butter

Take half a pound of butter; braid into it two table-spoonfuls of flour; put it into a saucepan, and add one teacup of boiling water; set it on the fire, stirring it all the time until it almost boils.

Elizabeth H. Putnam, *Miss Putnam's Receipt Book, and Young Housekeeper's Assistant*, 1869

Remarks on Boiled Turkey

This is a dish I rarely have, as I never could relish it boiled as it generally is, by putting it into that pure and chaste element water, into which has been thrown some salt, the quantity of which differs as much as the individuals that throw it in. I often reflect to myself, why should this innocent and well-brought up bird have its remains condemned to this watery bubbling inquisition, especially when alive it has the greatest horror of this temperate fluid; it is really for want of reflection that such mistakes occur: the flavor of a roasted turkey, hot or cold, is as superior to the boiled as it is possible to be.

Alexis Soyer, *The Modern Housewife*, 1857

To Roast Canvas-Back Duck

Having trussed the ducks, put into each a thick piece of soft bread that has been soaked in port wine. Place them before a quick fire and roast them from three quarters to an hour. Before they go to table, squeeze over each the juice of a lemon or orange, and serve them up very hot with their own gravy about them. Eat them with currant jelly. Have ready also, a gravy made by stewing slowly in a sauce-pan the giblets of the ducks in butter rolled in flour, and as little water as possible. Serve up this additional gravy in a boat.

Eliza Leslie, *Miss Leslie's New Cookery Book*, 1857

Galantine of Turkey

Select a nice fat hen turkey weighing about twelve pounds. Singe, but do not draw. Bone as directed. Turn the legs and wings inside out, and draw them inside of the turkey. Now bone a chicken, turn the legs and wings in the same way, dredge both with salt and pepper. Place the chicken inside the turkey, with the rump of the chicken toward the neck of the turkey so that the white meat will not all be in the same place. Mix one pound of sausage meat or lean ham with one cup of bread crumbs and two well-beaten eggs. Form into a roll the shape of the turkey carcass, place it inside the chicken, draw the skin of the turkey together, and sew it up. Then press and roll with the hands until the galantine is an even roll. Tie at the extremities, and also across in two places. Now wrap tightly in a cloth, and tie as before. Put into a soup-kettle the bones from the turkey and chicken, one onion, one carrot sliced, six whole cloves, two bay leaves, a large sprig of parsley and three quarts of cold water, stand it over a moderate fire and bring slowly to a boil; skim, put in the galantine, and *simmer* gently for four hours. At the end of that time take the kettle from the fire and let the galantine cool in the liquor, then take it out and place on a flat dish; put a meat board on top of it, and two flat irons on top of the board, and stand away over night. In the morning remove the cloth carefully, brush the galantine over with a beaten egg, dust with bread crumbs and parsley chopped very fine, place in a very hot oven to brown, then stand away until very cold. This can be garnished with aspic jelly, or a jelly made from the bones, same as Boned Chicken. It is to be sliced thin when eaten, helping a small portion of the jelly with each slice.

Sarah Tyson Rorer, *Mrs. Rorer's Philadelphia Cook Book*, 1886

Roasted Partridges, Pheasants, and Quails

Make a stuffing of fat bacon finely minced, and boiled chestnuts or grated sweet potato boiled, mashed, and seasoned with pepper only. Fill the birds with this. Cover them with thin slices of bacon, and wrap them well in young vine leaves. Roast them well, and serve them up in the bacon and vine leaves, to be taken off when they come to table. For company, have orange sauce to eat with them. If you roast pigeons, &c., without a covering of bacon and vine leaves, do them with egg and bread-crumbs all over.

If these birds have a bitter taste when cooked, do not eat them. It is produced by their feeding on laurel berries in winter, when their food is scarce. Laurel berries are poisonous, and people have died from eating birds that have fed on them.

Eliza Leslie, *Miss Leslie's New Cookery Book*, 1857

Roast Goose

This requires keeping the same as fowls, some days before cooking. The goose is best in the autumn and early part of winter—never good in spring. What is called a green goose is four months old. It is insipid after, although tender. Pick well and singe the goose; then clean carefully. Put the liver and gizzard on to cook as the turkey's. When the goose is washed and ready for stuffing, have boiled three white potatoes, skin and mash them; chop three onions very fine, throw them into cold water; stir into the potatoes a spoonful of butter, a little salt and black pepper, a tablespoonful of finely rubbed sage leaves; drain off the onions, and mix with the potato, sage, &c. When well mixed, stuff the goose with the mixture, have ready a coarse needle and thread, and sew up the slit made for cleaning and introducing the stuffing. A full grown goose requires one hour and three quarters. Roast it as a turkey, dredging and basting. The gravy is prepared as for poultry, with the liver and gizzard. Apple sauce is indispensable for roast goose.

A Practical Housekeeper, *Cookery As It Should Be*, 1856

Apple Sauce

Get fine juicy apples—bellflowers are the best for cooking. Sweet apples cook very badly—becoming tough, dry and tasteless. Green apples, if full grown, cook well, and have a pleasant acid.

For sauce, pare, core, and quarter or slice the apples. Wash the pieces in a cullender, and put them to stew, with only water enough to wet them a little. Apple stews that are thin and watery are disgraceful to the cook, or to the cook's mistress. Let them stew till you can mash them easily all through. Then take them off the fire, and sweeten them, adding the seasoning while the apples are warm. Season with rose-water, lemon juice, nutmeg; or with all these if for company. If you can get fresh lemon-peel, cut it into very thin slips, and put it in to stew with the apples at first. It is still better, and little more trouble, to grate the lemon-peel.

Eliza Leslie, *Miss Leslie's New Cookery Book*, 1857

ENTREES

Entrees are the middle dishes of the feast, and not the principal course, as many suppose; they are a series of dainty side dishes, in the preparation of which the cook demonstrates the extent of her capabilities.

Thomas J. Murray, *The Book of Entrees*, 1889

Ragout

Cut *one pint* of *cold meat* into half-inch dice; remove the fat, bone, and gristle. Put the meat in a stewpan; cover with *boiling water*, and simmer slowly two or three hours, or till very tender; then add *half a can* of *mushrooms*, cut fine, *two tablespoonfuls* of *Madeira wine*, *salt* and *pepper* to taste. Wet *one tablespoonful* of *flour* to a smooth paste with a little *cold water*, stir it into the boiling liquor; add *a teaspoonful* of *caramel*, if not brown enough. Cook ten minutes, and serve plain or in a border of *mashed potatoes*. The seasoning may be varied by using *one teaspoonful* of *curry powder, a few grains* of *cayenne pepper*, or *half a tumbler* of *currant jelly*, and *salt* to taste.

Mrs. D. A. Lincoln, *Mrs. Lincoln's Boston Cook Book*, 1889

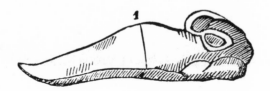

Beef Tongue

Soak the tongue twenty-four hours before boiling. It will require from three to four hours, according to size. The skin should always be removed as soon as it is taken from the pot. An economical method is to lay the tongue, as soon as the skin is removed, in a jar, coiled up, with the tip outside the root, and a weight upon it. When it is cold, loosen the sides with a knife, and turn it out. The slices being cut horizontally all round, the fat and lean will go together.

Jane Warren, *The Economical Cook Book*, ca. 1882

Fried Corned Beef

This is a very homely and economical dish, but it is liked by many persons. Cut thin slices from a cold round of beef, and season them with pepper. Fry them brown over a quick fire, and put them in a covered dish to keep hot. Then wash the frying-pan, cleaning it well from the fat, and put into it plenty of cold boiled cabbage, cut small, and some cold carrots, sliced thin, adding some thin sliced suet, or beef dripping to fry them in. When done, dish the meat with the vegetables laid around it; adding the gravy. This is the dish called in England, Bubble-and-Squeak, perhaps from the noise it makes when frying. It is only designed for strong healthy people with good appetites.

It is sometimes made of salt pork or bacon; sliced potatoes being added to the cabbage.

Eliza Leslie, *Miss Leslie's New Cookery Book*, 1857

Connecticut Thanksgiving Chicken Pie

In sufficient water to prevent burning, stew old not young fowls, jointed, all but tender enough for the table. Pour all into a dish, and season with salt and pepper to the taste. When about cold, place the parts in your pudding dish, lined with a thin common paste, adding about half a pound of butter to three pounds of fowl, in alternate layers. Take more of the paste; roll it *nine times*, studding it each time with butter, (it must be made very rich;) to be careful to roll out, each time, from you, and to roll up towards you, leaving it, at least, an inch thick. Add the upper crust; cut a lip in it; and ornament it with some of the reserved paste, having first lightly sprinkled the chickens with flour, after almost filling the dish with the liquor in which the chickens were stewed. Pin tight around the rim of the dish a cloth bandage, to prevent the escape of the juices; and bake from an hour to an hour and a half, in a quick oven. If the top burns, lay a paper over it.

Mrs. A. L. Webster, *The Improved Housewife*, 1853

Chicken Curry

Fine-grained poultry do not make good curry, as the curry powder is unable to permeate the centre of the flesh. A coarse-grained bird will be found the best for this purpose. Boil the chicken in the usual manner, saving the broth. When cold cut it neatly, and rub the curry powder into the meat. Cut up one large sour apple and half an onion, fry these in butter; add the meat, toss it about a moment, and add half a pint of the chicken broth and a tablespoonful of chutney, simmer until thoroughly amalgamated and serve with rice or shredded maize. A little sugar is an improvement and may thicken the sauce, but I like it without flour.

Chicken Fricassee with Mushrooms

Take a dry-picked chicken, separate the joints, cut each joint into pieces, remove the skin. Put the pieces into a saucepan with one onion, salt and pepper, and a few soup herbs, and water enough to cover them; simmer gently three-quarters of an hour, remove scum as it arises; when the chicken is quite tender remove it, strain the liquid. Put into a saucepan an ounce of butter, heat it, and whisk it thoroughly; thicken a cupful of the broth with a teaspoonful of flour, add it to the butter; do not let it boil, whisk it well, add gradually half the quantity of broth, draw the pan from the fire. Beat up the yolks of two eggs with a little cream, and add it to the remaining warm broth. Now add this to the sauce containing the butter, let stand a moment on back of range while you cut up a dozen button mushrooms, add these to the sauce, now add the chicken, and, when all is quite warm, serve.

Thomas J. Murray, *The Book of Entrees*, 1889

Chicken Croquettes

Half a pound of *chicken* chopped very fine, and seasoned with *half a teaspoonful* of *salt, half a teaspoonful* of *celery salt, a quarter* of *a saltspoonful* of *cayenne pepper, one saltspoonful* of *white pepper,* a few drops of *onion juice, one teaspoonful* of *chopped parsley,* and *one teaspoonful* of *lemon juice.* Make *one pint* of very *thick cream sauce.* When thick, add *one beaten egg,* and mix the sauce with the chicken, using only enough to make it as soft as can be handled. Spread on a shallow plate to cool. Shape into rolls. Roll in *fine bread crumbs,* then dip in *beaten egg,* then in *crumbs* again, and fry one minute in *smoking hot fat.* Drain, and serve with a *thin cream sauce.* Many prefer to cut the chicken into small dice. If this be done, use less of the sauce, or the croquettes will be difficult to shape. The white meat of chicken will absorb more sauce than the dark. Mushrooms, boiled rice, sweetbreads, calf's brains, or veal may be mixed with chicken. Cold roast chicken, chopped fine, may be mixed with the stuffing, moistened with the gravy, and shaped into croquettes.

Mrs. D. A. Lincoln, *Mrs. Lincoln's Boston Cook Book*, 1889

Jambalaya

Cut up, and stew till half done, a fowl, brown or white; then add rice, and a piece of ham well minced; this must be left on the fire till the rice has taken up the liquid; the roundness of the grain must be preserved, yet the dish must not be hard and dry. It is served in a heap, on a flat dish. Pepper and salt the only seasoning.

Southern children are very fond of this essentially home-dish. It is said to be of Indian origin. Wholesome as it is palatable, it makes part of almost every Creole dinner.

Sarah Josepha Hale, *The New Household Receipt-Book*, 1853

Filet Gumbo

Cut up a pair of fine plump fowls into pieces, as when carving. Lay them in a pan of cold water, till all the blood is drawn out. Put into a pot, two large table-spoonfuls of lard, and set it over the fire. When the lard has come to a boil, put in the chickens with an onion finely minced. Dredge them well with flour, and season slightly with salt and pepper; and, if you like it, a little chopped marjoram. Pour on it two quarts of boiling water. Cover it, and let it simmer slowly for three hours. Then stir into it two heaped tea-spoonfuls of sassafras powder. Afterwards, let it stew five or six minutes longer, and then send it to table in a deep dish; having a dish of boiled rice to be eaten with it by those who like rice.

This gumbo will be much improved by stewing with it three or four thin slices of cold boiled ham, in which case omit the salt in the seasoning. Whenever cold ham is an ingredient in any dish, no other salt is required.

A dozen fresh oysters and their liquor, added to the stew about half an hour before it is taken up, will also be an improvement.

If you cannot conveniently obtain sassafras-powder, stir the gumbo frequently with a stock of sassafras root.

This is a genuine southern receipt. Filet gumbo may be made of any sort of poultry, or of veal, lamb, venison, or kid.

Eliza Leslie, *Miss Leslie's New Cookery Book*, 1857

Veal Croquettes with String Beans

Chop up two pounds of cold roast veal with two boiled sweet-breads; moisten them with a little clear soup, and bind together with yolks of two eggs; season with a teaspoonful of chopped parsley, salt, and cayenne; roll the mass into cones, dip them in beaten egg, roll in crumbs, dip again in egg, and again roll in crumbs, and fry in hot fat. Arrange neatly on a dish with small ends upright, around them put a border of string-beans boiled and nicely seasoned, and serve.

RECIPES

Thomas J. Murray, *The Book of Entrees*, 1889

Veal Relish

Three pounds of uncooked veal, quarter of a pound of pork; chop these fine; add two eggs, one cupful pounded crackers, one teaspoonful of salt, two of pepper; sage and summer savory to suit the taste; press hard in a pudding-dish, and bake one and a half hours; cut in thin slices when cold.

Jane Warren, *The Economical Cook Book*, ca. 1882

Potted Pigeons

Draw and clean. Break the legs just above the feet; leave enough below the joint to tie down to the tail. Wash and wipe. If old and tough, cover them with *vinegar*, spiced and flavored with *onion*, and let them stand several hours. This makes them tender. Drain and wipe; stuff, if you like, with *cracker crumbs* highly seasoned and moistened with *butter*. Dredge with *salt, pepper*, and *flour*. Fry several slices of *salt pork*; cut *one large onion* fine, and fry in the salt pork fat. Put the crisp fat in the stewpan, add the fried onion, then brown the pigeons all over in the fat left in the pan. Put them in the stewpan; add *boiling water* or *stock* enough to half cover them; add *a pinch* of *herbs* tied in a bag. Simmer from one to three hours, or till the pigeons are tender. Remove the fat from the broth, season to taste, and thicken with *flour* and *butter* cooked together. Strain over the pigeons, and serve hot.

Mrs. D. A. Lincoln, *Mrs. Lincoln's Boston Cook Book*, 1889

Potted Cheese

This is a useful luncheon dish, and being in a glass jar, it looks light and pretty on the table. One pound of cheese must be well beaten in a mortar, and to it must be added two ounces of liquid butter, one glass of sherry, and a very small quantity of Cayenne pepper, mace, and salt. All should be well beaten together and put in a pretty shaped glass potting-jar, with a layer of butter at the top. It makes a delicious relish for bread or toast.

Godey's Lady's Book, January 1866

Macaroni

Macaroni, as an article of food, is rather more valuable than bread, as it contains a larger proportion of gluten. It is the bread of the Italian laborer. In this country, it is a sort of a luxury among the upper classes; but there is no good reason, considering its price, why it should not enter more extensively into the food of our working classes.

In selecting, choose that of a brownish color, rather than the pure white.

Spighetti is the most delicate form of macaroni that comes to this country.

Macaroni à l'italienne

¼ pound of macaroni
¼ pound of grated cheese
Salt and white pepper to taste

½ pint of milk
Butter the size of a walnut

Break the macaroni in convenient lengths. Put it in a two-quart kettle and nearly fill the kettle with boiling water; add a teaspoonful of salt and boil rapidly twenty-five minutes; then drain; throw into cold water to blanch for ten minutes. Put the milk into a farina boiler; add to it the butter, then the macaroni and cheese; stir until thoroughly heated, add the salt and pepper, and serve.

Sarah Tyson Rorer, *Mrs. Rorer's Philadelphia Cook Book*, 1886

Welsh Rarebit

½ pound of English cheese
3 eggs, well beaten
1 scant cup of fine bread-crumbs

3 table-spoonfuls of butter, melted
2 teaspoonfuls of made mustard
1 saltspoonful of salt

Mix all well together, and beat to a smooth paste. Have ready some slices of toasted bread, from which the crust has been pared; spread them thickly with the mixture, and set them upon the upper grating of the oven until they are slightly browned. Serve at once.

Marion Harland, *Breakfast, Luncheon and Tea*, 1875

Fried Frogs

The hind legs of frogs are the only part used as food. They are usually sold skinned in the markets; but if you get them out of town, they must be skinned and thrown into boiling water for five minutes; take out and put them in cold water until cold, then wipe dry. Season with salt and pepper, dredge with flour and fry a nice brown in butter. Serve with fried parsley around them, or with cream sauce.

Sarah Tyson Rorer, *Mrs. Rorer's Philadelphia Cook Book*, 1886

Fried Liver

Put into a frying-pan some nice thin slices of ham or bacon, that have soaked all night, and fry them in their own fat. Have ready your calf's liver, cut into slices not too thin, as that will render them hard. Take out the ham as soon as it is done, put it into a hot dish, and cover it closely. Lay the slices of liver into the gravy of the bacon that is left in the frying-pan, sprinkling it well with chopped parsley. It must be thoroughly done. Then dish with the bacon.

To those who like them, some onions will be thought an improvement to fried liver. First parboil the onions: then slice them, season them with a little salt and pepper, and fry them with the liver.

If lettuces are in season, quarter a fresh one, and lay it under the liver when you dish it, having previously removed the thickest part of the stalk. The liver of beef or sheep is not seen at good tables. It is very inferior to that of calf's, being hard and coarse.

Eliza Leslie, *Miss Leslie's New Cookery Book*, 1857

Kidneys

To dress kidneys: Cut them through the centre; take out the core; pull the kernels apart; put them into the saucepan without any water, and set them on the fire where they may get hot, not boil; in half an hour put the kidneys into cold water, wash them clean, and put them back into the saucepan, with just enough water to cover them; boil them one hour, then take them up; clean off the fat and skin; put into the frying-pan some butter, pepper and salt; dredge in a little flour, half a pint of hot water, and the kidneys; let them simmer twenty minutes; stir them often; do not let them fry, because it hardens them. This is a very nice dish for breakfast.

S. Annie Frost, *The Godey's Lady's Book Receipts and Household Hints*, 1870

Vol-au-Vent

Roll off a nice puff paste, about the eighth of an inch in thickness; then with a tin cutter, the size of the dish intended to lay the pastry on, cut out an oblong shape; lay this on a baking plate with a sheet of white paper beneath the paste; rub the paste over with the yolk of an egg; then roll out another piece of paste an inch in thickness; cut this also with the cutter the same size as the other; lay this on the other piece of paste, then with a cutter two sizes smaller, press nearly through the two pieces of paste in the centre; be careful not to cut entirely through the bottom of the paste; rub the top with the yolk of an egg; bake it in a quick oven twenty minutes, a light brown color; when cooked take out very carefully the centre piece marked by the small cutter; keep the paste warm until ready for table; then fill in the centre with nicely fricasseed chicken hot, or stewed oysters, or nicely-minced seasoned veal; then lay on the top piece, and serve hot.

A Practical Housekeeper, *Cookery As It Should Be*, 1856

Sausage Dumplings

Make one pound of flour and two ounces of dripping, or chopped suet, into a firm paste, by adding just enough water to enable you to knead the whole together. Divide this paste into twelve equal parts, roll each of these out sufficiently large to be able to fold up one of the beef sausages in it, wet the edge of the paste to fasten the sausage securely in it, and, as you finish off each sausage dumpling, drop it gently into a large enough saucepan, containing plenty of *boiling* water, and when the whole are finished, allow them to boil gently by the side of the fire for one hour, and then take up the dumplings with a spoon free from water, on to a dish, and eat them while they are hot.

Beef Cakes

Pound some beef that is under-done with a little fat bacon or ham; season with pepper, salt, and a little shallot or garlic; mix them well, and make into small cakes three inches long, and half as wide and thick; fry them a light brown, and serve them in a good thick gravy.

S. Annie Frost, *The Godey's Lady's Book Receipts and Household Hints*, 1870

VEGETABLES

OBSERVATIONS ON DRESSING VEGETABLES

Vegetables should be carefully cleaned from insects and nicely washed. Boil them in plenty of water, and drain them the moment they are done enough. If overboiled they will lose their beauty and crispness. Bad cooks sometimes dress them with meat; which is wrong, except carrots with boiling beef.

An American Lady, *The American Home Cook Book*, 1854

Saratoga Potatoes

It requires a little plane, or potato or cabbage cutter, to cut these potatoes. Two or three fine, large potatoes (ripe new ones are preferable) are selected and pared. They are cut, by rubbing them over the plane, into slices as thin or thinner than a wafer. These are placed for a few moments in ice, or very cold water, to become chilled. Boiling lard is now tested, to see if it is of the proper temperature. The slices must color quickly; but the fat must not be so hot as to give them a dark color.

Place a salt-box on the hearth; also a dish to receive the cooked potatoes at the side; a tin plate and perforated ladle should be at hand also. Now throw, separately, five or six slices of the cold potato into the hot lard; keep them separated by means of the ladle until they are of a delicate yellow color; skim them out into the tin plate; sprinkle over some salt, and push them on the dish. Now pour back any grease that is on the tin plate into the kettle, and fry five or six slices at a time until enough are cooked. Two potatoes fried will make a large dishful.

It is a convenient dish for a company dinner, as it may be made early in the day; and by being kept in a dry, warm place (for instance, a kitchen-closet), the potato-slices will be crisp and nice five or six hours afterward. They are eaten cold, and are a pretty garnish around game, or, in fact, any other kind of meat.

Mary F. Henderson, *Practical Cooking, and Dinner Giving*, 1878

RECIPES

Old Potatoes

Old potatoes are best to boil until soft, then peel and mash fine, with a little salt, butter, and a very little milk, beat well together with a spoon; then put into a dish, smooth over with a knife, sprinkle a little flour over it; put in the oven to brown.

Jane Warren, *The Economical Cook Book*, ca. 1882

Cold Potato Puffs

Take cold mashed or chopped potatoes and stir in milk and melted butter. Beat two eggs and mix, and then bake till browned. It is very nice, and the children love it as well as their elders. This may be baked in patties for a pretty variety.

Catharine E. Beecher, *Miss Beecher's Housekeeper and Healthkeeper*, 1874

Onion Custard

Peel and slice ten or twelve mild onions, and fry them in fresh butter, draining them well when you take them up. Then mince them as fine as possible. Beat four eggs till very thick and light, and stir them gradually into a pint of milk, in turn with the minced onion. Season the whole with plenty of grated nutmeg, and stir it very hard. Then put it into a deep white dish, and bake it about a quarter of an hour. Send it to table as a side dish, to be eaten with poultry. It is a French preparation, and will be found very nice, by those who have no dislike to onions.

Lima Beans

Shell the lima beans into a pan of cold water. Let them lie in it an hour. Put them in boiling water, little more than enough to cover them, and boil them till soft and tender. When done, drain and serve them up in a deep dish, adding among them a good piece of butter. The Lima beans now raised in North America have become coarse and white, requiring a renewal of fresh stock or new seeds from Peru. They will then be green and delicate again, as formerly.

Scolloped Tomatoes

Take fine large tomatos, perfectly ripe. Scald them to loosen the skins, and then peel them. Cover the bottom of a deep dish thickly with grated bread-crumbs, adding a few bits of fresh butter. Then put in a layer of tomatos, seasoned slightly with a little salt and cayenne, and some powdered mace or nutmeg. Cover them with another layer of bread-crumbs and butter; then another layer of seasoned tomatoes; and proceed thus until the dish is full, finishing at the top with bread-crumbs. Set the dish into a moderate oven, and bake it near three hours. Tomatos require long cooking, otherwise they will have a raw taste, that to most persons is unpleasant.

Eliza Leslie, *Miss Leslie's New Cookery Book*, 1857

Baked Tomatoes

Cut a thin slice off the top of each of four medium-sized tomatoes, sprinkle over them a little salt, cayenne, and very little cracker-crumbs. Add a small square of butter and bake a delicate brown on top. Tomatoes prepared in this way are very nice for those who dislike the trouble of preparing stuffed tomatoes.

Thomas J. Murray, *The Book of Entrees*, 1889

Fried Parsnips

[These] make a nice breakfast dish. They must first be parboiled; then split, and cut into long pieces, and fried brown in fresh butter, or in nice dripping[s] of veal or beef.

Eliza Leslie, *Miss Leslie's New Cookery Book*, 1857

Sackatash, or Corn and Beans

Boil three pints of shelled beans, or a quarter of a peck of string beans, half an hour, pour off the water. Cut the corn off of four dozen ears—put it in the pot among the beans, add salt and pepper, and cover them with boiling water—boil all together twenty minutes. Rub flour into a large piece of butter and stir it in, then let it boil up once. Pour it into your tureen and send it to table.

Sarah Josepha Hale, *The New Household Receipt-Book*, 1853

Pease

American mode: First boil the pods, which are sweet and full of flavor, in a little water; skim them out, and add the pease, which boil until tender; add then a little butter, cream, pepper, and salt. If they are served as a garnish, do not add the juice; but, if served alone, the juice is a savory addition.

Time to cook, about half an hour.

The American canned pease should be rinsed before cooking, as the juice is generally thick. The pease are then thrown into a little boiling water seasoned with salt, and a little sugar; butter is added when done.

Mary F. Henderson, *Practical Cooking, and Dinner Giving*, 1878

Canned Green Peas

The canned French peas (*pois verts*) are a tolerable substitute for fresh, but very expensive. The American are, when simply boiled—*in*tolerable, and cost less than half

as much as the imported. They may, however, be made palatable in the winter dearth of green food by two or three processes. First and best, I write down

Green Pea Pancakes

Mash the peas while hot, and work in butter, pepper, and salt. (If the peas are cold, heat the butter and pound the peas smooth with a potato-beetle.) Beat in two eggs, a cupful of milk, half a teaspoonful of soda, and twice as much cream of tartar sifted *three times* through half a cupful of flour. Beat up well, and bake as you would griddlecakes.

If you use prepared flour, omit soda and cream of tartar. Never forget to open the can several hours before cooking the peas. Throw away the liquor, and leave the peas in very cold clean water until you are ready for them. This freshens them to taste as well as sight.

Canned Corn Fritters

Canned corn, when simply stewed, is a wretched substitute for that most delicious and succulent of American esculents—green maize on the ear. Chopped fine it may take the place of the summer delicacy in the above receipt with more credit to itself than

would be believed by those who have never seen it thus manipulated. Open and empty the can some hours before the corn is to be used, drain dry and mince faithfully, then proceed as with the fresh.

Marion Harland, *The Cottage Kitchen*, 1883

Stuffed Artichokes

Trim and wash four artichokes; remove the "choke" found in the center; make a stuffing of bread-crumbs nicely seasoned with a preparation made as follows: Mince half a pound of ham, warm it, and add a dozen canned mushrooms chopped fine, a teaspoonful of chopped parsley, a few blades of chives, salt, and pepper. Add the crumbs, and moisten with clear soup or hot water; work all to a paste, and fill the artichokes with it. Tie each artichoke neatly; put them in a pan with a little butter, to prevent burning, and a pint of clear soup; cover the pan, and let them steam in their own vapors until tender.

The artichoke has been used as a vegetable over 300 years. The flower-heads in their immature state contain the thick, fleshy part called artichoke bottoms, which is the part most highly prized; the lower parts of the thick, imbricated scales are also eaten.

The blue flower of the artichoke, either fresh or dried, turns milk into an excellent curd for cheese.

Thomas J. Murray, *The Book of Entrees*, 1889

To Cook Beans in a French Style

Choose small young beans, and strip off the ends and stalks, throwing them, as prepared, into a dish full of cold spring water, and, when all are finished, wash and drain them well. Boil them in salted boiling water, in a large saucepan, and drain them, after which put them into an enamelled stewpan, and shake them over the fire until they are quite hot and dry; then add about three ounces of fresh butter, and a tablespoonful of veal or chicken broth; the butter must be broken up into small lumps. Season with white pepper, salt, and the juice of half a lemon strained. Stir them well over a hot fire for five minutes, and serve them in a vegetable dish very hot.

S. Annie Frost, *The Godey's Lady's Book Receipts and Household Hints*, 1870

Egg Plant

Cut them in slices half an inch thick; sprinkle them with salt, and let them stand a few minutes to extract the bitter taste; wash them in cold water, and wipe them dry; season with salt and pepper; dip them in flour, and fry them in butter.

Another way of cooking them is to cut them in thin slices, and bake them on a bake-iron that is hot enough to bake cakes.

Elizabeth F. Lea, *Domestic Cookery, Useful Receipts, and Hints to Young Housekeepers*, 1865

Salsify, or Oyster Plant

After scraping off the outside, parboil it, slice it, dip the slices into a beaten egg and fine bread crums, and fry in lard. It is very good boiled, and then stewed a few minutes in milk, with a little salt and butter. Or, make a batter of wheat flour, milk, and eggs; cut the salsify in thin slices, first boiling it tender; put them into the batter with a little salt; drop the mixture into hot fat by spoonfuls. Cook them till of a light brown.

Boston Baked Beans

Take two quarts of middling sized white beans, three pounds of salt pork, and one spoonful of molasses. Pick the beans over carefully, wash and turn about a gallon of soft water to them in a pot; let them soak in it lukewarm over night; set them in the morning where they will boil till the skin is very tender and about to break, adding a teaspoonful of salæratus. Take them up dry, put them in your dish, stir in the molasses, gash the pork, and put it down in the dish so as to have the beans cover all but the upper surface; turn in cold water till the top is just covered; bake and let the beans remain in the oven all night.

Beans are good prepared as for baking, made a little thinner, and then boiled several hours with the pork.

Mrs. A. L. Webster, *The Improved Housewife*, 1853

SALADS

There is hardly a vegetable which is not used, either cooked or raw, in salad, the usual dressing being one third or fourth vinegar, and two-thirds or three-fourths oil, with, of course, salt and pepper. For the bean salads, mustard is sometimes used.

Maria Parloa, *Home Economics*, 1898

French Dressing

Ingredients: One table-spoonful of vinegar, three table-spoonfuls of olive-oil, one salt-spoonful of pepper, one salt-spoonful of salt, one even tea-spoonful of onion scraped fine. Many use tarragon vinegar, *i.e.*, vinegar in which tarragon has been soaked.

Pour the oil, mixed with the pepper and salt, over the salad; mix them together; then add the vinegar and mix again.

This is the usual mode of mixing the salad; but I prefer to mix the pepper and salt, then add the oil and onion, and then the vinegar; and, when well mingled, to pour the mixture over the salad, or place the salad over it, and mix all together. It seems to me to be more evenly distributed in this manner.

Mayonnaise Sauce

Put the uncooked yolk of an egg into a cold bowl; beat it well with a silver fork; then add two salt-spoonfuls of salt, and one salt-spoonful of mustard powder; work them well a minute before adding the oil; then mix in a little good oil, which must be poured in very slowly (a few drops at a time) at first, alternated occasionally with a few drops of vinegar. In proportion as the oil is used, the sauce should gain consistency. When it begins to have the appearance of jelly, alternate a few drops of lemon-juice with the oil. When the egg has absorbed a gill of oil, finish the sauce by adding a very little pinch of Cayenne pepper and one and a half tea-spoonfuls of good vinegar; taste it to see that there are salt, mustard, cayenne, and vinegar enough. If not, add more very carefully. These proportions will suit most tastes; yet some like more mustard and more oil. Be cautious not to use too much cayenne.

Lettuce Salad

Rub garlic in the dish in which lettuce, with French dressing (without onion), is to be served. Leave no pieces of the garlic—merely rubbing the dish will give flavor enough. The French often use garlic in salads. I would advise, however, the use of the simple French dressing with onion to be mixed with the lettuce leaves, and dispense with the garlic. Use the plain or the tarragon vinegar. Nasturtium blossoms have a most pleasant piquant flavor, and make a beautiful garnish for a salad.

Cold Slaw

Cut the cabbage not too fine; sprinkle pepper and salt over it, and set it on ice, or in a cool place, to keep it crisp.

Dressing: Beat the yolks of three eggs, or the whole of two eggs, with five tablespoonfuls of good strong vinegar, two heaping tea-spoonfuls of sugar (three, if the vinegar is very strong), half a tea-spoonful of made mustard, and butter size of an almond. Put these ingredients into a tin cup, and stir them over the fire until they are about to boil, or until they become a smooth paste. Put the mixture one side to become cold, and to remain until just before it is wanted at table; then mix it well with the cold cabbage, and garnish the top with slices of hard-boiled egg.

Cold slaw is especially nice served with fried oysters. Place it in the centre of the warm platter on a folded napkin (a too warm platter would injure it), then make a circle of fried oysters around it. This makes a nice course for dinner.

Tomatoes à la Mayonnaise

This is a truly delicious dish; it would, in fact, be good every day during the tomato season.

Select large fine tomatoes and place them in the ice-chest; the colder they are, the better, if not frozen; skin them without the use of hot water, and slice them, still retaining the form of the whole tomato. Arrange them in uniform order on a dish, with a spoonful of *Mayonnaise* sauce thick as a jelly on the top of each tomato. Garnish the dish with leaves of any kind. Parsley is very pretty.

Some marinate the tomato slices, *i.e.*, dip them into a mixture of three spoonfuls of vinegar to one spoonful of oil, pepper, and salt; and then, after draining well, mix them in the *Mayonnaise* sauce.

String-Beans in Salad

String the beans and boil them whole; when boiled tender, and they have become cold, slice them lengthwise, cutting each bean into four long slices; place them neatly, the slices all lying in one direction, crosswise on a platter. Season them an hour or two before serving, with a marinade of a little pepper, salt, and three spoonfuls of vinegar to one spoonful of oil. Just before serving, drain from them any drops that may have collected, and carefully mix them with a French dressing. This makes a delicious salad.

Mary F. Henderson, *Practical Cooking, and Dinner Giving,* 1878

Chicken Salad for an Evening Party

Boil a pair of young tender chickens one hour, or less if they are very tender; cut into small pieces, but do not chop; [add] as much celery and the white tender parts of a cabbage as will measure as much as the meat; chop the cabbage. Boil until hard six eggs; chop the whites and mash the yolks to a pulp, with two tablespoonfuls of made mustard, one teaspoonful of black and a half teaspoonful of Cayenne pepper. Scald a coffeecupful of best cider vinegar, into which stir very gradually a teacupful of fresh, unsalted butter and the yolks of three beaten eggs; when thick, take immediately from the fire and cool; then stir into the other ingredients, with four-tablespoonfuls of good olive oil; mix into the meat several hours before using. If the vinegar is not sour, add a little citric acid.

Aunt Carey, *The Ladies' Floral Cabinet and Pictorial Home Companion,* March 1874

A Nice and Handsome Salad

Select two good heads of lettuce, split them in half, then wash them in cold water and shake them dry in a napkin, lay them in the salad bowl, cut lengthwise some well-cooked red beets, and lay them between the heads of lettuce, boil three eggs very hard, remove the whites from the yolks, and cut up the whites into squares, and scatter over the salad, then cut some squares of the beets and scatter over; of the yolks make the sauce, by rubbing very smoothly the yolk with a spoon, add a little cayenne, salt, a large spoonful of dry mustard, and a teasponful of pulverized white sugar, mix these well together in a basin, with a spoon, then slowly add two large spoonsful of olive oil, and when a smooth paste, add three spoonsful of the best vinegar. This sauce must be served with the salad.

RECIMES

. ———— .

A Practical Housekeeper, *Cookery As It Should Be,* 1856

A Family French Salad for Summer

I can assure you that, when in France during the hot weather, I used to enjoy the following salads immensely, having them usually twice a week for my dinner; they are not only wholesome, but cheap and quickly done. Cut up a pound of cold beef into thin slices, which put into a salad-bowl with about half a pound of white fresh lettuce, cut into pieces similar to the beef, season over with a good teaspoonful of salt, half that quantity of pepper, two spoonfuls of vinegar, and four of good salad oil, stir all together lightly with a fork and spoon, and when well mixed it is ready to serve.

Alexis Soyer, *The Modern Housewife*, 1857

Egg Salad

Boil six eggs fifteen minutes; while they are boiling, make a French dressing and add to it one tablespoonful of tarragon vinegar, one tablespoonful of onion juice and one tablespoonful of finely chopped parsley. When the eggs are done remove the shells, cut them into slices, and arrange them on a salad dish so that one overlaps the other; pour the dressing over while the eggs are still hot, stand away in a cold place for one or two hours, garnish with parsley, and serve.

Sarah Tyson Rorer, *Mrs. Rorer's Philadelphia Cook Book*, 1886

Lobster Salad

Cut one pint of lobster meat in dice, season with a *French dressing*, and keep it on ice until ready to serve, then mix with half of the *Mayonnaise dressing*. Make nests or cups of the crisp *lettuce* leaves; break the poorer lettuce leaves and mix with the lobster. Put *a large spoonful* of the lobster in each leaf, with *a tablespoonful* of the *Mayonnaise* on the top. Garnish with *capers* and *pounded coral*, sprinkled over the dressing, and with lobster claws and parsley round the edge.

Mrs. D. A. Lincoln, *Mrs. Lincoln's Boston Cook Book*, 1889

Roll Sandwiches

Take finger-rolls that are at least half a day old. Cut them in two, lengthwise. Scoop out the crumb and fill the hollow thus left with minced chicken, tongue, or ham. Tie the two halves together with a narrow ribbon. It is a pretty idea to indicate the filling used by different-colored ribbons. Thus, the tongue sandwiches may be tied with a red ribbon, the ham with pink, and the chicken with light-yellow.

Almost any sort of filling that is good in other sandwiches may be used for rolls. The old method of laying slices of meat between the sides of biscuit or pieces of bread makes graceful eating extremely difficult, and it is always best to chop the filling for all meat sandwiches.

Ham Sandwiches

Mince the ham very fine, putting a little fat with the lean. Work into this a suspicion of made mustard, and spread upon thin white buttered bread. Always cut the crust from the bread, unless it is very delicate.

Sardine Sandwiches

Lay the sardines upon tissue-paper for a few moments to free them from the oil in which they come. Reject all bits of skin or bone, and break the sardines to bits with a fork. Work into them a little melted butter and a few drops of lemon-juice and spread them upon buttered bread or rolls.

Egg and Anchovy Sandwiches

Mince two anchovies fine, and add them to your egg paste. Spread rolls or biscuit with this. Anchovy paste also makes a good filling for sandwiches, and is excellent to spread thinly upon buttered crackers.

Cheese and Lettuce Sandwiches (very good)

Cut Boston brown bread into thin slices, butter one of these lightly, and spread it with Neufchatel or Philadelphia cream cheese. On this lay a leaf of lettuce which has been dipped for a moment in French salad dressing. Place another buttered slice of brown bread upon this, and cut the round into three triangular sandwiches. Watercress may be used in place of lettuce.

Cold meat or fowl or game may be used as filling; pâtés of all sorts are excellent for the purpose, and sweetbread and oyster sandwiches are delicious.

Sandwiches should always be wrapped neatly in white tissue-paper, six, eight, or a dozen in each parcel, and tied with narrow ribbon. The extra care and expense are trifling, and are repaid by the daintiness of the result.

Rolled Bread and Butter

Bread a day old, and of rather close texture, must be used for this. Cut off the crust, butter the end of the loaf, and shave off the thinnest possible slice with a very sharp knife. Roll with the butter inside, and lay each roll with the overlapping end down, to keep it in place. These rolls are sometimes tied with ribbon, but it is hardly feasible except at a very small picnic party.

Lobster Mayonnaise Sandwiches

Chop cold boiled lobster fine, and moisten it with a thick mayonnaise dressing. Select white bread, a day old, butter each slice on the loaf, and cut very thin. Spread one slice with the lobster mixture and lay another slice over it. Do not have the sandwich the size of the whole slice, but cut it into squares, oblongs, or triangles that are easily managed. Salmon mayonnaise or chicken mayonnaise sandwiches are also very good.

Veal Loaf

Two pounds lean veal, raw, chopped very fine; quarter-pound ham or salt pork, also chopped fine; half-cup bread-crumbs; two eggs; half-teaspoonful salt; quarter-teaspoonful each of black pepper, minced thyme, and ground cloves and allspice; one teaspoonful onion juice. Mix the ingredients thoroughly and pack them closely into a brick-shaped tin, first greasing this. Cover this closely, set it in an outer pan of boiling water, and bake in a steady oven for two or three hours. Let it cool in the pan, turn it out, and cut into slices. This is readily managed with a fork, after it is once sliced, or the slice may be laid sandwich-wise between two pieces of bread or the halves of a roll or biscuit.

Christine Terhune Herrick, *The Outlook*, 26 August 1893

KICKSHAWS, PICKLES, AND RELISHES

The kickshaws are of two kinds, hot and cold—oysters, raw and cooked, anchovies, shrimps, sardines, horseradish, butter, rolls, and pickles of various kinds.

A Practical Housekeeper, The American Practical Cookery-Book, *1861*

A dinner or lunch without pickles of some kind is incomplete. When used judiciously and made properly, they give one an appetite and are wholesome. Home-made ones are much more healthful and better. Dealers wish to preserve the natural color of cucumbers and other green pickles and often resort to unscrupulous methods to color them, such as heating the vinegar in copper or brass kettles or adding poisonous substances.

Good Housekeeping, *20 July 1889*

Pickles

Do not keep pickles in common earthen ware, as the glazing contains lead, and combines with the vinegar.

Vinegar for pickling should be sharp, but not the sharpest kind, as it injures the pickles. If you use copper, bell metal, or brass vessels for pickling, never allow the vinegar to cool in them, as it then is poisonous. Add a tablespoonful of alum and a tea-cup of salt to each three gallons of vinegar, and tie up a bag with pepper, ginger-root, and spices of all sorts in it, and you have vinegar prepared for any kind of common pickling.

Keep pickles only in wood, or stone ware.

Catharine E. Beecher, *Mrs. Beecher's Domestic Receipt Book, 1858*

Green Tomato Pickles

I sliced onions & green tomatoes & put in a crock in alternate layers with salt sprinkled in—& put away, then tomorrow will put these into the culander [sic] & pour scalding water on until cooked, then scald vinegar & pour on—thus they will be pickled adding spices.

Almira Virginia MacDonald Diary, 1873

Pickled Walnuts

Take a hundred nuts, an ounce of cloves, an ounce of allspice, an ounce of nutmeg, an ounce of whole pepper, an ounce of race ginger, an ounce of horseradish, half pint of mustard seed, tied in a bag, and four cloves of garlic.

Wipe the nuts, prick with a pin, and put them in a pot, sprinkling the spice as you lay them in; then add two tablespoonfuls of salt; boil sufficient vinegar to fill the pot, and pour it over the nuts and spice.

Cover the jar close, and keep it for a year, when the pickles will be ready for use.

Butternuts may be made in the same manner, if they are taken when green, and soft enough to be stuck through with the head of a pin. Put them for a week or two in weak brine, changing it occasionally. Before putting in the brine, rub them about with a broom in brine to cleanse the skins. Then proceed as for the walnuts.

The vinegar makes an excellent catsup.

Pickled Peppers

Take green peppers, take the seeds out carefully, so as not to mangle them, soak them nine days in salt and water, changing it every day, and keep them in a warm place. Stuff them with chopped cabbage, seasoned with cloves, cinnamon, and mace; put them in cold spiced vinegar.

Ripe Pickels [sic]

peel and take out the core
lay them in salt and water overnight
drain them dry
cinnamon and cloves and a quarter of a pond [sic]
  of sugar to a quart of vinegar
boil till soft and cover them tight when they
  are cooking and when they are in the jar

Sarah Cooper Comfort, Geneva, New York, penciled inside the cover of her copy of *Miss Beecher's Domestic Receipt Book*, 1858

Piccalilli

One peck of green tomatoes, half a dozen green peppers, one solid head of cabbage; chop the tomatoes and squeeze them through a bag, chop the cabbage and mix all together, sprinkle over with half a pint of salt and let it stand all night; then drain through a colander and pack in a jar. Take two pounds of brown sugar, two tablespoonfuls of ground cinnamon, two of whole white mustard seed, half a pint of grated horse-radish and add enough cider vinegar to cover the pickle, heat boiling hot and pour on the pickle. After it is cold cover with horse-radish leaves which prevents pickles from moulding and put a small plate or saucer inside the jar, upside down over the pickle to keep all under vinegar.

Good Housekeeping, 20 July 1889

Horse-radish

Let the horse-radish lie one or two hours in cold water; then scrape off the skin, grate it, and moisten it with vinegar, serve it with roast meat.

Sarah Josepha Hale, *The New Household Receipt-Book*, 1853

Celery

Celery should be scraped and washed and then put in iced water, to be made crisp, at least an hour before it goes on the table. It is now served in long, flat glass dishes. It should be put on the table with the meat and other vegetables, and is to be removed before the dessert is served.

Maria Parloa, "Everything About the House," *Ladies' Home Journal*, November 1891

Nasturtiums Pickled
(A traditional accompaniment for roast mutton)

| Nasturtiums | Allspice and |
| Vinegar | Mustard Seed |

Select the seeds which are ripe as soon as the flowers have fallen off; gather them on a dry day; let them lie spread out in the sun for a few days, then put them in a jar and cover with the vinegar that has had the spices boiled in it and strained. Nasturtiums thus pickled are an excellent substitute for capers.

Godey's Lady's Book, September 1885

Tomato Catchup

Take a peck of large ripe tomatos. In the middle States they are in perfection the last of August. Late in the autumn they are comparatively insipid and watery. Cut a slit down the side of every tomato. Put them into a large preserving kettle without any water. Their own juice is sufficient. On no account boil tomatoes in brass or copper, their acid acting on those metals produces verdigris, and renders them poisonous. Boil them till they are quite soft, and easily mashed, stirring them up frequently from the bottom. Press and mash them through a hair sieve, till all the pulp has run out into the pan below, leaving in the sieve only the skins and seeds. Season the liquid with a little salt, some cayenne, and plenty of powdered nutmeg and mace. Mix it well, and when cold put up the catchup in small jars, the covers pasted all round with bands of white paper. This catchup, when done, should be very thick and smooth.

Eliza Leslie, *Miss Leslie's New Cookery Book*, 1857

Mushroom Catsup

Sprinkle with salt one bushel of mushrooms freshly picked, let them remain three days, stirring daily; then put them into a stone jar tightly covered to prevent evaporation; set them in not too warm an oven for five hours, then strain them through a hair sieve. To every gallon of juice add one quart of mixed wines, one part red cooking wine, one of port wine, and one of brown sherry all mixed, making in all the required quart; salt to the taste; one ounce of blades of mace, one ounce of cloves, half an ounce of black pepper corns, one pod of garden pepper, two table-spoonsful of dry American mustard, one root of green ginger cut up, and the juice of three fresh lemons; let these simmer until reduced to one-third, then strain and put into half pint bottles tightly corked and sealed. This improves with age, and is a very superior catsup.

English Oyster Catsup

Select fine fresh oysters; drain off the liquor; pound the oysters in a mortar; to a pint of these mashed or rubbed oysters, add a pint of white wine, one ounce of table-salt, one quarter of an ounce of mace, half an ounce of good cayenne pepper; mix these with the oysters and wine; let it simmer only for ten minutes, skim it well; then pour it into a sieve and rub through; when quite cold, bottle it and cork closely and seal; put it into small bottles; this is very fine for seasoning when oysters are not edible, and will keep for months.

Pepper Sauce

Take twenty-five peppers, without the seeds, cut them pretty fine, then take more than double the quantity of cabbage, cut like slaw, one root of horseradish grated, a handful of salt, rather more than a tablespoonful of mustard-seed, a tablespoonful of cloves, the same of allspice, ground; simmer a sufficient quantity of vinegar to cover it, and pour over it, mixing it well through.

A Practical Housekeeper, *Cookery As It Should Be*, 1856

Walnut Catsup

Take one hundred green walnuts that are young enough to be pierced through easily with a pin. Pierce each walnut in five or six places, then put them in an earthen vessel,* cover with a half-pound of salt and two quarts of vinegar. Cover and stand aside for six days, mashing with a potato masher and stirring every day. At the end of that time, strain off and squeeze every drop of liquor from the walnuts. Add a half-pint of vinegar to the remaining husks, beat them with a potato masher and squeeze again. Turn all this liquor into a porcelain-lined kettle, add to it one ounce of whole pepper-corns, forty whole cloves slightly bruised, a quarter-ounce of whole mace, a quarter-ounce of nutmeg cut in thin slices, a small root of horse-radish cut in slices, one blade of garlic chopped, one long red pepper, a half-pound of anchovies, and a quarter-ounce of green ginger-root cut in slices. Bring this mixture slowly to a boil, cover the kettle closely, and boil slowly a half-hour. Then strain through a cloth and stand aside to cool. When cold, add one pint of port wine; bottle, cork tightly, and seal. This should stand three or four months before using.

Sarah Tyson Rorer, *Mrs. Rorer's Philadelphia Cook Book*, 1886

* This probably means a stoneware crock with a salt glaze, which would contain no lead to combine with the vinegar.—Ed.

Fine French Mustard

Take a gill or two large wine-glasses of tarragon vinegar, (strained from the leaves,) and mix with it an equal quantity of salad oil, stirring them well together. Pound in a mortar, two ounces of mustard seed till it becomes a fine smooth powder, and mix it thoroughly. Add to it one clove of garlic (not more) peeled, minced and pounded. Make the mixture in a deep white-ware dish. If the mustard affects your eyes, put on glasses till you have finished the mixture. When done, put it up in white bottles, or gallipots. Cork them tightly, and seal the corks. Send it to table in those bottles.

This mustard is far superior to any other, the tarragon imparting a peculiar and pleasant flavor. It is excellent to eat with any sort of roast meat, particularly beef or mutton, and an improvement to almost all plain sauces, stews, soups, &c.

French mustard is to be purchased very good, at all the best grocery stores.

Eliza Leslie, *Miss Leslie's New Cookery Book*, 1857

Home-made Vinegar

Fourteen pounds of corse brown sugar, 10 gallons water, 1 cupful of brewers' or bakers' yeast. Boil the sugar with 3 parts of the water, and skim. Remove from the fire, and pour in the cold water. Strain into a ten gallon keg. Put in some small pieces of toast with the yeast. Stir every day for a week. Then tack gauze over the orifice. Set where the sun will shine on it, and let remain six months, by which time, if made in the spring, it will be vinegar.

Always save all the currants, skimmings, pieces, etc., left after making jelly, place in a stone jar, cover with soft water previously boiled to purify it, let stand several days; in the meantime, take your apple peelings, without the cores, and put on in porcelain kettle, cover with water, boil twenty minutes, drain into a large stone jar; drain currants also into this jar, add all the rinsings from your molasses jugs, all dribs of syrups, etc., and when jar is full, drain off all that is clear into vinegar keg (where, of course, you have some good cider vinegar to start with). If not sweet enough, add brown sugar or molasses, cover the bung hole with a piece of coarse netting, and set in the sun or by the kitchen stove. In making vinegar always remember to give it plenty of air, and it is better to have the cask or barrel (which should be of oak) only half full, so that the air may pass over as large a surface as possible. Vinegar must also have plenty of material, such as sugar, molasses, etc., to work upon. Never use alum or cream of tartar, as some advise, and never let your vinegar freeze. Paint your barrel or cask if you would have it durable.

Apple Vinegar (economical and good)

Have an earthen jar ready for use. Into this put your apple peelings and cores if good. Cover generously with water. Cover the jar tight, and let stand in cool place. Every day parings may be added, putting on more water each time. When cold tea is left, pour into this jar and also add molasses to the proportion of a cup to a gallon of water.

In the course of two or three weeks you will have an excellent vinegar made of nothing. When ready to use, strain through cheese cloth and stand away. This has been tried with good results, and with a little thought economical housekeepers can make enough in one summer to last all winter.

Beet Vinegar

The juice of 1 bushel of sugar beets, will make from five to six gallons of the best vinegar, equal to cider. Wash the beets, grate them, and express the juice. Put the liquid in an empty barrel, cover the orifice with gauze, and set in the sun. In twelve or fifteen days it will be fit for use.

Grace Townsend, *Dining Room and Kitchen*, 1891

Nugmeg, cinnamon, mace, cloves, mustard, allspice, ginger, curry powder, and pepper were usually stored in spice boxes, away from the deteriorating effects of light and air.

RECIPES

2 6 9

India Pickle

Put two hundred gherkins, three pints of small onions, one quart of nasturtiums, one quart of radish-pods, 1 quartern of string-beans, six cauliflowers, and two hard, white cabbages, sliced, into a pan, and sprinkle them with salt—the onions having been previously peeled, and laid in salt and water for a week, to take off their strength. Then, after a day or two, take them out of the pan, and dry them thoroughly in a warm place, in the shade: they must be spread out separately. To two gallons of vinegar, put one ounce and a half of allspice, the same of long pepper and of white, and two ounces of ginger, tied up in muslin bags. When cold, mix with the vinegar one pound and a half of flour of mustard, and two table-spoonfuls of Cayenne pepper. Boil it well together, and pour it on the pickle. The vegetables mentioned, not being all procurable at the same time, may be added separately, at different periods, but they must all undergo the salting and drying process.

In choosing those vegetables, some discrimination may also be used. When in season, few things add a higher flavor to the pickle than the buds and flowers of the elder.

Sarah Josepha Hale, *The New Household Receipt-Book,* 1853

Celery Vinegar

This is fine to keep in the castor stand. . . . Pound two gills of celery seed, and add sharp vinegar. Shake every day for a week or two. The flavor of sweet herbs and sage can be obtained by pouring vinegar onto them, and for three successive days taking them out, and putting in a fresh supply of herbs. It must be kept corked and sealed.

Catharine E. Beecher, *Miss Beecher's Domestic Receipt Book,* 1858

A Cheap and Good Vinegar

To a gallon of water, put two pounds of coarse sugar; boil and skim it for about half an hour. Put it into a tub, and when almost cold, add to it a slice of bread soaked in fresh yeast. In a week put it into stone bottles or a cask, and keep uncorked, either in the heat of the sun, or near the fire, for six months. To keep out insects, paste a piece of crape or gauze over the bunghole.

A Practical Housekeeper, *The American Practical Cookery-Book*, 1861

Epicurean Sauce

Pound in a mortar five or six anchovies; a heaped table-spoonful of minced tarragon leaves; a shalot, or very small onion, two or three pickled gherkins, finely minced; the yolks of four hard-boiled eggs, a quarter of a pound of fresh butter, and a large table-spoonful of French mustard. If you have no good butter, mix a sufficient portion of olive oil to moisten it well. Let the whole be thoroughly mixed. Put it into a bowl, and set it on ice till wanted. Then mould it into pats of equal size. Arrange them on small glass or china plates, and send them to table for dinner company, to eat with the cheese.

Eliza Leslie, *Miss Leslie's New Cookery Book*, 1857

Devilled Sardines

Try devilled sardines for breakfasts, teas, and "snacks." They are easily done. Broiled lightly, a dash of lemon-juice, a pinch of cayenne, and there you are, don't know!

Jessup Whitehead, *The Steward's Handbook*, 1899

Chow-Chow

A peck of tomatoes, two quarts of green peppers, half a peck of onions, two cabbages cut as for slaw, and two quarts of mustard seed. Have a large firkin, put in a layer of sliced tomatoes, then one of onions, next one of peppers, lastly cabbage; sprinkle over some of the mustard seed, repeat the layers again, and so on until you have used up the above quantity. Boil a gallon of vinegar, with a bit of alum, two ounces of cloves and two of allspice tied in a little bag, and boiled with the vinegar; skim it well and turn into the firkin. Let it stand twenty-four hours, then pour the whole into a large kettle, and let it boil five minutes; turn into the firkin, and stand away for future use.

Jane Warren, *The Economical Cook Book*, ca. 1882

FRUIT AND PRESERVES

It is fashionable, and therefore considered a wise sanitary measure, to eat oranges as a prelude to the regular business of the morning meal. Grapes are eaten so long as they can be conveniently obtained. It may be because my own taste and digestion revolt at the practice of forcing crude acids upon an empty, and often faint stomach, that I am disposed to doubt the healthfulness of the innovation upon the long-established rule that sets fruit always in the place of dessert. I have an actual antipathy to the pungent odor of raw orange-peel, and have been driven from the breakfast-table at a hotel more than once by the overpowering effect of the piles of yellow rind at my left, right, and opposite to me. A cluster of grapes taken before breakfast would put me, and others whom I know, *hors de combat* for the day with severe headache. In the consciousness of this, I can be courageous in declining the "first course" of an *à la mode* breakfast, and at my own table, withholding the fruit until the stomach has regained its normal tone under the judicious application of substantial viands.

Marion Harland, *Breakfast, Luncheon and Tea*, 1875

How They Eat Oranges in Havana

A fork is pierced partly through the centre of an orange, entering it from the stem side; the fork serves for a handle, which is held in the left hand, while with a sharp knife the peel and thin skin are cut off in strips from the top of the orange to the fork handle; now, holding it in the right hand, the orange can be eaten, leaving all the fibrous pulp on the fork.

Mary F. Henderson, *Practical Cooking, and Dinner Giving*, 1878

To Keep Oranges and Lemons

Take small sand and make it very dry; after it is cold, put a quantity of it into a clean vessel; then take your oranges, and set a laying of them in the same, the stalk-end downwards, so that they do not touch each other, and strew in some of the sand, as much as will cover them two inches deep; then set your vessel in a cold place, and you will find your fruit in high preservation at the end of several months.

Sarah Josepha Hale, *The New Household Receipt-Book*, 1853

Frosted Peaches

12 large rich peaches—freestones
Whites of three eggs, whisked to a standing froth

2 table-spoonfuls water
1 cup powdered sugar

Put water and beaten whites together; dip in each peach when you have rubbed off the fur with a clean cloth, and then roll in powdered sugar. Set up carefully, on the stem end, upon a sheet of white paper, laid on a waiter in a sunny window. When half dry, roll again in the sugar. Expose to the sun and breeze until perfectly dry, then, put in a cool, dry place until you are ready to arrange them in the glass dish for table.

Garnish with green leaves.

Marion Harland, *Breakfast, Luncheon and Tea*, 1875

Mixed Fruits

Always choose a raised dish for fruits. Arrange part of the clusters of grapes to fall gracefully over the edge of the dish. Mix any kind of pretty green leaves or vines, which may also fall, and wind around the stem of the dish. Although the colors of the fruits should blend harmoniously, and the general appearance should be fresh and *négligé*, arrange them firmly, so that when the dish is moved there will be no danger of an avalanche.

Water-Melon

A water-melon should be thoroughly chilled; it should be kept on the ice until about to be served. It may be simply cut in two, with a slice cut from the convex ends, to enable the halves to stand firmly on the platter. When thus cut, the pulp is scooped out in egg-shaped pieces with a table-spoon and served; or it may be cut [so that] slices with the rind attached may be served.

Mary F. Henderson, *Practical Cooking, and Dinner Giving,* 1878

Rich Sweet Apple Pudding

Half a pound of bread crumbs, half a pound of suet, half a pound of currants, half a pound of apples, half a pound of moist sugar, six eggs, twelve sweet almonds, half a salt-spoonful of grated nutmeg, one wineglassful of brandy. Chop the suet very fine; wash the currants, dry them, and pick away the stalks and pieces of grit; pare, core and chop the apple, and grate the bread into fine crumbs, and mince the almonds. Mix all these ingredients together, adding the sugar and nutmeg; beat up the eggs, omitting the whites of three; stir these to the pudding, and when all is well mixed add the brandy, and put the pudding into a buttered mould; tie down with a cloth, put it into boiling water, and let it boil for three hours.

S. Annie Frost, *The Godey's Lady's Book Receipts and Household Hints,* 1870

Iced Currants

One-quarter pint of water, the whites of 2 eggs, currants, pounded sugar. Select very fine bunches of red or white currants, and well beat the white of the eggs. Mix these with water; then take the currants, a bunch at a time, and dip them in; let them drain for a minute or two, and roll them in finely pounded sugar. Let them to dry on paper when the sugar will crystalize round each currant, and have a very pretty effect. All fresh fruit may be prepared in the same manner.

Grace Townsend, *Dining Room and Kitchen*, 1891

Apples and Rice Ornamented

First, turn or peel smoothly about two dozen golden pippins (after the cores have been removed); boil these very gently in some light syrup for about ten minutes, when they will be sufficiently done. Then prepare some rice in the same manner as for a cake, observing that for this purpose, it must be kept firmer. Prepare also a circular or oval raised pie-case . . . about three inches high, taking care that its diameter suits the dish it is meant for. When the case is baked, fill it with the prepared rice, and pile the apples up in a pyramidal form, . . . placing some of the rice in the centre of these. Mask the whole with some diluted apricot-jam, place a preserved cherry in the hole of each apple, and insert some pieces of angelica, cut in the form of pointed leaves, in between the apples. This dish should be served hot, and must, therefore, be dished up only a short time previously to its being served.

Charles Elmé Francatelli (late *mâitre d'hôtel*
and chief cook to Her Majesty the Queen), *The Modern Cook*, 1877

Directions for Making Sweetmeats

For preserving most kinds of fruit, a pound of sugar to a pound of fruit is sufficient. Some kinds of fruit require more, and some will do with less, than their weight of sugar. Good brown sugar, if clarified before putting in the fruit, does very well, for most kinds of fruit; and for family use, three-quarters of a pound of sugar to a pound of fruit does very well. The nicest white sugar needs not be clarified. All kinds of fire-proof ware, except iron ware, will do to preserve in. Enameled kettles of iron lined with china, called preserve kettles, are best. The fruit should be turned out of the preserving kettle as soon as done, and set away. It should be looked to often, to see that it does not ferment. Whenever it does, the sirup should be turned off and scalded, and turned back while hot.

Mrs. A. L. Webster, *The Improved Housewife*, 1853

RECIPES

2 7 5

Cement for Jars

One third of yellow bees-wax, and two-thirds of finely pounded rosin; put them together into a clean saucepan, and set it near the fire to melt slowly; when all is melted remove it from the fire, and stir in finely powdered red brick dust until it becomes the consistency of sealing wax; then dip the corked jars in twice.

Covering for Jars

For Jellies or preserves, a nice way is after laying on the brandied paper next to the jelly, to cut soft nice paper an inch and a half larger round than the jar, then coat the under side with the white of an egg and whilst moist put it on, pressing down the edges well, which will adhere tightly better than paste, and excludes insects as well as air.

A Practical Housekeeper, *Cookery As It Should Be,* 1856

Brandy Peaches

Take large juicy *freestone* peaches, not so ripe as to burst or mash on being handled. Rub off the down from every one with a clean thick flannel. Prick every peach down to the stone with a large silver fork, and score them all along the seam or cleft. To *each* pound of peaches allow a pound of double-refined loaf sugar, broken-up small, and a half pint of water mixed with half a white of egg, slightly beaten. Put the sugar into a porcelain kettle, and pour the water upon it. When it is quite melted give it a stirring, set it over the fire, and boil and skim it till no more scum rises. Next put in the peaches, and let them cook (uncovered) in the syrup till they look clear, or for about half an hour, or till a straw will penetrate them. Then take the kettle off the fire. Having allotted a pint of the very best white brandy to each pound of peaches, mix it with the syrup, after taking out the fruit with a wooden spoon, and draining it over the kettle. Put the peaches into a large tureen. Let the syrup remain in the kettle a little longer. Mix the brandy with it, and boil them together ten minutes, or more. Transfer the peaches to large glass jars, (two thirds full,) and pour the brandy and syrup over them, filling quite up to the top. When cool, cover them closely, and tie some bladder over the lids.

Eliza Leslie, *Miss Leslie's New Cookery Book,* 1857

Preserved Limes

Take green limes and put them into salt and water, strong enough to bear an egg, for six weeks; at the end of six weeks make an incision in each one of them the length of the lime, take out all the seeds, and put them into cold water twenty-four hours, changing the water several times; then boil them in soda water till tender enough to put a straw through; say one teaspoonful to six quarts of water. Put them again in cold water for twenty-four hours, changing the water several times. To each pound of limes, two pounds and a half of crushed sugar, and three pints of water. Boil syrup fifteen minutes, then put in limes; boil them slowly for fifteen minutes. They are then clear. Let the syrup boil fifteen minutes more, and they are all done. One hundred limes make about two pounds weight. These preserves are delicious.

A Practical Housekeeper, *Cookery As It Should Be*, 1856

Preserved Green Gages

Get the largest and ripest green gages, or egg plums. Scald them in boiling water to make them peel easily; the skins of all sorts of plums becoming very hard and tough when preserved. Remove the stems; they are no ornament, and render them troublesome to eat. Make a syrup in the usual way, allowing to each pound of plums a pound of the finest loaf sugar, half a pint of water, and half a white of egg. When well skimmed and boiled put in the plums, and boil them gently till quite clear and soft, but not till broken. All plums may be done in this manner. If not as ripe as possible, they will require to each pound of fruit a pound and a half of the best sugar.

Eliza Leslie, *Miss Leslie's New Cookery Book*, 1857

Preserved Pine-Apple

A pound of sugar to a pound of pine-apple; put the slices in water, and boil a quarter of an hour; then remove them, and add the sugar to the water; put in the apple and boil fifteen minutes. Boil the syrup till thick.

Jane Warren, *The Economical Cook Book*, ca. 1882

Cherries Preserved

Take fine large cherries, not very ripe; take off the stems, and take out the stones; same whatever juice runs from them; take an equal weight of white sugar; make the syrup of a teacup of water for each pound, set it over the fire until it is dissolved and boiling hot, then put in the juice and cherries, boil them gently until clear throughout; take them from the syrup, with a skimmer, and spread them on flat dishes to cool; let the syrup boil until it is rich and quite thick; set it to cool and settle: take the fruit into jars and pots, and pour the syrup carefully over; let them remain open till the next day; then cover as directed. Sweet cherries are improved by the addition of a pint of red currant-juice, and half a pound of sugar to it, for four or five pounds of cherries.

Godey's Lady's Book, June 1866

Orange Marmelade

Take equal weights of sour oranges and sugar. Grate the yellow rind from one-fourth of the oranges. Cut all the fruit in halves at what might be called the "equator." Pick out the pulp and free it of seeds. Drain off as much juice as you conveniently can, and put it on to boil with the sugar. Let it come to a boil; skim, and *simmer* for fifteen minutes; then put in the pulp and grated rind, and boil fifteen minutes longer. Put away in jelly tumblers.

Sarah Tyson Rorer, *Mrs. Rorer's Philadelphia Cook Book*, 1886

Crab Apple Jam

Pare the crab apples when quite ripe, put them into a stone jar, cover it well, and put it in a pan of boiling water for an hour and a half. Then prepare the syrup with two pounds of sugar in half a pint of water for every pound of the apples. Clarify the syrup. Then put the apples into it and boil the whole to a jam.

S. Annie Frost, *The Godey's Lady's Book Receipts and Household Hints*, 1870

They may be prepared if of a small size whole, or in quarters if large; pair and core them, and lay them as they are pared into cold water to prevent their becoming dark; when all are pared and cored, put the cores and parings into a preserving kettle and cover them with cold water; let them simmer four hours, keeping the quinces in the cold water during the time; then strain off the juice from the parings and cores, and into it put the quinces to cook; let the quinces simmer in it until they are perfectly tender, then remove them carefully and lay in a sieve to drain, and make the syrup as directed;' when the syrup boils lay in the quinces, and let them cook slowly fifteen minutes and no more, or they will become hard and dark; then take them out of the syrup and lay them on dishes to cool; return the syrup to the fire and evaporate all the watery particles by a smart boil for ten minutes; when the quinces are quite cool put them into small sized glass jars, as when large jars are used the frequent openings to take out preserves injure the fruit; when the syrup is quite cold pour it on the quinces and fill the jars well up; cover with a cloth and cork up tightly; keep them in a cool dry place; then take the juice in which the fruit was cooked and to every pint of juice add one pound of the best brown sugar; let it simmer slowly for thirty minutes and it will become a nice jelly, and is delightful with blanc-mange.

A Practical Housekeeper, *Cookery As It Should Be*, 1856

Preserved Watermelon Rinds

This is a fine article to keep well without trouble for a long time. Peel the melon, and boil it in just enough water to cover it till it is soft, trying with a fork. (If you wish it green, put green vine leaves above and below each layer, and scatter powdered alum, less than half a teaspoonful to each pound.)

Allow a pound and a half of sugar to each pound of rind, and clarify it.

Simmer the rinds two hours in this syrup, and flavor it with lemon peel grated and tied in a bag. Then put the melon in a tureen, and boil the syrup till it looks thick, and pour it over. Next day, give the syrup another boiling, and put the juice of one lemon to each quart of syrup. Take care not to make it bitter by too much of the peel.

Citrons are preserved in the same manner. Both these keep through hot weather with very little care in sealing and keeping.

Catharine E. Beecher, *Miss Beecher's Domestic Receipt Book*, 1858

DESSERTS

Dessert may consist of merely two dishes of fruit for the top and bottom [of the table]; dried fruits, biscuits, filberts, etc. for the sides and corners; and a cake for the center.

Elizabeth F. Ellet, *The New Cyclopaedia of Domestic Economy, and Practical Housekeeper*, 1873

Jelly Lemonade

Slice three fresh Seville oranges very thinly, and six fresh lemons; pour on them one quart of boiling water, cover tightly and let them steep; soak three ounces of good isinglass in a cup of cold water, when soft pour on it the lemon, orange and water; let the whole simmer for fifteen minutes; stir in one-fourth of a pound of crushed sugar, one pint of good wine, let it simmer three minutes, and strain through a bag or "jelly strainer," which is the best thing for jelly, and can be obtained at the tin furnishing stores; when it is clear pour into moulds.

A Practical Housekeeper, *Cooking As It Should Be*, 1856

Gelatine Blanc Mange

One quart of milk, one ounce gelatine, sugar to sweeten to taste; put it on the fire and keep stirring until it is all melted, then pour it into a bowl and stir it until it is cold; season with vanilla; pour into a mold, and put it into a cool place to stiffen. Soak the gelatine in the milk twenty minutes before you put it on to boil.

Jane Warren, *The Economical Cook Book*, ca. 1882

Plain Custard

Boil half a dozen peach leaves, or the rind of a lemon, or a vanilla bean in a quart of milk; when it is flavored, pour into it a paste made by a tablespoonful of rice flour, or common flour, wet up with two spoonfuls of cold milk, and stir it till it boils again. Then beat up four eggs and put in, and sweeten it to your taste, and pour it out for pies or pudding.

Rich Custards

One quart of cream
The yolks of six eggs
Six ounces of powdered white sugar
A small pinch of salt
Two tablespoonfuls of brandy

One spoonful of peach water
Half a tablespoonful of lemon brandy
An ounce of blanched almonds,
    pounded to a paste

•

Mix the cream with the sugar, and the yolks of the eggs well beaten, scald them together in a tin pail in boiling water, stirring all the time, until sufficiently thick. When cool, add the other ingredients, and pour into custard cups.

•

Catharine E. Beecher, *Miss Beecher's Domestic Receipt Book*, 1858

Lemon Custards

Beat the yolk of eight eggs until they are quite light; stir in one quart of boiling water; grate the rind of two lemons and their juice in a cup; pour it into the eggs and water; add a cup of sugar; mix these together well; then set the pan containing the mixture in a hot place; stir it until it thickens, then remove it, and add one wineglass of wine and one of good brandy; stir it well; when cool, put it into the jelly glasses for the table; whip the whites to a stiff froth with a knife, with three spoonfuls of fine white sugar; put a spoonful on each glass, and sprinkle small colored nonpareils on the top; this is a beautiful and nice dessert.

•

Sarah E. Scott, *Every-Day Cookery for Every Family*, 1868

Almond Custard

Take one pint of rich milk, one·of cream, half a pound of shelled sweet almonds, two ounces of shelled bitter almonds, four spoonfuls of rose-water, four ounces of white sugar, the yolks of eight eggs, and a little oil of lemon; blanch the almonds and pound them to a paste, mixing the rose-water gradually with them; powder the sugar, and beat the yolks till very light; mix the milk and cream together, and stir in gradually, the sugar, the pounded almonds, and the beaten yolks. Stir the whole very hard. Put the mixture into a skillet or sauce pan, and set it in a heated stove, or on a charcoal furnace. Stir it one way till it becomes thick, but take it off before it curdles. Set it away to get cold. Take half the whites of the eggs; beat them well, adding a little powdered sugar, and a few drops of oil of lemon. Put the custard into a glass bowl or dish, and heap the frothed white of an egg upon it. Ornament the top with nonpareils, or sugar sand. Or put the custard in small cups, piling some froth on each.

Mrs. A. L. Webster, *The Improved Housewife*, 1853

Directions for Freezing Ice Creams, Water Ices, Etc.

Break the ice in small pieces,—say about the size of an egg, or smaller,—and put some in the bottom of a tub; set the kettle in; then put in about a quart of coarse rock salt; then two quarts of ice; and so on until the tub is filled up to the top of the kettle. Sir it until the cream is frozen. In the old-fashioned freezer you must take off the cover frequently, and scrape off the cream from the sides until it freezes evenly.

If it is to be put into moulds, fill them quite full, shut them very tight, and put them in the ice and salt, covering them entirely; then throw over a piece of carpet to keep the air out. To take them out of the mould, have your dish ready, wipe the mould, and then turn over it some boiling water, wiping it again very quickly; then turn it on the dish. Remove the mould very slowly, for fear of breaking. When pure essences can be procured, they are quite equal to fresh fruits to flavor with.

Elizabeth H. Putnam, *Mrs. Putnam's Receipt Book, and Young Housekeeper's Assistant*, 1869

Philadelphia Ice Cream

Two quarts of milk (cream when you have it) | The whites of eight eggs well beaten
Three tablespoonfuls of arrowroot | One pound of powdered sugar

Boil the milk, thicken it with the arrowroot, add the sugar, and pour the whole upon the eggs. If you wish it flavored with va- | nilla, split half a bean, and boil it in the milk.

Catharine E. Beecher, *Miss Beecher's Domestic Receipt Book*, 1858

Raspberry Ices

Select fresh ripe berries; extract the juice by pressing them in a hair sieve with a wooden spoon; then squeeze gooseberries fully ripe also through a sieve; to one quart of the raspberry juice add one pint of gooseberry juice, and the juice of two lemons; put this on the fire to simmer slowly, and add two pounds of clarified sugar; let this | simmer for twenty minutes; then strain it through a hair sieve, and when quite cold freeze it in your freezer; other fruits may be prepared in the same way; currant juice is a good substitute for gooseberries, strawberries are even superior to raspberry with the addition of the currant.

A Practical Housekeeper, *Cookery As It Should Be*, 1856

Pine-apple Ice-cream Pudding

Add one pound of pine-apple grated fine to the yolks of eight eggs well beaten with one pound of sugar, one and a half pints of boiled cream, and a very little salt. Stir all together over the fire until it begins to thicken. When beginning to set in the freezer (having stirred it in the usual way), add a | pint of cream (whipped). This addition of the whipped cream is a great improvement, although it is generally omitted. Put it into a form. When ready to serve, press the tuft of leaves, cut from the pine-apple and trimmed, in the top of the cream. Surround it with whipped and sweetened cream.

Iced Rice-pudding (Francatelli)

Wash and parboil half a pound of rice; then put it into a stew-pan, with a quart of milk and a pint of cream, two sticks of vanilla, three-quarters of a pound of sugar, and a little salt. Allow the rice to simmer very gently over or by a slow fire, until the grains are almost dissolved, stirring it occasionally with a light hand. When the rice is done, and while it is yet hot, add the yolks of six eggs; then stir all well together for several minutes, in order to mix in the eggs, and also for the purpose of breaking up and smoothing the rice. Let this rice custard be frozen like an ordinary ice-cream, stirring it from the sides until it is set, when put it into a mold, and immerse it in the ice and salt.

While the above part of the process is going on, a *compôte* of twelve oranges should be prepared in the following manner: First,

separate them into sections, and remove every particle of the white pith with a small knife, laying the transparent pulp of the fruit quite bare. When all the oranges are ready, throw them into a stew-pan containing about a pint of sirup (made with one pound of sugar and nearly a pint of clear water); allow the pieces of oranges to boil up gently in this for two minutes, and then drain them in a sieve. Boil the sirup down to about one-half of its original quantity; then add two wine-glassfuls of curaçoa and three table-spoonfuls of peach marmalade or apricot jam; mix all together, and pour this preparation over the oranges in a basin. When about to send the pudding to table, turn it out of the mold on a platter, dress the *compôte* of oranges on the top and around the base, pour the sirup over it, and serve.

Mary F. Henderson, *Practical Cooking, and Dinner Giving*, 1878

Floating Island

Beat the whites of eight eggs to a stiff froth, then whip in four table-spoonsful of currant jelly, four spoonsful of fine pulverized white sugar, all this beaten to a firm consistency, then pour a small quantity of cream into a

glass dish, and drop with a spoon the mixture on the cream; on this sprinkle coloured nonpareils; in serving pour some cream into the saucer, and drop on the island.

A Practical Housekeeper, *Cookery As It Should Be*, 1856

To Make a Chantilly Cake

Cut a piece out of the top of a Savoy cake, and scoop out all the inside; put it on the dish or plate in which it is to be sent to table; pour Lisbon wine into the cake, and as the wine soaks out pour it over it again with a spoon: when it has absorbed as much wine as it can, pour the remainder off the dish, pour custard down the sides, and some in the middle; whip up some cream the same as for a trifle, and put it in the middle of the cake; blanch some almonds, cut them in quarters, and stick them round the edges and on the sides of the cake. It is a dish for a supper table.

Godey's Lady's Book, December 1850

A Charlotte Russe

Half a pint of milk, and half a vanilla bean boiled in it, and then cooled and strained.

Four beaten yolks of eggs, and a quarter of a pound of powdered loaf sugar stirred into the milk. Simmer five minutes, and cool it.

An ounce of Russia isinglas boiled in a pint of water till reduced one half, and strained into the above custard.

Whip a rich cream to a froth, and stir into the custard.

The preceding is for the custard that is to fill the form.

Prepare the form thus: Take a large round, or oval sponge cake, three or four inches thick, with perpendicular sides. Cut off the bottom about an inch thick, or a little less, and then turn it bottom upwards into a form of the same size and shape. Then dig out the cake till it is a shell, an inch thick, or less. Fill the opening with the custard, and cover it with the slice cut from the bottom. Then set it into a tub of pounded ice and salt, for forty minutes, being careful not to get any on to the cake. When ready to use it, turn it out of the form on to a flat oval dish, and ornament the top with frosting, or syringe on it candy sugar, in fanciful forms. This can be made by fitting slices of sponge cake nicely into a form, instead of using a whole cake.

Catharine E. Beecher, *Miss Beecher's Domestic Receipt Book*, 1858

Apple Snow

Put twelve good tart apples in cold water, and set them over a slow fire; when soft, drain off the water, strip the skins off the apples, core them, and lay them in a deep dish. Beat the whites of twelve eggs to a stiff froth; put half a pound of powdered white sugar to the apples, beat them to a stiff froth, and add the beaten eggs. Beat the whole to a stiff snow, then turn it into a dessert dish, and ornament it with myrtle or box.

Mrs. A. L. Webster, *The Improved Housewife*, 1853

Savoy Cakes

Four eggs, six ounces of pounded sugar, the rind of one lemon, six ounces of flour. Break the eggs into a basin, separating the whites from the yolks; beat the yolks well, mix with them the pounded sugar and grated lemon-rind, and beat these ingredients together for quarter of an hour. Then dredge in the flour gradually, and when the whites of the eggs have been whisked to a solid froth, stir them to the flour, etc.; beat the mixture well for another five minutes, then draw it along in strips upon thick cartridge paper to the proper size of the biscuit, and bake them in rather a hot oven; but let them be carefully watched, as they are soon done, and a few seconds over the proper time will scorch and spoil them. These biscuits, or ladies'-fingers, as they are called, are used for making Charlotte russes, and for a variety of fancy sweet dishes.

Godey's Lady's Book, May 1866

Trifle

Arrange macaroons and sponge cakes in a deep glass dish; place about them slices of currant jelly and little lumps of apricot jam, and pour as much white wine or brandy over them as they will drink. Take a quart of cream, flavor some sugar by rubbing it on a lemon until it takes the essence of the peel, and with it sweeten the cream to taste. Mill your cream to a strong froth; lay as much froth on a sieve as will fill the dish intended for the trifle. Put the remainder of the cream into a tossing-pan, with a stick of cinnamon, the yolks of four eggs, well beaten, and sugar to taste, and stir it over a slow fire until it is thick; pour it over the macaroons, and when it is cold put the frothed cream on the top, and decorate it with sweetmeats of various colors. Another good trifle is made by placing the cakes, and saturating them as above, and then pouring over them a *very thick* custard; this is left some hours to become firm, and is then covered with a layer of rich jam first and whipped cream all over.

Godey's Lady's Book, February 1866

Cranberry Tart

Take half a pint of cranberries, pick them from the stems and throw them into a saucepan with half a pound of white sugar and a spoonful of water; let them come to a boil; then retire them to stand on the hob while you peel and cut up four large apples; put a rim of light paste around your dish; strew in the apples; pour the cranberries over them; cover with a lid of crust, and bake for an hour. For a pudding, proceed in the same manner with the fruit, and boil it in a basin or cloth.

S. Annie Frost, *The Godey's Lady's Book Receipts and Household Hints*, 1870

Family Pie Paste

One coffee-cupful of flour will make the paste for a medium-sized pie. Use three-fourths of a cup of shortening to each cup of flour; you may use all butter or part lard if preferred. Take one-third of the shortening, a little salt, and rub well into the flour with the hand, then stir in as little water as possible and form with a spoon into a very stiff paste; put it on a pie board, roll lightly, and spread with one-third of the remaining shortening, sprinkle on a little flour, fold and roll out enough for the under crust. Take the rest of the paste, spread on half the remaining butter, fold and roll as before, repeat the process, roll thin and use it for the upper crusts. Always make a few slits in the centre of the upper crust, to allow the steam to escape. Never put in the filling until you are ready to bake them. A nice pie will be brown, tender and flaky.

Jane Warren, *The Economical Cook Book*, ca. 1882

Pumpkin Pie

Halve, seed, rinse, slice into small strips, and stew the pumpkin over a gentle fire, in just water enough to prevent burning to the bottom of the pot. After stewed soft, pour off the water, and steam the pumpkin about eighteen minutes, over a slow fire, seeing that it does not burn. Take it off, and strain it, when cool, through a sieve. Put to a quart of the pumpkin, twelve eggs and two quarts of milk, if you wish the pies very rich. Put to a quart of the pumpkin, three eggs and one quart of milk, if you wish them plain. If very plain, put to a quart, one egg, with a spoonful of flour, and very little milk. The more thinned the pumpkin, the greater the number of eggs required. Sweeten the pumpkin to the taste, with sugar beaten with the egg, and very little molasses. Lemon peel, nutmeg, and ginger, are good seasoning for the pies. As they require a hot oven, have the pumpkin scalding hot at the time of putting it into the plates, to prevent the rim of the pies getting burnt before the inside is sufficiently baked. Bake as soon as the plates are filled, to prevent the crust becoming clammy. The fewer the eggs in the pies, the longer the time required to bake them. Pumpkin may be kept several months in cold weather, by making it, after stewed, very sweet, and strong of ginger, and then scalding it well. Keep it in a cool place, in a stone jar. Take out what you want at any time, and put to it the milk and eggs.

Mrs. A. L. Webster, *The Improved Housewife*, 1853

Filling for Mince Pies

Take four pounds of beef, after it has been boiled and chopped, one of suet, two of sugar, two of raisins, and four of chopped apples; mix these together, with a pint of wine and cider, to make it thin enough; season to your taste with mace, nutmeg and orange peel; if it is not sweet enough, put in more sugar. Warm the pies before they are eaten. Where persons are not fond of suet, put butter instead, and stew the apples instead of so much cider.

Sarah E. Scott, *Every-Day Cookery for Every Family*, 1868

Rhubarb Pies

Peel with care the tender stalks of the pie plant; cut them about an inch in length; lay them in the baking dish, alternately a layer of the plant and thickly scattered good brown sugar and very thin slices of fresh lemon, until the dish is filled; but no water as the plant is very juicy; then cover with a nice paste; bake three-quarters of an hour; another nice way is to stew the plant to a rich jam, and fill puffs after it is cold, like cranberry tarts.

A Practical Housekeeper, *Cookery As It Should Be*, 1856

Washington Pie

One cup of sugar, one egg, one-third of a cup of butter, half a cup of sweet milk, half a teaspoonful of soda, one teaspoonful of cream of tartar, one and a third cups of flour; flavor with lemon. Bake on two round tins; when done spread one cake with nice apple sauce, then put the other cake on top, and sift powdered sugar over it.

Jane Warren, *The Economical Cook Book*, ca. 1882

Apple Pie

Fill a pudding dish with pared and cored apples—the tart baking apple; fill each hole of the apple with good brown sugar; cut very thinly the oily part of the rind of two lemons; then cut it into narrow strips, and lay on the top of the apples; squeeze the juice of the lemons into a cup and add a little cold water; pour this over the apples, and sprinkle over more sugar, quite thickly; then cover the whole with a nice puff paste, and bake it rather slowly one hour; serve hot. Peaches are very nice done in the same way, with the stones left in and only pared, but no lemon, and very little water as they make their own juice.

A Practical Housekeeper, *Cookery As It Should Be*, 1856

Golden Cake

Half a pound of flour, half a pound of sugar, one quarter pound of butter, yolk of seven eggs, yellow of one lemon, and the juice. Beat the butter and sugar together; add yolk, lemon, flour, half a teaspoonful of soda, with the same of cream of tartar. Bake in flat pans, and ice them. This and silver cake should be made together, to use all of the eggs.

Silver Cake

Half a pound of sugar, half a pound of flour, one quarter pound of butter, and the whites of seven eggs. Flavor with peach or almond water; bake as above. Ice this, placing alternately gold and silver cake in a silver cake basket, for the tea table.

Sarah E. Scott, *Every-Day Cookery for Every Family*, 1868

Iceing

This elegant finish to rich cake is made by beating the whites of two eggs to a very stiff froth, and adding, little by little, fine white pulverized sugar till quite thick. Lay it on immediately after the cake is baked, with a broad knife, returning it to the oven for a few minutes, leaving the oven door open.

A Practical Housekeeper, *Cookery As It Should Be*, 1856

Vermont Sugar Cake

Rub to a cream, one pound of butter with one and three-quarters of sugar; add seven well-beaten eggs, seven spoonfuls of milk, a little rose-water, and two and a half pounds of flour. Bake in an oven of but moderate heat, first grating over the cake a little loaf sugar. This cake will keep a long time good.

Jenny Lind Cake

Stir together 2 cups white sugar and 1 butter. Add 10 egg-whites, well beaten. Just before *setting in*, add half a teaspoonful soda dissolved in cup of cold milk, and 1 and half cream tartar mixed with 4 cups flour. Flavor with vanilla, or to taste. Line pans with buttered paper, and bake in moderate oven fifteen or twenty minutes. Frost it,— *Or:* the 10 yelks with the other ingredients as above, and the grated rind of 2 lemons for the flavoring, make a nice cake.

Mrs. A. L. Webster, *The Improved Housewife*, 1853

Thick Gingerbread

One quart of molasses, quarter of a pound of butter, quarter of a pound of coarse brown sugar, a pound and a half of flour, one ounce of ginger, half an ounce of ground allspice, a teaspoonful of carbonate of soda, quarter of a pint of warm milk, and three eggs. Put the flour into a bread-pan with the sugar, ginger and allspice; mix these together; warm the butter, and add it with the molasses, to the other ingredients. Stir well; warm the milk and dissolve the carbonate of soda in it; beat the eggs light, and mix the whole into a smooth dough. Pour the mixture into a buttered tin and bake about one hour in a moderate oven. Just before it is done, brush the top with the yelk of an egg beaten in a little milk, and replace it in the oven to glaze.

S. Annie Frost, *The Godey's Lady's Book Receipts and Household Hints*, 1870

Strawberry Shortcake

1 cup of powdered sugar	3 eggs
1 table-spoonful of butter,	1 cup prepared flour—a heaping cup
rubbed into the sugar	2 table-spoonfuls of cream
Bake in three jelly-cake tins	

When quite cold, lay between the cakes nearly a quart of fresh, ripe strawberries. Sprinkle each layer lightly with powdered sugar, and strew the same thickly over the uppermost cake. Eat while fresh.

Marion Harland, *Breakfast, Luncheon and Tea*, 1875

Lemon Cheese Cake

Grate with care the oily rind of three fresh lemons; rub this with one quarter of a pound of loaf sugar pounded, until perfectly incorporated with the sugar; then add by degrees half a pound of good fresh butter; beat very light the yolk of six eggs, and add; mix these well together; then line a dish with puff paste, and put in the above mixture. Bake three quarters of an hour. Serve hot.

Sarah E. Scott, *Every-Day Cookery for Every Family*, 1868

Apple Cheesecake

Half a pound of apple pulp | Four eggs
Quarter of pound of sugar | One Lemon
Quarter of a pound of butter | Puff paste

Pare, core, and boil sufficient apples to make half a pound of pulp when cooked; add to them the sugar and butter which must be melted, the eggs, leaving out the whites of two, and the grated rind and juice of the lemon. Stir the mixture well, line some patty pans with puff paste, put in the mixture and bake about twenty minutes.

Godey's Lady's Book, December 1885

Gingersnaps

One quarter of a pound of butter, and the same of lard, mixed in a quarter of a pound of brown sugar, a pint of West India molasses, ginger according to its strength, and cinnamon according to taste; add one quart of flour, two teaspoonfuls of soda, dissolved in a wineglass of milk and flour, to enable you to roll it thin. Bake in a moderate oven.

S. Annie Frost, *The Godey's Lady's Book Receipts and Household Hints*, 1870

Jumbles

Rub to a cream a pound of sugar and half a pound of butter; add eight well-beaten eggs, essence of lemon or rose-water to the taste, and flour to make the jumbles stiff enough for rolling out. Roll out, in powdered sugar, about half an inch wide and four inches long, and form them into rings, by joining the ends. Lay them on flat buttered tins, and bake in a quick oven.

Mrs. A. L. Webster, *The Improved Housewife*, 1853

Jumbles for Delicate Persons

Roll a heaped pint of light-brown sugar, and rub it in two pints of flour, half a pound of butter, and a dessert spoonful of cinnamon; beat an egg, and mix it with half a tea-cup of rich milk (in which a very small lump of salæratus has been dissolved;) stir all together with a wine glass of rose brandy; work it well, roll thin and cut them out— bake with moderate heat.

Elizabeth F. Lea, *Domestic Cookery, Useful Receipts, and Hints to Young Housekeepers*, 1865

Caraway Cookies

Two cups of sugar, one-half cup of butter, one cup of sweet milk, one teaspoonful of baking powder, caraway seeds, flour enough to roll. These are deliciously light and tender.

Jane Warren, *The Economical Cook Book*, ca. 1882

Directions About Puddings

A buttered earthen bowl, with a cloth tied up close over it, is a very good thing in which to boil a pudding or dumpling; but some persons think they are lighter boiled in a cloth. A large square of thick tow or hemp cloth does very well; but if a bag is preferred, it should be so cut that the bottom will be several inches narrower than the top, and the corners rounded. The seam should be stitched close with a coarse thread on one side, and then turned and stitched again on the other, in order to secure the pudding from the water. When used, let the seam be outside. A strong twine, a yard long, should be sewed at the middle to the seam, about three inches from the top of the bag. When the bag is to be used, wring it in cold water, and sprinkle the inside thick with flour,* and lay it in a dish; pour in the batter and tie up the bag quickly, drawing the string as tight as possible. Allow a little room for the pudding to swell. (An Indian pudding made with cold milk, swells more than any other.) Lay it immediately into the boiling pot, and after ten minutes, turn it over to prevent the flour from settling on one side. If there is fruit in the pudding, it should be turned three or four times during the first half hour. Keep it covered by adding water from the tea-kettle if necessary, and be careful that it boils steadily. If it does not, the pudding will be watery. When you take it up, plunge it for a moment in a pan of cold water; then pour off the water, untie the twine, and gently lay back the top of the bag. Have a dish ready, and turn the pudding out upon it. A batter pudding without berries cooks very nicely in a tin pudding pan, set upright in a kettle of boiling water.

Mary Hooker Cornelius, *The Young Housekeeper's Friend*, 1864

* Some persons prefer to spread the inside with butter and then flour it. Perhaps this method excludes the water most effectually. Either way does well. Always butter the dish in which a pudding is to be baked.

Rich Boiled Indian Pudding

Warm a pint of molasses and a pint of milk, and stir them well together; beat four eggs, and stir them gradually into the molasses and milk, in turn with a pound of beef suet chopped very fine, and Indian meal sufficient to make a thick batter; add a teaspoonful of pulverized cinnamon and nutmeg, and a little grated lemon peel, then stir all together very hard,—if you have *too much* Indian meal, the pudding will be heavy.

Dip your cloth into boiling water, shake it out, and flour it a little. Turn in the mixture, and tie up, leaving room for the pudding to swell. Boil it three hours; serve it up hot, and eat it with sauce made of drawn butter, wine and nutmeg. It is nice, cut in slices and fried, when cold.

Mrs. A. L. Webster, *The Improved Housewife*, 1853

Yankee Pumpkin Pudding

Take a pint of stewed pumpkin. Mix together a pint of *West India* molasses and a pint of milk, adding two large table-spoonfuls of brown sugar, and two table-spoonfuls of ground ginger. Beat three eggs very light, and stir them, gradually, into the milk and molasses. Then, by degrees, stir in the stewed pumpkin. Put it into a deep dish, and bake it without a crust. This is a good farm-house pudding, and *equally* good for any healthy children.

For a large family, double the quantities of ingredients—that is, take a quart of milk, a quart of molasses, four spoonfuls of brown sugar, four spoonfuls of ginger, six eggs, and a quart of stewed pumpkin.

You had best have at hand *more than a quart* of pumpkin, lest when mixed it should not hold out. This pudding is excellent made of winter squash.

Eliza Leslie, *Miss Leslie's New Cookery Book*, 1857

Mush, or Hasty Pudding

Wet up the Indian meal in cold water, till there are no lumps, stir it gradually into boiling water which has been salted, till so thick that the stick will stand in it. Boil slowly, and so as not to burn, stirring often. Two or three hours' boiling is needed. Pour it into a broad, deep dish, let it grow cold, cut it into slices half an inch thick, flour them, and fry them on a griddle with a little lard, or bake them in a stove oven.

Catharine E. Beecher, *Miss Beecher's Domestic Receipt Book*, 1858

After-Thought Pudding

One pint of nice apple sauce sweetened to taste. The yolks of two eggs beaten with it. Put into a buttered dish and bake ten or fifteen minutes. Beat the whites of the eggs stiff, and add half a cup of fine sugar. Spread this meringue on the top and return to the oven to brown.

Bird's-nest Pudding

Pare six apples and take out the cores without breaking them. Fill the holes where the cores came out, with sugar, after placing the apples in an earthen pudding dish. Make a batter of one pint of milk, two tablespoonfuls of flour, and three eggs. Pour this over the apples, and bake until the fruit is soft. Serve with "Cream Sauce."

Christmas Pudding

One pound of grated or chopped bread, one pound of stoned raisins, one pound of currants, half a pound of citron, cut in small bits, half a pound of suet, chopped fine, quarter of a pound of sugar, one teaspoonful of salt, one teaspoonful of clove, two teaspoonfuls of cinnamon, half a teaspoonful of mace, one nutmeg, the juice and grated peel of a lemon. Mix all these ingredients together and then add the yolks of six eggs, beaten, and mixed in a large cup of milk. Last of all, add the beaten whites of the eggs. Boil in a buttered mold six hours. Serve with "Foaming Sauce" or "Madeira Sauce."

Madeira Sauce

Whites of two eggs, one and a half cups of sugar, five tablespoonfuls of boiling milk, one wineglassful of Madeira wine, two tablespoonfuls of brandy. Beat the whites to a stiff froth, and beat in thoroughly the sugar. Pour over the boiling milk and stir rapidly, adding the wine and sugar.

Susan Anna Brown, *The Book of Forty Puddings*, 1882

A Rich Wine Sauce

Rub to a cream four large spoonfuls of sugar, and two large spoonfuls of butter; stir it into a teacup of hot water; pour this into a very clean saucepan, and set it on some coals; stir it steadily until it boils, then add either rosewater or lemon juice, to flavor it; then give it another quick boil, and add a wineglass of wine and brandy mixed; if stirred properly a rich foam will be on the top; before sending to table, grate on the sauce a little nutmeg, after it is in the tureen. The reason why the stirring is necessary while cooking, is to prevent the butter becoming oily.

Sarah E. Scott, *Every-Day Cookery for Every Family*, 1868

Raspberry Charlotte

Butter a pudding dish and cover the bottom with dry breadcrumbs. Put over this a layer of ripe raspberries, sprinkle with sugar, and then add another layer of crumbs; proceed in this way until the dish is full, having the last layer crumbs. Put bits of butter over the top and bake, with a plate over it, half an hour. Remove the plate and let it brown just before serving. Use only half the quantity of crumbs that you do of the fruit. Eat with cream.

Susan Anna Brown, *The Book of Forty Puddings*, 1882

Plum Pudding

Six ounces of finely chopped suet
Six ounces stoned raisins
Three ounces Sultanas
Six ounces of washed currants
Half a pound of peeled and chopped apples
Four ounces of sugar
Three ounces of bread crumbs
Three ounces of flour

Half-ounce of blanched almonds
Half a pint of brandy
Half-ounce of cloves, cinnamon and nutmeg
Three ounces of chopped citron
Half a pint of milk
Two wine-glasses of brandy
Six eggs.

Beat up the eggs and spices well together; mix the milk with them by degrees, then the other ingredients, working them to a smooth paste. Dip a cloth in boiling water, put it in a sieve, flour it, tie the pudding well up in it, and boil in plenty of water from ten to twelve hours. If made some time before, boil for ten hours. When wanted, plunge it into boiling water and boil for three hours more; pour half a pint of brandy in the dish, set fire to it as it is put on table; serve, also, brandy butter with it.

Brandy Butter

Three-quarters of a pound of butter | Quarter of a pound of sugar
One and a half wine-glasses of brandy

Beat the butter to a cream, add the sugar, and, very slowly, the brandy; continue beating until well mixed.

Godey's Lady's Book, December 1885

TREATS

White Candy

Libbie sent for us to come up & make candy this evening—we went & made *White candy* first. The rule I write down—to a pint of white sugar, granulated, ½ cup of water let boil *without stirring* at all—when nearly candy add 1 tablespoon vinegar, & butter large as hickory nut—when done which is in ½ an hour usually—add vanilla & then pull it & cut in flat sticks like cream candy.

Almira Virginia MacDonald Diary, 8 March 1871

Peppermint Drops

There are various ways of making them; a simple one is the following: take a quantity of sugar and put it in a dish, with water enough to hardly dissolve all the sugar; put on a quick fire and boil; then put in a few drops of peppermint (only a few drops), drop on a tin plate to suit yourself; stir the solution until ready to make the drops.

Jane Warren, *The Economical Cook Book*, ca. 1882

Molasses Candy

1 cup of New Orleans molasses
1 tablespoonful of vinegar

1 cup of brown sugar
1 ounce of melted butter

Mix all together, and boil without stirring until it hardens when dropped in cold water; then add a teaspoonful of baking soda, and pour into buttered tins.

Or, when cool, pull and cut into sticks. While pulling, brush the hands with butter or moisten them with ice-water.

How to Pull Candy

After boiling candy, turn it on a marble slab or a large meat-plate to cool. When cool, but not cold, grease your hands lightly with olive oil or butter, take the candy in your hands, throw it over a large hook and pull it towards you, and so continue until the candy is creamy. Make the candy move, and not your hands, or you will blister them quickly.

Taffy

½ pint of water
3 ounces of butter
1½ pounds of sugar (confectioners' A)

½ teaspoonful of lemon-juice
2 teaspoonfuls of vanilla

Stir the water and sugar over the fire until the sugar is dissolved, then boil until it arrives at the ball stage; that is, when small quantity is cooled in water and rolled between the thumb and finger, it forms a soft ball. Now add the butter and lemon juice and boil to the "crack," that is, it hardens quickly when dropped into cold water, and will not stick to the teeth. Add the vanilla, and turn out in greased shallow pans to cool.

Sarah Tyson Rorer, *Mrs. Rorer's Philadelphia Cook Book*, 1886

Lemon Taffy

Put into a porcelain-lined preserving kettle three pounds of the best loaf sugar, and pour on it a pint and a half of very clear water. When it has entirely dissolved, set it over the fire, and add a table spoonful of fine cider vinegar to assist in clearing it as it boils. Boil and skim it well, and when no more scum rises add the juice of four large lemons or oranges. Let it boil till it will boil no longer, stirring it well. When done transfer it to square tin pans, that have been made very clean and bright, and that are slightly greased with sweet oil. Set the taffy away to cool, first marking it with a knife, while soft. Mark it in straight lines the broad or crossway of the pans. If marked lengthways, the pieces will be too long. When the taffy is cold, cut it according to the lines, in regular slips. . . . It is for a handsome supper party. Serve it up in glass dishes.

Orange taffy is made in the same manner. These candies should be kept in tin boxes.

Eliza Leslie, *Miss Leslie's New Cookery Book*, 1857

Cream Candy

1 pound of granulated sugar | ½ teaspoon of cream of tartar
1 tablespoonful of gum-arabic water | 1 cup of water
1 teaspoonful of vanilla

Mix all the ingredients except the vanilla, and stir over the fire until the sugar is dissolved; then boil without stirring until it hardens when dropped in cold water. It must not be brittle. When done, turn out on a greased plate or marble slab; pour over it the vanilla; when nearly cold, begin to pull, and pull continuously until it is perfectly white. Cut it into sticks or pieces as soon as you are done pulling, or it may be braided; then put it in a tureen, cover and let stand two hours, and it is ready to use.

Chocolate Caramels

¼ pound of chocolate | 1 pound of brown sugar
2 tablespoonfuls of molasses | Butter the size of an egg
½ cup of milk | 1 teaspoonful of vanilla

Put the whole into a granite or copper saucepan; let it heat slowly, and stir until thoroughly dissolved. Then boil until it hardens. Try by dropping a few drops in a cup of cold water; if it hardens quickly, it is done. Turn into a greased square pan, and, when partly cool, mark into squares with a dull knife. Stand in a cool, dry place to harden.

Sarah Tyson Rorer, *Mrs. Rorer's Philadelphia Cook Book*, 1886

Pop Corn

Put some nice fresh lard into a pan; when boiling, drop in the corn and cover tightly, to prevent it popping out of the pan; when done popping, remove the corn from the pan and put them into a colander to drain; have ready some nice steam syrup, heat it and flavour with either seville orange juice or lemon juice; when simmering drop in the corn; let it simmer for ten minutes; take it out in large lumps and lay on buttered dishes to cool.

A Practical Housekeeper, *Cookery As It Should Be*, 1856

Pop Corn Balls

To six quarts of popped corn, boil one pint of molasses about fifteen minutes; then put the corn into a large pan, pour the boiled molasses over it, stirring briskly until thoroughly mixed. Then, with clean hands, make into balls of the desired size.

Jane Warren, *The Economical Cook Book*, ca. 1882

NOTES

BIBLIOGRAPHY

PICTURE CREDITS

&

INDEX

NOTES

1. PROPER AND PROSPEROUS: THE VICTORIAN MIDDLE CLASS

1. Clipping from unidentified newspaper, Rochester, New York, 2 March 1895, in "Scrapbook of Society Events" from 1 October 1887 to 19 October 1895, 149; Local History Division, Rochester Public Library.

2. William Dean Howells, *A Modern Instance* (1882), in *Novels: Eighteen Seventy-Five to Eighteen Eighty-Six*, ed. Edwin H. Cady (New York: Library of America, 1982), 270–71.

3. Norbert Elias, *The History of Manners*, vol. 1 of *The Civilizing Process* (1939; reprint, New York: Pantheon Books, 1982), 9–10.

4. "Scrapbook of Society Events," 149.

5. John A. Ruth, *Decorum: A Practical Treatise on Etiquette and Dress of the Best American Society* (New York: Union Publishing House, 1883), 231. For a comprehensive analysis of the importance of etiquette to Victorian Americans, see Karen Halttunen, *Confidence Men and Painted Women: A Study of Middle-Class Culture in America, 1830–1870* (New Haven, Conn.: Yale University Press, 1982).

6. Calvert A. Vaux, *Villas and Cottages: A Series of Designs Prepared for Execution in the United States* (New York: Harper & Brothers, 1857), 134–35, 277–78.

7. Mrs. Lydia Maria Child, "Our Treasury: Hints About Furniture," *Godey's Lady's Book* 47 (May 1853): 467–68.

8. Wedding list of Frances Munn Field, 1872, Munn-Pixley Family Papers, Box 9:12, Department of Rare Books and Special Collections, Rush Rhees Library, University of Rochester.

9. Wedding list of Lucy Rice Reynolds, 1853, Reynolds Family Papers, private collection.

10. Louise Bolard More, *Wage-Earners' Budgets* (1907; reprint, New York: Arno Press, 1971), 201.

11. Elias, 50, 92.

12. Susan Coolidge, "Angels Unaware," *Ladies' Home Journal* 8 (October 1891): 2.

13. Amelia Simmons, *American Cookery*, 3rd. ed. (Albany, N.Y.: Charles R. & George Webster, 1804), 47.

14. Ruth, 99.

15. Van Wyck Brooks, *Howells: His Life and World* (New York: E. P. Dutton & Co., 1959), 109, 135.

2. THE MANDATES OF MANNERS: ETIQUETTE OF THE TABLE

1. John A. Ruth, *Decorum: A Practical Treatise on Etiquette and Dress of the Best American Society*, rev. S. L. Louis (New York, Union Publishing House, 1883), 92–93.

2. William Dean Howells, *The Rise of Silas Lapham* (1885), in *Novels: Eighteen Seventy-Five to Eighteen Eighty-Six*, ed. Edwin H. Cady (New York: Library of America, 1982), 1037.

3. John H. Young, *Our Deportment* (Detroit: F. B. Dickerson & Co., 1883), 106; Eliza Leslie, *The Ladies' Guide to True Politeness and Perfect Manners; or, Miss Leslie's Behavior Book* (Philadelphia: T. B. Peterson & Brothers, 1864); Agnes H. Morton, *Etiquette: An Answer to the Riddle, When? Where? How?* (Philadelphia: Penn Publishing Co., 1894), 1.

4. Ruth, 2.

5. Norbert Elias, *The History of Manners*, vol. 1 of *The Civilizing Process* (1939; reprint, New York: Pantheon Books, 1982), 56.

6. Leslie, *The Ladies' Guide*, 131–32.

7. "Silver and Silver Plate," *Harper's New Monthly Magazine* 37 (September 1868), 434.

8. Morton, 11.

9. Howells, *Silas Lapham*, 988.

10. Sarah Josepha Hale, *The New Household Receipt-Book* (New York: H. Long & Brother, 1853), 210.

11. William Dean Howells, *A Modern Instance*, in *Novels*, 371.

12. Elias, 11, 15.

13. Brillat-Savarin, *The Handbook of Dining; or, Corpulency and Leanness Scientifically Considered* (New York: D. Appleton & Co., 1865), 34.

14. Elizabeth F. Ellet, *The New Cyclopaedia of Domestic Economy, and Practical Housekeeper* (Norwich, Conn.: Henry Bill Pub. Co., 1873), 126–29.

15. Mary F. Henderson, *Practical Cooking, and Dinner Giving* (New York: Harper & Brothers, 1878), 351–64.

16. Ruth, 105.

17. Leslie, *The Ladies' Guide*, 136.

18. Ruth, 16.

19. Morton, 14.

20. *Ibid.*, 8.

21. Leslie, *The Ladies' Guide*, 37.

22. *Godey's Lady's Book* 110 (March 1885): 349.

23. Morton, 58.

24. "The Third Bridesmaid," *Godey's Lady's Book* 23 (July–December 1841): 201–6.

25. Lyman Beecher, "Propriety and Importance," *American National Preacher* 3 (March 1829):154.

26. Robert Laird Collier, *English Home Life* (Boston: Ticknor & Co. 1886), 70–71.

27. Fannie Munn Field Diary, 17 September 1886, Box 9:18, Munn-Pixley Family Papers, Department of Rare Books and Special Collections, Rush Rhees Library, University of Rochester.

28. Margaret E. Sangster, *Good Manners for All Occasions* (New York: Christian Herald, 1904), 186. This Scottish grace would have been widely known in a culture that was still predominantly Anglo-Saxon in origin. Its popularity in 1904 may be explained by the ongoing revival of interest in the ethnic and historical roots of established Americans.

29. Elsie Smith to Mrs. A. Ericson Perkins, ca. 1879–1889. Papers of Mrs. A. Ericson Perkins, Strong Museum Library, Rochester, N.Y.

30. Ethel May Rafter to John Ralston Williams, 1897, collection of the author; Fannie Munn Field Diary, 15 September 1886.

31. *The Successful Housekeeper* (Detroit: M. W. Ellsworth & Co., 1883), 481; Ruth, 277–78, 3.

32. Howells, *Silas Lapham*, 1027–30, 1035.

33. *Ibid.*, 1037.

34. Ruth, 96.

35. Almira Virginia MacDonald Diary, 15 March 1892, Osborne Family Papers, Strong Museum Library, Rochester, N.Y.

36. Leslie, *The Ladies' Guide*, 50.

37. A Practical Housekeeper, *Cookery As It Should Be: A New Manual of the Dining Room and Kitchen, for Persons of Moderate Circumstances* (Philadelphia: Willis P. Hazard, 1856), 16.

38. Leslie, *The Ladies' Guide*, 127.

39. *Ibid.*, 50.

40. Helen Sprackling, *Customs on the Tabletop: How New England Housewives Set Out Their Tables* (Sturbridge, Mass.: Old Sturbridge Village, 1958), 15; Leslie, *The Ladies' Guide*, 49.

41. Leslie, *The Ladies' Guide*, 127.

42. Ruth, 214.

43. *Ibid.*, 99, 101.

44. Leslie, *The Ladies' Guide*, 135.

45. *Ibid.*, 128.

46. Howells, *A Modern Instance*, 188–89.

47. Morton, 81.

48. Ruth, 103.

49. *Ibid.*, 214.

50. *Ibid.*, 213.

51. *The Successful Housekeeper*, 470.

52. Ruth, 213.

53. Leslie, *The Ladies' Guide*, 130.

54. *Ibid.*

55. *Ibid.*

56. Norman H. Clark, quoted in Joseph F. Kett, "Review Essay: Temperance and Intemperance as Historical Problems," *Journal of American History* 67 (March 1981): 878–85.

57. W. J. Rorabaugh, *The Alcoholic Republic* (New York and Oxford: Oxford University Press, 1979), 101.

58. Leslie, *The Ladies' Guide*, 131–32.

59. Karin Calvert, "Cradle to Crib: The Revolution in Nineteenth Century Children's Furniture," in Mary Lynn Stevens Heininger, et al., *A Century of Childhood, 1820–1920* (Rochester, N.Y.: Strong Museum, 1984), 46.

60. Ruth, 97.

61. Leslie, *The Ladies' Guide*, 128.

3 . THE ALTAR OF GASTRONOMY:
DINING ROOMS AND THEIR FURNISHINGS

1. Maria Parloa, *Home Economics* (New York: Century Co., 1898), 37.

2. Louise Conway Belden, *The Festive Tradition: Table Decoration and Desserts in America, 1650–*

1900 (New York: W. W. Norton & Co., 1983), 6, 10. This study is particularly useful for its analysis of American eating and drinking customs of the seventeenth and eighteenth centuries.

3. Gwendolyn Wright, *Building the Dream: A Social History of Housing in America* (New York: Pantheon Books, 1981), 34–36.

4. Robert Laird Collier, *English Home Life* (Boston: Ticknor & Co. 1886), 71.

5. For a more complete discussion of the moral and ethical aspects of household aesthetics, see Clifford E. Clark, Jr., "Domestic Architecture as an Index to Social History: The Romantic Revival and the Cult of Domesticity in America, 1840–1870," *Journal of Interdisciplinary History* 7 (1976):42–47; and Harvey Green, *The Light of the Home: An Intimate View of the Lives of Women in Victorian America* (New York: Pantheon Books, 1983), 93–111.

6. *Catalogue of Genteel Household Furniture, for Sale at Auction by Henry H. Leeds & Co., on Friday, April 29, 1853,* (New York, 1853), Strong Museum Library, Rochester, N.Y.

7. Mrs. William Parkes, *Domestic Duties; or, Instructions to Young Married Ladies on the Management of Their Households, and the Regulation of Their Conduct in the Various Relations and Duties of Married Life*, 3rd ed. (New York: J. & J. Harper, 1829), 173.

8. Calvert A. Vaux, *Villas and Cottages: A Series of Designs Prepared for Execution in the United States* (New York: Harper & Brothers, 1857), 82.

9. George E. and F. W. Woodward, *Woodward's Country Homes*, 5th ed. (New York: George E. & F. W. Woodward, 1866), 38.

10. H. Hudson Holly, *Holly's Country Seats* (New York: D. Appleton & Co., 1863), Design 3, 41.

11. *Ibid.*, 52.

12. Wright, 64.

13. Vaux, 145, 146.

14. Margaret Byington, cited in Lizabeth Cohen, "Material Culture in Working Class Homes," in Thomas J. Schlereth, ed., *Material Culture Studies in America* (Nashville, Tenn.: American Association for State and Local History, 1982), 301.

15. Marion Harland, *Breakfast, Luncheon and Tea* (New York: Charles Scribner's Sons, 1875), 11.

16. Kate Taylor to Annjennet Huntington, 3 October 1880, Huntington-Hooker Papers, Department of Rare Books and Special Collections, Rush Rhees Library, University of Rochester.

17. Katherine E. Bragdon Diary, 21 March 1861, Bragdon Family Papers 1819–1980, Department of Rare Books and Special Collections, Rush Rhees Library, University of Rochester.

18. Parloa, *Home Economics*, 75.

19. Ella Rodman Church, *How to Furnish a Home* (New York: D. Appleton & Co., 1881), 20; Julia Holmes Cook Diary, 19 August 1880, vol. 1 1880–89, box 1, Cook Papers, Department of Rare Books and Special Collections, Rush Rhees Library, University of Rochester.

20. Sarah Josepha Hale, *The New Household Receipt-Book* (New York: H. Long & Brother, 1853), 211.

21. Parloa, *Home Economics*, 150.

22. Mary Jane Anderson Loftie, *The Dining-Room* (1878; reprint, New York: Garland Publishing, 1978), 60–61.

23. *Godey's Lady's Book* 40 (January–June 1850): 153.

24. Cook Diary, 23 May and 2 June 1881.

25. Loftie, 63.

26. Hale, 20.

27. Parloa, *Home Economics*, 149.

28. Loftie, 66–67.

29. A Practical Housekeeper, *Cookery As It Should Be: A New Manual of the Dining Room and Kitchen, for Persons of Moderate Circumstances* (Philadelphia: Willis P. Hazard, 1856), 336.

30. Alcesta Huntington to Annjennet Huntington, 1 February 1868, Huntington-Hooker Papers, Department of Rare Books and Special Collections, Rush Rhees Library, University of Rochester.

31. Maria Parloa, "Everything about the House," *Ladies' Home Journal* 9 (August 1892): 25.

32. For a historical and structural analysis of the nineteenth-century sideboard, see Kenneth Ames, "Murderous Propensities: Notes on the Dining Iconography of the Mid-Nineteenth Century," unpublished manuscript, Winterthur Museum, Winterthur, Del., 1975.

33. Belden, 24.

34. Parloa, *Home Economics*, 37.

35. Loftie, 63.

36. Parloa, *Home Economics*, 37.

37. Charles Wyllys Elliott, "Household Art. [Part] V.—The Dining Room," *Art Journal* [American ed.] 2 (1876): 120.

38. *Catalogue of the Publications of L. Prang & Co., Fine Art Publishers* (Boston, 1883), 9.

39. A Lady, *The Workwoman's Guide* (London: Simpkin, Marshall & Co., 1840), 179.

40. Elizabeth F. Ellet, *The New Cyclopaedia of Domestic Economy, and Practical Housekeeper* (Norwich, Conn.: Henry Bill Pub. Co., 1873), 25.

41. Belden, 17.

42. *The Workwoman's Guide*, 184.

43. Mrs. John A. Logan, *The Home Manual* (Chicago: H. J. Smith Co., 1889), 18.

44. Agnes H. Morton, *Etiquette: An Answer to the Riddle, When? Where? How?* (Philadelphia: Penn Publishing Co., 1894), 71.

45. Sarah Hadley, "Dainty Designs in Point Lace," *Ladies' Home Journal* 10 (June 1893): 13.

46. Martha Buell Munn Diary, 1886; Munn Ledger, vol. 1, 1886–1887; Munn-Pixley Family Papers, Department of Rare Books and Special Collections, Rush Rhees Library, University of Rochester.

47. Louise Bolard More, *Wage-Earners' Budgets* (1907; reprint, New York: Arno Press, 1971), 182–83, 193.

48. *The Successful Housekeeper* (Detroit: M. W. Ellsworth & Co., 1883), 467.

49. Ledger, vol. 1, 1886–1887, Munn-Pixley Family Papers; Elizabeth F. Lea, *Domestic Cookery, Useful Receipts, and Hints to Young Housekeepers* (Boston: Cushings & Bailey, 1865), 195; Green, 72–75.

50. Catharine E. Beecher, *Miss Beecher's Domestic Receipt Book: Designed as a Supplement to Her Treatise on Domestic Economy*, 3rd ed. (New York: Harper & Brothers, 1858), 236.

51. Foster Coates, "How Delmonico Sets a Table," *Ladies' Home Journal* 8 (November 1891): 10.

52. *Good Housekeeping* 8 (2 March 1889): 199; Morton, 70; Belden, 14–15; Beecher, 237.

53. Maria Parloa, "Everything About the House," *Ladies' Home Journal* 10 (October 1892): 25.

54. Morton, 78. The custom of folding bread into the napkin has descended from table settings of the sixteenth century, when the goblet and knife were placed on the right, and the bread on the left at each place. Bread was an integral part of the place setting, and remained so through the nineteenth century.

55. *The Workwoman's Guide*, 183.

56. Norbert Elias, *The History of Manners*, vol. 1 of *The Civilizing Process* (1939; reprint, New York: Pantheon Books, 1982), 104–5.

57. Historian Richard D. Brown has theorized that societies undergoing the process of modernization—as America was during the nineteenth century—are characterized by "social and political change in the direction of rational, complex, integrated structures"; cited in Clark, 47.

58. Montgomery Ward & Company, *Catalogue and Buyers' Guide No. 57, Spring and Summer, 1895*, 528–29.

59. Ellet, 25.

60. Todd S. Goodholme, ed., *A Domestic Cyclopedia of Practical Information* (New York: Henry Holt, 1877), 187.

61. T. A. Lockett, *Davenport Pottery and Porcelain, 1794–1887* (Rutland, Vt.: Charles E. Tuttle, 1972), 66; George L. Miller, "Classification and Economic Scaling of Nineteenth-Century Ceramics," *Historical Archeology* 14 (1980): 24–34.

62. Beecher, *Domestic Receipt Book*, 237.

63. Invoice, John Collamore, Jr., & Co. to Captain Richard H. Tucker, 20 November 1858, Tucker Family Papers, Castle Tucker, Wiscasset, Me.

64. Jean McClure Mudge, *Chinese Export Porcelain for the American Trade* (Newark: University of Delaware Press, 1962), 128.

65. Parloa, *Home Economics*, 152.

66. Invoice, A. E. & E. A. Potter, Bath, Me., to Captain Richard H. Tucker, 20 March 1869, Tucker Family Papers, Castle Tucker, Wiscasset, Me.

67. Morton, 72; Ellet, 102; Hale, 33.

68. Ellet, 24–25.

69. Morton, 73.

70. Munn household inventory, 1886–87.

71. Morton, 86.

72. Estate inventory, Jonathan C. Babcock, Henrietta, N.Y., 1858; Estate inventory, Henry T. Rogers, Rochester, N.Y., 1879.

4. THE BOUNTIFUL PANTRY:
FASHIONS IN FOOD AND DRINK

1. Mary Hooker Cornelius, *The Young Housekeeper's Friend* (Boston: Taggard & Thompson, 1864), 8.

2. Siegfried Giedion, *Mechanization Takes Command* (1948; reprint ed., New York: W. W. Norton & Co, 1969), 203–6.

3. Mrs. N. K. M. Lee, *The Cook's Own Book and Housekeeper's Register* (New York: C. S. Francis, 1842), iv.

4. Elizabeth F. Holt, *From Attic to Cellar* (Salem, Mass.: Salem Press, 1892, 1, 3–5, 6–7; cited in Harvey Green, *The Light of the Home: An Intimate View of the Lives of Women in Victorian America* (New York: Pantheon Books, 1983), 70.

5. Waverley Root and Richard De Rochemont, *Eating in America: A History* (New York: Ecco Press, 1976), 159.

6. Edmund Morris, *Ten Acres Enough*, 6th ed. (New York: J. Miller, 1864), 121.

7. Root and De Rochemont, 190.

8. *Philadelphia Cash Grocer* 9 (1882): 12.

9. Fabens & Graham advertisement, *The Boston Directory*, no. 70 (Boston: Sampson, Davenport & Co., 1882).

10. *Ibid.*, 1552.

11. Root and De Rochemont, 191; Green, 62–63.

12. Eliza Leslie, *Miss Leslie's New Cookery Book* (Philadelphia: T. B. Peterson & Brothers, 1857), 217.

13. Root and De Rochemont, 192.

14. "Washington Market at Christmas-Time," *Harper's Weekly* 9 (30 December 1865): 823.

15. Giedion, 220–22.

16. Sarah Granger Hollister Diary, 6 March 1884, Hollister Papers, Department of Rare Books and Special Collections, Rush Rhees Library, University of Rochester.

17. Fannie Merritt Farmer, *The Original Boston Cooking-School Cook Book*, (1896; facsimile ed., New York: Weathervane Books, n.d.), 10.

18. Root and De Rochemont, 160.

19. Louise Bolard More, *Wage-Earners' Budgets* (1907; reprint, New York: Arno Press, 1971), 173.

20. Elizabeth F. Ellet, *The New Cyclopaedia of Domestic Economy, and Practical Housekeeper* (Norwich, Conn.: Henry Bill Pub. Co., 1873), 126–29.

21. Mrs. William Parkes, *Domestic Duties; or, Instructions to Young Married Ladies on the Management of Their Households, and the Regulation of Their Conduct in the Various Relations and Duties of Married Life*, 3rd ed. (New York: J. & J. Harper, 1829), 62.

22. Leslie, *New Cookery Book*, 36.

23. Faye E. Dudden, *Serving Women: Household Services in Nineteenth Century America* (Middletown, Conn.: Wesleyan University Press, 1983), 136–37.

24. *The Boston Directory*, 1451; Leslie, *New Cookery Book*, 333–34.

25. Ellet, 41.

26. Dorothy T. and H. Ivan Rainwater, *American Silverplate* (Nashville, Tenn.: Thomas Nelson, 1968), 323.

27. Eliza Leslie, *The Ladies' Guide to True Politeness and Perfect Manners; or, Miss Leslie's Behavior Book* (Philadelphia: T. B. Peterson & Brothers, 1864), 128.

28. Wiltsea Papers, Department of Rare Books and Special Collections, Rush Rhees Library, University of Rochester; Almira Virginia MacDonald Diary, 1897, Osborne Family Papers, Strong Museum Library, Rochester, N.Y.

29. Rainwater, 325.

30. Rainwater, 320; W. Atlee Burpee Co. claimed the honor of introducing the "Gold Self-

Blanching" celery to the United States in 1884, according to Ken Kraft, *Garden to Order* (Garden City, N.Y.: Doubleday & Co., 1962).

31. Rainwater, 348–50.

32. Ellen Conway, "Twelve Lenten Lunches," *Ladies' Home Journal* 7 (March 1891): 25.

33. Caroline Talcott Lyon wedding list, Edmund Lyon Papers, Department of Rare Books and Special Collections, Rush Rhees Library, University of Rochester.

34. Marion Harland, *Breakfast, Luncheon and Tea* (New York: Charles Scribner's Sons, 1875), 12.

35. Ellet, 386.

36. Jessup Whitehead, *The Steward's Handbook and Guide to Party Catering*, 4th ed. (Chicago: J. Whitehead & Co., 1899), 326–28, 386–88, 353–54, 279–80, 348–50, 422, 436–39.

37. Sarah Granger Hollister Diary, 1 February 1884; A Practical Housekeeper, *The American Practical Cookery-Book; or, Housekeeping Made Easy* (Philadelphia: J. W. Bradley, 1861) 218; Leslie, *The Ladies' Guide*, 129.

38. Farmer, 287; Robert F. Becker, "Vegetable Gardening in the United States: A History, 1565–1900," *HortScience* 19 (October 1984): 626.

39. Robert Buist, *The Family Kitchen Gardener* (New York: C. M. Saxton & Co., 1855), 50.

40. Almira Virginia MacDonald Diary, 6 March 1879, Osborne Family Papers, Strong Museum Library, Rochester, N.Y.

41. Catharine E. Beecher, *Miss Beecher's Domestic Receipt Book: Designed as a Supplement to Her Treatise on Domestic Economy*, 3rd ed. (New York: Harper & Brothers, 1858), 170.

42. Leslie, *The Ladies' Guide*, 325.

43. Ellet, 139.

44. Mary F. Henderson, *Practical Cooking, and Dinner Giving* (New York: Harper & Brothers, 1878), 42.

45. Harland, *Breakfast, Luncheon and Tea*, 12; "My Wife's 'First Family Party,'" *Peterson's Magazine* 74 (July 1878): 62.

46. Beecher, *Domestic Receipt Book*, 107, 168.

47. *The Encyclopaedia Britannica*, 11th ed., vol. 7 (New York: Encyclopaedia Britannica Co., 1910), s.v. "Dairy," 738–54.

48. Ellet, 472.

49. This would still have been considered a bargain when contrasted with the prevailing 30.5 cents/pound wholesale price for butter in New York City the previous year. *Historical Statistics of the United States, Colonial Times to 1870* (Bicentennial ed., 1970; Washington: U.S. Department of Commerce, Bureau of the Census, 1975), 523–54; Julia Holmes Cook Diary, 6 May 1880, 24 May 1880, 6 September 1880, Cook Papers, Department of Rare Books and Special Collections, Rush Rhees Library, University of Rochester.

50. Leslie, *The Ladies' Guide*, 36.

51. Rainwater, 241–48.

52. Catharine E. Beecher, *Miss Beecher's Housekeeper and Healthkeeper* (New York: Harper & Brothers, 1874), 109.

53. Beecher, *Domestic Receipt Book*, 59.

54. Isabella Beeton, *Mrs. Beeton's Book of Household Management* (1859–1861; facsimile ed., London: Chancellor Press, 1982), 759, 760.

55. Fannie Munn Field Diary, 1885–1886, Munn-Pixley Family Papers, Department of Rare Books and Special Collections, Rush Rhees Library, University of Rochester.

56. Ellet, 533.

57. Alice Morse Earle, *Home Life in Colonial Days* (1898; reprint ed., Stockbridge, Mass.: Berkshire Traveller Press, 1974), 155–56.

58. Maria Parloa, *Home Economics* (New York: Century Co., 1898), 201; Root and De Rochemont, 232.

59. William Dean Howells, *A Modern Instance*, in *Novels*, 269.

60. W. J. Rorabaugh, *The Alcoholic Republic* (New York and Oxford: Oxford University Press, 1979), 99.

61. Sarah Josepha Hale, *The New Household Receipt-Book* (New York: H. Long & Brother, 1853), 33.

62. Leslie, *The Ladies' Guide*, 35, 42.

63. Farmer, 37.

64. Leslie, *The Ladies' Guide*, 41–42.

65. The net import of coffee was 5.6 pounds per capita, as contrasted with only about one pound of tea; Rorabaugh, 99.

66. Joseph B. and Laura E. Lyman, *The Philosophy of House-keeping* (Hartford, Conn.: Goodwin & Betts, 1867), 322.

67. Farmer, 40.

68. Lyon wedding list.

69. Howells, *A Modern Instance*, 407.

70. Rorabaugh, 7–10.

71. Hale, 258.

72. Martha Buell Munn Journal of European trip, May 1877–July 1878, 29 November 1877, box 9:11, Munn-Pixley Family Papers, Department of Rare Books and Special Collections, Rush Rhees Library, University of Rochester.

73. Leslie, *The Ladies' Guide*, 129–30.

74. Hale, 30–31.

75. Nancy Harris Brose et al., *Emily Dickinson: Profile of the Poet as Cook* (Amherst, Mass.: Hamilton I. Newall, 1976, 1981), 9.

76. Trade card, Danville Bottling Co., Danville, Pa., Strong Museum Library, Rochester, N.Y.; Richard J. Hooker, *Food and Drink in America: A History* (Indianapolis and New York: Bobbs-Merrill Co., 1981), 276; MacDonald Diary, 13 July 1870.

77. Hooker, 274.

78. "Hire's Improved Root Beer" trade card, Strong Museum Library, Rochester, N.Y.

79. Rainwater, 248–69; Maria Parloa, "Everything About the House," *Ladies' Home Journal* 8 (November 1891): 29.

80. Agnes H. Morton, *Etiquette: An Answer to the Riddle, When? Where? How?* (Philadelphia: Penn Publishing Co., 1894), 84.

81. Parloa, "Everything about the House," 29.

82. Alice C. Steele, *Aunt Teeks in Memory Land*, vol. 2 (Windsor, Mass.: Progressive Club, November 1960), 38.

1. William Dean Howells, *A Modern Instance*, in *Novels*, 376, 379, 381–82.

2. Patricia Easterbrook Roberts, *Table Settings, Entertaining, and Etiquette: A History and Guide* (New York: Bonanza Books, n.d.), 201–3; Joyce W. Carlo, *Trammels, Trenchers, & Tartlets: A Definitive Tour of the Colonial Kitchen* (Old Saybrook, Conn.: Peregrine Press, 1982), 39.

3. Almira Virginia MacDonald Diary, 5 July 1884, Osborne Family Papers, Strong Museum Library, Rochester, N.Y.; Michael Slater, *Dickens on America and Americans* (Austin: University of Texas Press, 1978), 154–55; Fannie Munn Field Diary, 1886, Munn-Pixley Family Papers, Department of Rare Books and Special Collections, Rush Rhees Library, University of Rochester; Eliza Leslie, *The Ladies' Guide to True Politeness and Perfect Manners; or, Miss Leslie's Behavior Book* (Philadelphia: T. B. Peterson & Brothers, 1864), 103.

4. John A. Ruth, *Decorum, A Practical Treatise on Etiquette and Dress of the Best American Society*, rev. S. L. Louis (New York: Union Publishing House, 1882), 212.

5. Noah Webster, *An American Dictionary of the English Language* (Springfield, Mass.: G & C. Merriam, 1860), 681, 335.

6. Roberts, 202–3.

7. Howells, *A Modern Instance*, 370.

8. MacDonald Diary, 21 August 1879, 3 September 1883, 25 November 1884, 4 November 1884.

9. Ruth, 215.

10. *The Oxford English Dictionary*, vol. 6 (Oxford: Clarendon Press, 1970), 502.

11. Joseph Job, *Extended Travels in Romantic America* (Lausanne: Edita, 1966), 193–94.

12. Agnes H. Morton, *Etiquette: An Answer to the Riddle, When? Where? How?* (Philadelphia: Penn Publishing Co., 1894), 93.

13. MacDonald Diary, 10 March 1885.

14. In 1853, high-society Philadelphians, according to the English traveler and historian William Thackeray, dined at four and supped at ten. Christopher Mulvey, *Anglo-American Landscapes: A Study of Nineteenth Century Anglo-American Travel Literature* (Cambridge and New York: Cambridge University Press, 1983), 172.

15. Webster, 1110.

16. "The Dining Room," *Godey's Lady's Book* 111 (September 1885), 293.

17. A Practical Housekeeper, *The American Practical Cookery-Book; or, Housekeeping Made Easy* (Philadelphia: J. W. Bradley, 1861), 215–19.

18. Sarah Josepha Hale, *The New Household Receipt-Book* (New York: H. Long & Brother, 1853), 211.

19. Louise Conway Belden, *The Festive Tradition: Table Decoration and Desserts in America, 1650–1900* (New York: W. W. Norton & Co., 1983), 33.

20. John H. Young, *Our Deportment* (Detroit: F. B. Dickerson & Co., 1883), 113.

21. *The American Practical Cookery-Book*, 217.

22. Gwendolyn Wright, *Building the Dream: A Social History of Housing in America* (New York: Pantheon Books, 1981), 111.

NOTES

· —— ·

23. Catharine E. Beecher, *Domestic Receipt Book: Designed as a Supplement to Her Treatise on Domestic Economy*, 3rd ed. (New York: Harper & Brothers, 1858), 240.

24. *The American Practical Cookery-Book*, 219.

25. Julia Holmes Cook Diary, 3 February 1881, Cook Papers, Department of Rare Books and Special Collections, Rush Rhees Library, University of Rochester.

26. Faye E. Dudden, *Serving Women: Household Services in Nineteenth-Century America* (Middletown, Conn.: Wesleyan University Press, 1983), 123.

27. Mrs. V. Shelley Haller, "Dining-Room," *Godey's Lady's Book* 110 (February 1885), 214.

28. Elizabeth F. Ellet, *The New Cyclopaedia of Domestic Economy, and Practical Housekeeper* (Norwich, Conn.: Henry Bill Pub. Co., 1873), 26.

29. *Ibid.*

30. Wright, 172.

31. Maria Parloa, *Home Economics* (New York: Century Co., 1898), 156–57; Ruth, 101; Morton, 90–91.

31. Between 1880 and 1924, immigrants from southern and eastern Europe arrived in America in greater numbers than ever before. The fear that the assimilation of these newly arrived immigrant groups threatened the positions of Anglo-Saxons in society coincided with reports of declining birth rates among the families of established Americans. Harvey Green, "Popular Science and Political Thought Converge: Colonial Survival Becomes Colonial Revival, 1830–1900," *Journal of American Culture* 6 (Winter 1983): 3–24.

32. Marion Harland, *Breakfast, Luncheon and Tea* (New York: Charles Scribner's Sons, 1875), 66.

33. Ruth, 212.

34. *Ibid.*, 212; Harland, *Breakfast, Luncheon and Tea*, 66.

35. Hale, 253.

36. Montgomery Ward & Company, *Catalogue and Buyers' Guide No. 57, Spring and Summer, 1895*, 534.

37. Harland, *Breakfast, Luncheon and Tea*, 18; Hale, 253.

38. Grace Townsend, *Dining Room and Kitchen* (Chicago: L. P. Miller, 1891), 23.

39. Mary F. Henderson, *Practical Cooking, and Dinner Giving* (New York: Harper & Brothers, 1878), 35.

40. *Ibid.*, 36–37.

41. Sarah Granger Hollister Diary, 1 February 1883, 23 February 1884, Hollister Papers, Department of Rare Books and Special Collections, Rush Rhees Library, University of Rochester.

42. MacDonald Diary, 7 February 1889, 27 August 1895.

43. "In Society Here and There," Saturday, 8 October 1890, in "Scrapbook of Society Events" from 1 October 1887 to 19 October 1895, 40; Local History Division, Rochester Public Library.

44. *The Successful Housekeeper* (Detroit: M. W. Ellsworth & Co., 1883), 487; Louise Bolard More, *Wage-Earners' Budgets* (1907; reprint, New York: Arno Press, 1971), 187–88, 201.

45. Ruth, 91.

46. Constance B. Hiett and Sharon Butler, *Pleyn Delit: Medieval Cookery for Modern Cooks* (Toronto: University of Toronto Press, 1976), xi.

47. Fannie Munn Field Diary, 15 September 1886.

48. Frank Hanford to Ella Hanford, 13 January 1884; Hanford Papers, Department of Rare Books and Special Collections, Rush Rhees Library, University of Rochester.

49. Jessup Whitehead, *The Steward's Handbook and Guide to Party Catering*, 4th ed. (Chicago: J. Whitehead & Co., 1899), 411.

50. Isabella Beeton, *Mrs. Beeton's Book of Household Management* (1859–1861; facsimile ed., London: Chancellor Press, 1982), 605–6.

51. MacDonald Diary.

52. Howells, *A Modern Instance*, 267–68.

53. C. W. Gesner, "Concerning Restaurants," *Harper's New Monthly Magazine* 32 (April 1866), 591–92.

54. MacDonald Diary, 7 March 1879.

55. *The American Practical Cookery-Book*, 219.

56. *Ibid.*, 220.

57. Beeton, 760.

58. *The Boston Directory*, no. 78 (Boston: Sampson, Davenport & Co., 1882), 1466.

59. Ethel M. Rafter letter to John R. Williams, 1 October 1898, collection of the author.

60. Invoice, A. M. & E. A. Potter, Bath, Me., to Captain Richard H. Tucker, 20 March 1869, Tucker Family Papers, Castle Tucker, Wiscasset, Me.

61. Lyman Beecher, D.D., *Autobiography, Correspondence, Etc.*, vol. 1, ed. Charles Beecher (New York: Harper & Brothers, 1865), 27.

62. Harvey Green, *The Light of the Home: An Intimate View of the Lives of Women in Victorian America* (New York: Pantheon Books, 1983), 7, 93, 59.

63. Harland, *Breakfast, Luncheon and Tea*, 357–58.

64. Parloa, *Home Economics*, 153.

65. MacDonald Diary, 13 August 1880; *1095 Menus: Breakfast, Dinner, and Tea* (Philadelphia: E. Bradford Clarke Co., 1891).

66. Eliza Leslie, *The Ladies' Guide to True Politeness and Perfect Manners; or, Miss Leslie's Behavior Book* (Philadelphia: T. B. Peterson & Brothers, 1864), 45–46.

67. Catharine E. Beecher, *Miss Beecher's Housekeeper and Healthkeeper* (New York: Harper & Brothers, 1874), 111.

68. Mrs. Burton Kingsland, "A Talk about Teas," *Ladies' Home Journal* 9 (October 1892): 4.

69. MacDonald Diary, 23 November 1876.

70. Kingsland, 4.

71. Timothy Dwight, *Travels in New England and New York*, The John Harvard Library, vol. 4 (Cambridge, Mass.: Belknap Press of Harvard University Press, 1969), 249; cited in Carlo, 41.

72. MacDonald Diary, 4 March 1887, 12 March 1887, 26 March 1887.

73. Kenneth Ward Hooker, *Susan Huntingdon Hooker: A Memoir* (New York: privately published, 1952), 52.

74. Henderson, 39.

75. Menu, complimentary supper, 9 June 1881, Strong Museum Library, Rochester, N.Y.

76. "The Napier Ball," *Harper's Weekly* 3 (26 February 1859): 134.

77. Cook Diary, Thanksgiving 1881.

78. "Washington Market at Christmas-Time," *Harper's Weekly* 9 (30 December 1865): 823.

79. MacDonald Diary, 22–24 November 1870.

80. Maria Parloa, "Everything About the House," *Ladies' Home Journal* 8 (November 1891): 29.

81. MacDonald Diary, 30 November 1882.

82. Fannie Merritt Farmer, *The Original Boston Cooking-School Cook Book* (1896; facsimile ed., New York: Weathervane Books, n.d.), 520.

83. *Godey's Lady's Book* 61 (December 1885): 620.

84. Sarah Tyson Rorer, "The Table on Christmas Day," *Ladies' Home Journal* 15 (December 1897): 34.

85. Robert F. Becker, "Vegetable Gardening in the United States," *HortScience* 19 (October 1984): 626.

86. May Bragdon Diary, 25 December 1893, Bragdon Family Papers, Department of Rare Books and Special Collections, Rush Rhees Library, University of Rochester.

87. Rorer, "The Table on Christmas Day," 34.

88. May Bragdon Diary, 1 January 1896.

89. Katherine Bragdon Diary, 4 July 1861, Bragdon Family Papers.

90. MacDonald Diary; Grace Townsend, *Dining Room and Kitchen* (Chicago: L. P. Miller, 1891), 382–83.

91. Hollister Diary, 25 January 1885.

92. MacDonald Diary, 12 December 1873.

93. MacDonald Diary, 22 February 1894.

BIBLIOGRAPHY

An American Lady [pseud.]. *The American Home Cook Book*. New York: Dick & Fitzgerald, 1854.

———. *True Politeness: A Handbook of Etiquette for Ladies*. New York: Leavitt, 1853 (?).

Ames, Kenneth. "Murderous Propensities: Notes on the Dining Iconography of the Mid-Nineteenth Century." Unpublished manuscript. Winterthur Museum, Winterthur, Del., 1975.

Becker, Robert F. "Vegetable Gardening in the United States: A History, 1565–1900." *HortScience* 19 (October 1984): 626.

Beecher, Catherine E. *Miss Beecher's Domestic Receipt Book: Designed As a Supplement to Her Treatise on Domestic Economy*. 3rd ed. New York: Harper & Brothers, 1858.

———. *Miss Beecher's Housekeeper and Healthkeeper*. New York: Harper & Bros., 1874.

Beecher, Lyman. "Propriety and Importance." *American National Preacher* 3 (March 1829): 154.

Beeton, Isabella. *Mrs. Beeton's Book of Household Management*. 1859–1861. Facsimile ed. London: Chancellor Press, 1982.

Belden, Louise Conway. *The Festive Tradition: Table Decoration and Desserts in America, 1650–1900*. New York: W. W. Norton & Co., 1983.

Bon Ton, Mlle. [pseud.]. "Hints for the Hostess." *Godey's Lady's Book* 110 (March 1885): 349.

Bordin, Ruth. *Women and Temperance: The Quest for Power and Liberty, 1873–1900*. Philadelphia: Temple University Press, 1981.

The Boston Directory. Boston: Sampson, Davenport & Co., 1882.

Bragdon Family Papers. Department of Rare Books and Special Collections, Rush Rhees Library, University of Rochester, Rochester, N.Y.

Brillat-Savarin, Anthelme. *The Handbook of Dining; or, Corpulency and Leanness Scientifically Considered*. Translated by L. F. Simpson. New York: D. Appleton & Co., 1865.

Brooks, Van Wyck. *Howells: His Life and World*. New York: E. P. Dutton & Co., 1959.

Brose, Nancy Harris, Juliana McGovern Dupre, Wendy Tocher Kohler, and Jean McClure Mudge. *Emily Dickinson: Profile of the Poet As Cook*. Amherst, Mass.: Hamilton I. Newall, 1976, 1981.

Brown, Susan Anna. *The Book of Forty Puddings*. New York: Charles Scribner's Sons, 1882.

Buist, Robert. *The Family Kitchen Gardener*. New York: C. M. Saxton & Co., 1853.

Calvert, Karin. "Cradle to Crib: The Revolution in Nineteenth Century Children's Furniture." In *A Century of Childhood, 1820–1920*, by Mary Lynn Stevens Heininger, Karin Calvert, Barbara Finkelstein, Kathy Vandell, Anne Scott MacLeod, and Harvey Green. Rochester, N.Y.: Strong Museum, 1984.

Carlo, Joyce W. *Trammels, Trenchers, and Tartlets: A Definitive Tour of the Colonial Kitchen*. Old Saybrook, Conn.: Peregrine Press, 1982.

Catalogue of Genteel Household Furniture, for Sale at Auction by Henry H. Leeds & Co., on Friday, April 29, 1853. New York, 1853. Strong Museum Library, Rochester, N.Y.

Catalogue of the Publications of L. Prang & Co., Fine Art Publishers. Boston, 1883.

Child, Lydia Maria. *The American Frugal Housewife: Dedicated to Those Who Are Not Ashamed of Economy.* 16th ed. Boston: Carter, Hendee & Co., 1835.

———. "Our Treasury: Hints About Furniture." *Godey's Lady's Book* 47 (May 1853): 467–68.

Church, Ella Rodman. *How to Furnish a Home.* New York: D. Appleton & Co., 1881.

Clark, Clifford E., Jr. "Domestic Architecture as an Index to Social History: The Romantic Revival and the Cult of Domesticity in America, 1840–1870." *Journal of Interdisciplinary History* 7 (1976): 42–47.

Coates, Foster. "How Delmonico Sets a Table." *Ladies' Home Journal* 8 (November 1891): 10.

Cohen, Lizabeth. "Material Culture in Working Class Homes." In *Material Culture Studies in America,* compiled and edited by Thomas J. Schlereth. Nashville, Tenn.: American Association for State and Local History, 1982.

Colbrath, M. Tarbox. *What to Get for Breakfast: With More Than One Hundred Different Breakfasts, and Full Directions for Each.* Boston: James H. Earle, 1886.

Collier, Robert Laird. *English Home Life.* Boston: Ticknor & Co., 1886.

Conway, Ellen. "Twelve Lenten Lunches." *Ladies' Home Journal* 8 (March 1891): 25.

Cook Papers. Department of Rare Books and Special Collections, Rush Rhees Library, University of Rochester, Rochester, N.Y.

Coolidge, Susan. "Angels Unaware." *Ladies' Home Journal* 8 (October 1891): 2.

Cornelius, Mary Hooker. *The Young Housekeeper's Friend.* Rev. and enl. ed. Boston: Taggard & Thompson, 1864.

Dewing, Mrs. W. T. *Beauty in the Household.* New York: Harper & Brothers, 1882.

Dudden, Faye E. *Serving Women: Household Service in Nineteenth Century America.* Middletown, Conn.: Wesleyan University Press, 1983.

Dwight, Timothy. *Travels in New England and New York.* John Harvard Library, vol. 4. Cambridge, Mass.: Belknap Press of Harvard University Press, 1969.

Earle, Alice Morse. *Home Life in Colonial Days.* 1898. Reprint. Stockbridge, Mass.: Berkshire Traveller Press, 1974.

Elias, Norbert. *The History of Manners.* Vol. 1 of *The Civilizing Process.* Translated by Edmund Jephcott. 1939. Reprint. New York: Pantheon Books, 1982.

Ellet, Elizabeth F., ed. *The New Cyclopaedia of Domestic Economy, and Practical Housekeeper.* Norwich, Conn.: Henry Bill Publishing Co., 1873.

Elliott, Charles Wyllys. "Household Art. [Part] V.—The Dining Room." *Art Journal* [American ed.] 2 (1876): 116–21.

The Encyclopaedia Britannica. 11th ed. 29 vols. New York: Encyclopaedia Britannica Co., 1910.

Farmer, Fannie Merritt. *The Original Boston Cooking-School Cook Book, 1896: A Facsimile of the Boston Cooking-School Cookbook.* New York: Weathervane Books, n.d.

Francatelli, Charles Elmé. *The Modern Cook: A Practical Guide to the Culinary Art in All Its Branches.* Philadelphia: T. B. Peterson & Brothers, 1877.

Frost, S. Annie. *The Godey's Lady's Book Receipts and Household Hints.* Philadelphia: Evans, Stoddart & Co., 1870.

Gesner, C. W. "Concerning Restaurants." *Harper's New Monthly Magazine* 32 (April 1866): 591–92.

Giedion, Siegfried. *Mechanization Takes Command: A Contribution to Anonymous History.* 1948. Reprint. New York: W. W. Norton & Co., 1969.

Goodholme, Todd S., ed. *A Domestic Cyclopedia of Practical Information.* New York: Henry Holt, 1877.

Green, Harvey, *The Light of the Home: An Intimate View of the Lives of Women in Victorian America.* New York: Pantheon Books, 1983.

———. "Popular Science and Political Thought Converge: Colonial Survival Becomes Colonial Revival, 1830–1900." *Journal of American Culture* 6 (Winter 1983): 3–24.

Hadley, Sarah. "Dainty Designs in Point Lace." *Ladies' Home Journal* 10 (June 1893): 13.

Hale, Sarah Josepha. *The New Household Receipt-Book.* New York: H. Long & Brother, 1853.

Haller, Mrs. V. Shelley. "Dining Room." *Godey's Lady's Book* 110 (February 1885): 214.

Halttunen, Karen. *Confidence Men and Painted Women: A Study of Middle-Class Culture in America, 1830–1870.* New Haven, Conn.: Yale University Press, 1982.

Hanford Papers. Department of Rare Books and Special Collections, Rush Rhees Library, University of Rochester, Rochester, N.Y.

Harland, Marion. *Breakfast, Luncheon and Tea.* New York: Charles Scribner's Sons, 1875.

———. *The Cottage Kitchen: A Collection of Practical and Inexpensive Receipts.* New York: Charles Scribner's Sons, 1883.

Henderson, Mary F. *Practical Cooking, and Dinner Giving.* New York: Harper & Brothers, 1878.

Herrick, Christine Terhune. "Provisions for Picnics." *The Outlook,* 26 August 1893.

Hiett, Constance B., and Sharon Butler. *Pleyn Delit: Medieval Cookery for Modern Cooks.* Toronto: University of Toronto Press, 1976.

Hollister Papers. Department of Rare Books and Special Collections, Rush Rhees Library, University of Rochester, Rochester, N.Y.

Holly, Henry Hudson. *Holly's Country Seats.* New York: D. Appleton & Co., 1863.

Holt, Elizabeth F. *From Attic to Cellar.* Salem, Mass.: Salem Press, 1892.

Hooker, Margaret Huntington. *Ye Gentlewoman's Housewifery.* New York: Dodd, Mead & Co., 1896.

Hooker, Richard J. *Food and Drink in America: A History.* Indianapolis and New York: Bobbs-Merrill Co., 1981.

Howells, William Dean. *A Modern Instance.* 1882. In *Novels: Eighteen Seventy-Five to Eighteen Eighty-six,* edited by Edwin H. Cady. New York: Library of America, 1982.

———. *The Rise of Silas Lapham.* 1885. In *Novels: Eighteen Seventy-Five to Eighteen Eighty-Six,* edited by Edwin H. Cady. New York: Library of America, 1982.

Huntington-Hooker Papers. Department of Rare Books and Special Collections, Rush Rhees Library, University of Rochester, Rochester, N.Y.

Illustrated Catalogue and Price List, Rogers, Smith and Company, New Haven, Conn. 1867. Strong Museum Library, Rochester, N.Y.

Illustrated Catalogue of Fine Silver Plated Ware Manufactured and Imported by J. F. Curran & Co. 18 John Street, New York. 1868. Strong Museum Library, Rochester, N.Y.

Job, Joseph. *Extended Travels in Romantic America.* Lausanne: Edita, 1966.

Kett, Joseph F. "Review Essay: Temperance and Intemperance as Historical Problems." *Journal of American History* 67 (March 1981): 878–85.

Kingsland, Mrs. Burton [Florence]. "A Talk About Teas." *Ladies' Home Journal* 9 (October 1892): 4.

Kraft, Ken. *Garden to Order.* Garden City, N.Y.: Doubleday & Co., 1962.

A Lady [pseud.]. *The Workwoman's Guide.* 2nd ed., rev. and corr. London: Simpkin, Marshall & Co., 1840.

Lea, Elizabeth F. *Domestic Cookery, Useful Receipts, and Hints to Young Housekeepers.* Baltimore: Cushings & Bailey, 1865.

Lee, Mrs. N. K. M. *The Cook's Own Book and Housekeeper's Register.* New York: C. S. Francis, 1842.

Leslie, Eliza. *The Ladies' Guide to True Politeness and Perfect Manners; or, Miss Leslie's Behavior Book.* Philadelphia: T. B. Peterson & Brothers, 1864.

————. *Miss Leslie's New Cookery Book.* Philadelphia: T. B. Peterson & Brothers, 1857.

Lincoln, Mrs. D. A. *Mrs. Lincoln's Boston Cook Book.* Boston: Roberts Brothers, 1889.

Lockett, T. A. *Davenport Pottery and Porcelain, 1794–1887.* Rutland, Vt.: Charles E. Tuttle, 1972.

Loftie, Mary Jane Anderson. *The Dining-Room.* In *The Dining-Room by M. J. Loftie. The Drawing-Room by Lucy Orrinsmith. The Bedroom and the Boudoir by Lady Barker.* Art at Home Series. London: Macmillan & Co., 1878. Reprint. The Aesthetic Movement and the Arts and Crafts Movement Series. New York: Garland Publishing, 1978.

Logan, Mrs. John A. *The Home Manual.* Chicago: H. J. Smith Co., 1889.

Long, Clarence D. *Wages and Earnings in the United States, 1860–1890.* New York: Arno Press, 1975.

Lyman, Joseph B., and Laura E. Lyman. *The Philosophy of House-keeping.* Hartford, Conn.: Goodwin & Betts, 1867.

Lyon Papers, Department of Rare Books and Special Collections, Rush Rhees Library, University of Rochester, Rochester, N.Y.

Miller, George L. "Classification and Economic Scaling of Nineteenth-Century Ceramics." *Historical Archeology* 14 (1980): 24–34.

Montgomery Ward & Company. *Catalogue and Buyer's Guide No. 57, Spring and Summer, 1895.* Reprint. New York: Dover Publications, 1969.

More, Louise Bolard. *Wage-Earners' Budgets.* 1907. Reprint. New York: Arno Press & The New York Times, 1971.

Morris, Edmund. *Ten Acres Enough.* 6th ed. New York: J. Miller, 1864.

Morton, Agnes H. *Etiquette: An Answer to the Riddle, When? Where? How?* Philadelphia: Penn Publishing Co., 1894.

Mudge, Jean McClure. *Chinese Export Porcelain for the American Trade.* Newark: University of Delaware Press, 1962.

Mulvey, Christopher. *Anglo-American Landscapes: A Study of Nineteenth Century Anglo-American Travel Literature.* Cambridge and New York: Cambridge University Press, 1983.

Munn-Pixley Family Papers. Department of Rare Books and Special Collections, Rush Rhees Library, University of Rochester, Rochester, N.Y.

Murray, Thomas J. *The Book of Entrees.* New York: Frederick A. Stokes & Brother, 1889.

"My Wife's 'First Family Party.'" *Peterson's Magazine* 74 (July 1878): 62–64.

"The Napier Ball." *Harper's Weekly* 3 (26 February 1850): 134.

"New Furniture." *Godey's Lady's Book* 40 (February 1850): 152–53.

1095 Menus: Breakfast, Dinner, and Tea. Philadelphia: E. Bradford Clarke Co., n.d. (ca. 1891).

Osborne Family Papers. Strong Museum Library, Rochester, N.Y.

The Oxford English Dictionary. 12 vols. 1933. Reprint. Oxford: Clarendon Press, 1970.

Parkes, Mrs. William. *Domestic Duties; or, Instructions to Young Married Ladies on the Management of Their Households, and the Regulation of Their Conduct in the Various Relations and Duties of Married Life*. 3rd ed. New York: J. & J. Harper, 1829.

Parloa, Maria. "Everything About the House." *Ladies' Home Journal* 8 (November 1891): 29.

———. "Everything About the House." *Ladies' Home Journal* 9 (August 1892): 25.

———. "Everything About the House." *Ladies' Home Journal* 10 (October 1892): 25.

———. "From Soup Tureen to Pudding Dish." *Good Housekeeping* 8 (2 March 1889): 199–200.

———. *Home Economics*. New York: Century Co., 1898.

Mrs. A. Ericson Perkins Papers. Strong Museum Library, Rochester, N.Y.

"Practical Hints for the Household: The Dining Room." *Godey's Lady's Book* 111 (September 1885): 293.

A Practical Housekeeper [pseud.]. *The American Practical Cookery-Book; or, Housekeeping Made Easy, Pleasant and Economical in All Its Departments*. Philadelphia: J. W. Bradley, 1861.

———. *Cookery As It Should Be: A New Manual of the Dining Room and Kitchen, for Persons of Moderate Circumstances*. Philadelphia: Willis P. Hazard, 1856.

Putnam, Elizabeth H. *Mrs. Putnam's Receipt Book, and Young Housekeeper's Assistant*. New and enl. ed. New York: Sheldon & Co., 1869 (c 1867).

Rafter, Ethel M., to John R. Williams, 1 October 1898. Collection of the author.

Rainwater, Dorothy T., and H. Ivan Rainwater. *American Silverplate*. Nashville, Tenn.: Thomas Nelson, 1968.

"Recipes." *Godey's Lady's Book* 61 (December 1885): 620–21.

Reynolds Family Papers. Private collection.

Roberts, Patricia Easterbrook. *Table Settings, Entertaining, and Etiquette: A History and Guide*. New York: Bonanza Books, n.d.

Root, Waverley, and Richard De Rochemont. *Eating in America: A History*. New York: Ecco Press, 1976.

Rorabaugh, W. J. *The Alcoholic Republic*. New York: Oxford University Press, 1979.

Rorer, Sarah Tyson. *Mrs. Rorer's Philadelphia Cook Book*. Philadelphia: Arnold & Co., 1886.

———. "The Table on Christmas Day." *Ladies' Home Journal* 15 (December 1897): 34.

Ruth, John A. *Decorum: A Practical Treatise on Etiquette and Dress of the Best American Society*. Revised by S. L. Louis. New York: Union Publishing House, 1883.

Sangster, Margaret E. *Good Manners for All Occasions*. New York: Christian Herald, 1904.

Scott, Sarah E. *Every-Day Cookery for Every Family: Containing 1,000 Receipts Adapted to Moderate Incomes*. Philadelphia, Davis & Brother, 1868 (c 1866).

"Silver and Silver Plate." *Harper's New Monthly Magazine* 37 (September 1868): 434.

Simmons, Amelia. *American Cookery*. 3rd ed. Albany, N.Y.: Charles R. & George Webster, 1804.

Slater, Michael. *Dickens on America and Americans*. Austin: University of Texas Press, 1978.

Soyer, Alexis. *The Modern Housewife, or Ménagère*. New York: D. Appleton & Co., 1857 (c 1849).

Sprackling, Helen. *Customs on the Table Top: How New England Housewives Set Out Their Tables*. Old Sturbridge Village Booklet Series, no. 8. Sturbridge, Mass.: Old Sturbridge Village, 1958.

Steele, Alice C. *Aunt Teeks in Memory Land*. 2 vols. Windsor, Mass.: Progressive Club, 1960.

The Successful Housekeeper. Detroit: M. W. Ellsworth & Co., 1883.

Susman, Warren I. "History and the American Intellectual: Uses of a Usable Past." In *The American Experience*, edited by Hennig Cohen. Boston: Houghton Mifflin Co., 1968.

"The Third Bridesmaid." *Godey's Lady's Book* 23 (July–December 1841): 201–6.

Townsend, Grace. *Dining Room and Kitchen*. Chicago: L. P. Miller, 1891.

Tucker Family Papers. Castle Tucker, Wiscasset, Maine.

Twelfth Appendix to Illustrated Catalogue and Price List of Electro Silver Plate, on Nickel Silver and White Metal. Meriden Britannia Co., West Meriden, Conn., 1879. Strong Museum Library, Rochester, N.Y.

U.S. Bureau of the Census. *Historical Statistics of the United States, Colonial Times to 1870*. Bicentennial ed. Washington: U.S. Department of Commerce, Bureau of the Census, 1975.

Vaux, Calvert A. *Villas and Cottages: A Series of Designs Prepared for Execution in the United States*. New York: Harper & Brothers, 1857.

Warren, Jane. *The Economical Cook Book*. New York: Hurst & Co., 1882(?).

"Washington Market at Christmas-Time." *Harper's Weekly* 9 (30 December 1865): 823.

Webster, Mrs. A. L. *The Improved Housewife, or Book of Receipts; with Engravings for Marketing and Carving*. Boston: Phillips, Sampson & Co., 1853.

Webster, Noah. *An American Dictionary of the English Language*. Springfield, Mass.: G. & C. Merriman, 1860.

Whitehead, Jessup, *The Steward's Handbook and Guide to Party Catering: In Five Parts*. 4th ed. Chicago: J. Whitehead & Co., 1899.

Wiltsea Papers. Department of Rare Books and Special Collections, Rush Rhees Library, University of Rochester, Rochester, N.Y.

Woodward, George E., and F. W. Woodward. *Woodward's Country Homes*. 5th ed., rev. and enl. New York: George E. & F. W. Woodward, 1866.

Wright, Gwendolyn. *Building the Dream: A Social History of Housing in America, 1650–1900*. New York: Pantheon Books, 1981.

Young, John H. *Our Deportment*. Detroit: F. B. Dickerson & Co., 1883.

PICTURE CREDITS AND DESCRIPTIONS

1. PROPER AND PROSPEROUS: THE VICTORIAN MIDDLE CLASS

PAGE 1: *Ladies' Home Journal* 10 (February 1893): 5. PAGE 3: *Ladies' Home Journal* 19 (November 1892): 3. PAGE 5: Hand-painted stereograph, United States or England, ca. 1860. PAGE 7: Illustration by Charles Dana Gibson, 1902, from *The Gibson Book II* (New York: Charles Scribner's Sons; R. H. Russell, 1906). PAGE 13: Clockwise, beginning upper left: silver-plated toothpick holder, James W. Tufts Co., Boston, ca. 1890; "Burmese" glass toothpick holder, Mt. Washington Glass Co., New Bedford, Mass., ca. 1890; pressed-glass toothpick holder, United States, ca. 1900; pressed-glass toothpick holder, United States, ca. 1895; silver-plated toothpick holder, Meriden Silver Plate Co., Meriden, Conn., ca. 1886; box of toothpicks, Charles Forster, Strong, Maine, patented 24 March 1891; pressed-glass toothpick holder, United States, ca. 1890. Center: pressed-glass toothpick holder, United States or France, ca. 1890. PAGE 14: "The Kitchen," lithographed paper, L. Prang & Co., 1874; courtesy of Library of Congress.

2. THE MANDATES OF MANNERS: ETIQUETTE OF THE TABLE

PAGE 15: Lithographed trade card, United States, copyright 1883. PAGE 18: Selection of etiquette books and women's magazines: John H. Young, *Our Deportment*, 1883; Martha Louise Rayne, *Gems of Deportment*, 1882; John A. Ruth. *Decorum*, 1882; *Woman's Home Companion*, November 1899; *Peterson's Ladies' National Magazine*, June 1882. PAGE 23: Dining room at 309 Pinckney Street, Madison, Wis., ca. 1894; photograph by Frederick K. Conover; courtesy of the State Historical Society of Wisconsin. PAGE 29: Pressed-glass bread tray, "Sheaf of Wheat" pattern, United States, ca. 1865. Curtis family and friends, Manchester, Mass., 1883–1887; photograph by Mrs. Greely Curtis; courtesy of the Society for the Preservation of New England Antiquities. PAGE 31: Invitation, ink and watercolor on paper, Rochester, N.Y., ca. 1880; invitation, engraving and ink on paper, Rochester, N.Y., ca. 1880. PAGE 32: Invitation, engraving on paper, United States, 1888. Fashion plate reprinted from Stella Blum, *Victorian Fashions and Costumes from Harper's Bazaar 1867–1898* (New York: Dover Publications, 1974), 164–65; courtesy of Dover Publications, Inc. PAGE 36: "Served Him Right," woodcut from *Harper's Weekly* 3 (12 February 1859): 112. PAGE 37: Coin-silver fish slice, "Kings" pattern, William Gale Jr. & Co., New York,

1853–1870. PAGE 38: "On Carving," from A Practical Housekeeper, *Cookery As It Should Be* (Philadelphia: Willis P. Hazard, 1856), 16, 19. PAGE 39: Flow-blue sugar bowl, "Scinde" pattern, Thomas Walker, Staffordshire, England, 1845–1851, gift of Petra Williams; sterling silver sugar tongs, England, ca. 1850; revolving butter dish, France, ca. 1885; silver-plated butter knife, "Tipped" pattern, Meriden Britannia Co., Meriden, Conn., introduced 1862; sterling silver salt cellar and spoon, Bailey & Co., Philadelphia, Pa., 1857. PAGES 40–41: Mary Chambers, *Table Etiquette* (Boston: Boston Cooking School Magazine, 1929), 1–4. PAGE 41: Cut-glass finger bowl, "Chrysanthemum" pattern, T. G. Hawkes & Co., Corning, N.Y., ca. 1900; cotton damask doily, probably United States, ca. 1890. PAGE 43: Sterling silver pastry fork, "Iris" pattern, William B. Durgin Co., Concord, N.H., 1904. Thermoplastic napkin ring, United States, ca. 1880; silver-plated napkin ring, R. Wallace & Sons Manufacturing Co., Wallingford, Conn., 1871–1900; wooden napkin ring, United States, ca. 1890; silver-plated napkin ring, United States, ca. 1870. PAGE 45: Pressed-glass cup plate, New England, ca. 1835; transfer-printed earthenware teacup and saucer, Staffordshire, England, ca. 1820. PAGE 48: Sterling silver corn scraper, "Flanders" pattern, Simons, Brother & Co., Philadelphia, patented 1900.

3. THE ALTAR OF GASTRONOMY: DINING ROOMS AND THEIR FURNISHINGS

PAGE 49: Photograph courtesy of the Dewitt Historical Society, Dewitt, N.Y. PAGE 54: Photograph of General Peyton Wise dining room, Richmond, Va., 1880; courtesy of the Valentine Museum. PAGE 55: Photograph of dining room at 348 Beacon Street, Boston, Mass.; Soule Photographic Co., 1885–1895; courtesy of the Society for the Preservation of New England Antiquities. PAGE 56: Photograph, 1880s; courtesy of the Society for the Preservation of New England Antiquities. PAGE 57: Calvert A. Vaux, *Villas and Cottages* (New York: Harper & Brothers, 1857), pl. 19. PAGE 58: Lithographed paper trade card, White, Warner & Co., Taunton, Mass., ca. 1885. PAGE 61: Spring and Summer Catalogue, Jordan Marsh & Co. (Boston, 1885), 89. PAGE 62: Maple gate-leg table, United States, ca. 1900. Cherry and pine drop-leaf table, United States, ca. 1875. PAGE 64: Walnut and leather chair, United States, ca. 1880; walnut and cane chair, United States, ca. 1875. PAGE 65: Catalogue illustrations, Paine's Furniture Co. (Boston, ca. 1890), 92, 93, 98, 102. PAGE 66: Charles Locke Eastlake, *A History of the Gothic Revival* (London: Longmans, Green, 1877), 326. PAGE 67: Harriet Spoffard, *Art Decoration Applied to Furniture* (New York: Harper & Brothers, 1877), 193. PAGE 68: Oak, walnut, and rosewood sideboard, United States, ca. 1865. Lower shelf: linen and crocheted cotton sideboard cloth, ca. 1890; silver-plated tea set, Reed & Barton, Taunton, Mass., ca. 1867; cased-glass and silver-plated fruit bowl, Taunton Silverplate Co., Taunton, Mass., ca. 1870; pressed-glass decanters, "Diamond Point" pattern, New England, ca. 1850, courtesy of John Castle; silver-plated water pitcher and tray, James W. Tufts Co., Boston, ca. 1895. Upper shelf: silver-plated spoon warmer, England, ca. 1895; porcelain cups and saucers, France, ca. 1865; "Royal Flemish" glass cracker jar, Mt. Washington Glass Co., New Bedford, Mass., 1889–1899. PAGE 70: Oak china cabinet, United States, ca. 1900. Top shelf: cut-glass wine glasses, punch cups, sherry glasses, and tumblers, Nehemiah Packwood, Sandwich, Mass., 1888–1920, gift of Yvette Van Huysen and Shirley Bidelman; cut-glass cordial and wine glasses, "Chrysanthemum" pattern, T. G. Hawkes & Co.,

Corning, N.Y., ca. 1900. Second shelf: transfer-printed earthenware dinner service, "Etruscan Vase" pattern, Enoch Wood & Sons, Staffordshire, England, ca. 1840; pressed-glass wine glasses, "Grape and Festoon" pattern, Doyle & Co., Pittsburgh, Pa., ca. 1880. Third and fourth shelves: porcelain dinner service, France, ca. 1865; enameled bone-china dessert plates, England, ca. 1860, gift of Elizabeth F. Cheney. PAGE 71: "Still Life with Fish," oil on canvas, artist unknown, United States, ca. 1840; "Still Life with Game Birds," oil on canvas, artist unknown, United States, ca. 1840. PAGE 74: *Ladies' Home Journal* 8 (November 1891): 37. PAGE 77: Jessup Whitehead, *The Steward's Handbook* (Chicago: J. Whitehead & Co., 1899), appendix, p. 24. PAGE 78: Silver-plated napkin ring, Barbour Brothers, New Haven, Conn., ca. 1892; cotton damask napkin, probably United States, ca. 1890. Back: silver-plated napkin ring, United States, ca. 1900; silver-plated napkin ring, Wilcox Silverplate Co., Meriden, Conn., 1885. Front: silver-plated napkin ring, Aurora Silver Plate Manufacturing Co., Aurora, Ill., 1869–1900. PAGE 81: Porcelain dinner service, France, ca. 1865. PAGE 83: Invoice from papers of Captain Richard Tucker, Wiscasset, Maine; courtesy of Jane Tucker. PAGE 84: E. G. Webster & Brother, *Illustrated Catalogue and Price List of Fine Electro Silver Plate* (New York, ca. 1880), 25. PAGE 85: Pressed-glass dessert wares, "Cupid and Venus" pattern, Richards & Hartley Glass Co., Tarentum, Pa., ca. 1878; gift of Marion Folsom, Jr. PAGE 88: Silver-plated buckwheat-cake lifter, Tiffany & Co., New York, patented 1884; sterling silver ice-cream knife, "Twist Engraved" pattern, Joseph Seymour & Co., Syracuse, N.Y., pattern introduced 1867; sterling silver sugar sifter, United States, ca. 1870; sterling silver grape shears, United States, ca. 1900; coin-silver mustard ladle, H. Salisbury, New York, 1830–1838. PAGE 89: Silver-plated asparagus tongs, England, 1905–1906, gift of Elizabeth F. Cheney; sterling silver ice-cream fork, Frank W. Smith Silver Co., Gardner, Mass., ca. 1900, gift of Elizabeth F. Cheney; sterling silver lemonade sipper, United States, ca. 1900; silver-plate and mother-of-pearl fruit knife, United States, ca. 1890; silver-plated strawberry fork, William H. Glenney Co., Rochester, N.Y., after 1876. PAGE 90: *Harper's Weekly*, 14 (1870): 388.

4 . THE BOUNTIFUL PANTRY:
FASHIONS IN FOOD AND DRINK

PAGE 93: Lithographed paper advertising brochure, H. J. Heinz Co., Pittsburgh, Pa., 1895. PAGE 97: Lithographed paper can labels, United States, ca. 1890. PAGE 98: Lithographed paper trade card, T. A. Snider, Cincinnati, Ohio, printed by Henderson-Achert Krebs Lithography Co., ca. 1895. PAGE 99: *Rochester Directory* (Rochester, N.Y., 1871), 444. PAGE 101: *Harper's Weekly* 9 (30 December 1865): 828. PAGE 102: Courtesy of Pacific Fruit Express. PAGE 103: Lithographed paper trade card, New York Condensed Milk Co., New York, 1887. PAGE 104: Condensed milk can, Borden's Condensed Milk Co., New York, 1899, courtesy of Tony Knipp; pressed-glass and silver-plated condensed-milk server, E. G. Webster & Son, Brooklyn, N.Y., 1886–1928, courtesy of Thomas F. Gallagher. PAGE 106: Price list, Cobb, Aldrich & Co., Boston, ca. 1890 PAGE 107: Lithographed paper trade card, H. J. Heinz Co., Pittsburgh, Pa., 1895. PAGE 108: Pressed-glass banana bowl, "Medallion Sunburst" pattern, United States, ca. 1880. PAGE 109: Clockwise, beginning lower left: silver-plated orange cup, Wilcox Silver Plate Co., Meriden, Conn., ca. 1893, gift of Jay A. Lewis; silver-plated orange cup, United States, patented 1896, gift of Jay A. Lewis; silver-plated orange spoon, "Princeton" pattern, Rogers &

Brother, Waterbury, Conn., ca. 1897; silver-plated orange spoon, "Avon" pattern, Meriden Britannia Co., Meriden, Conn., ca. 1900.   PAGE 110: Engraved glass celery vase, United States or Bohemia, ca. 1870.   PAGE 111: Glass and silver-plated sardine box, United States, ca. 1890; silver-plated sardine tongs, Meriden Britannia Co., Meriden, Conn., ca. 1885; sterling silver sardine server, Sweden, ca. 1895.   PAGES 112–13: Trade catalogue, Simpson, Hall, Miller & Co., Wallingford, Conn., 1891.   PAGE 114: Sterling silver salad servers, "Love Disarmed" pattern, Reed & Barton, Taunton, Mass., ca. 1900; sterling silver lettuce fork, "Rose" pattern, Steiff Co., Baltimore, Md., pattern introduced about 1904.   PAGE 118: Trade catalogue, Simpson, Hall, Miller & Co., Wallingford, Conn., 1891.   PAGE 119: Lithographed paper trade cards, United States, ca. 1885.   PAGES 120–21: Trade catalogue, Simpson, Hall, Miller & Co., Wallingford, Conn., 1891.   PAGE 123: Redware turk's-head mold, United States, 1875–1900; tin jelly mold, United States or England, ca. 1880; ironstone blancmange mold, Grimwades Ltd., Staffordshire, England, 1930–1940.   PAGE 124: Cone of sugar, 1985; wrought-iron sugar nippers, England, ca. 1850.   PAGE 126: Price list, Cobb, Aldrich & Co., Boston, ca. 1890.   PAGE 127: Photograph courtesy of the Smithsonian Institution (private collection).   PAGE 128: Sterling silver coffee pot, Whiting Manufacturing Co., Newark, N.J., ca. 1885; porcelain demitasse cup and saucer, Charles Field Haviland & Cie., Limoges, France, ca. 1865; sterling silver coffee spoons, Whiting Manufacturing Co., Newark, N.J., ca. 1890.   PAGE 129: Silver-plated samovar, England, ca. 1890. PAGES 130–31: Chromolithographed paper trade cards, United States, last quarter of the nineteenth century.   PAGE 132: Porcelain chocolate pot, Limoges, France, ca. 1885; porcelain cup and saucer, Shelley Potteries, Ltd., Longton, England, ca. 1890; silver-plated souvenir spoon, United States, ca. 1890; lithographed tin "Huyler's Caracas Cocoa" can, S. A. Ilsley & Co., New York, ca. 1890.   PAGE 133: Salt-glazed stoneware beer pitcher, Germany, ca. 1900, gift of Cynthia Janes; earthenware beer mug, Villeroy & Boch, Mettlach, Germany, 1896; pressed-glass ladies' beer mug, "Argus" pattern, Bakewell, Pears & Co., Pittsburgh, Pa., ca. 1870; blown- and cut-glass ale glass, "Cut Mirror" pattern, United States, ca. 1860.   PAGE 135: Lithographed paper trade card, printed by Chapman & Bloomer, New York, 1886.   PAGE 136: Top row: cut-glass champagne pitcher, "Strawberry Diamond and Fan" pattern, United States, ca. 1900; cut-glass and silver-plated wine caster, England, ca. 1865. Bottom row: cut-glass wine glass, "Chrysanthemum" pattern, T. G. Hawkes & Co., Corning, N.Y., ca. 1900; cut-glass wine coaster, "Russian" pattern, United States, 1890–1900; pressed-glass wine, cordial, and champagne glasses, "Cupid and Venus" pattern, Richards & Hartley Glass Co., Tarentum, Pa., ca. 1878, gift of Marion Folsom, Jr. PAGE 138: Silver-plated root-beer pitcher, Colonial Silver Co., Portland, Maine, 1899–1943. Chromolithographed paper trade card, printed by J. Ottman, New York, 1870–1900.   PAGE 139: Silver-plated ice-water pitcher, Meriden Britannia Co., Meriden, Conn., ca. 1867.   PAGE 140: Trade catalogue, Simpson, Hall, Miller & Co., Wallingford, Conn., 1891.

5 . FROM SOUP TUREEN TO PUDDING DISH:
BREAKFAST, LUNCH, DINNER, TEA, AND SUPPER

PAGE 141: *Ladies' Home Journal* 10 (April 1893): 5.   PAGE 143: Photograph by S. Beer, New York, ca. 1860; courtesy of the Smithsonian Institution (private collection).   PAGE 145: "Oatmeal and the Morning Paper," illustration by Charles Dana Gibson.   PAGE 147: Painted tin lunchbox,

United States, ca. 1880. "Morning Bell," wood engraving by Winslow Homer, 1873. PAGE 149: Photograph by R. B. Whittaker, Liberty, N.Y.; courtesy of the Smithsonian Institution (private collection). PAGE 150: *Godey's Lady's Book* 58 (March 1859): 267. PAGE 151: *Ladies' Home Journal* 19 (November 1892): 3. PAGE 153: Silver-plated service bell, United States, ca. 1880. PAGE 154: Silver-plated crumb tray, "Assyrian" pattern, Meriden Britannia Co., Meriden, Conn., pattern introduced 1887. PAGE 157: *Harper's Weekly* 11 (7 December 1867): 781; "Studies in Expression," illustration by Charles Dana Gibson, 1902, from *The Gibson Book II* (New York: Charles Scribner's Sons; R. H. Russell, 1906). PAGE 159: Silver-plated toast rack, James Dixon & Sons, Sheffield, England, ca. 1880; glass and silver-plated breakfast caster, United States, ca. 1870; cotton damask napkin and tablecloth, ca. 1885; silver-plated napkin ring, Middletown Plate Co., Middletown, Conn., ca. 1875; sterling silver fork, Newton E. Crittendon, Leroy, N.Y., 1862–1872, gift of Marjorie E. McDowell in memory of Mr. and Mrs. Charles Hutchison; sterling silver butter knife, "Kings" pattern, Towle Silversmiths, Newburyport, Mass., ca. 1900; silver-plated spoon, "Plain Tipped" pattern, William H. Glenny & Co., Rochester, N.Y., ca. 1880; ironstone plate, T. & R. Boote, Burslem, England, 1890–1906; ironstone porridge bowl, J. & G. Meakin, Staffordshire, England, after 1890; ironstone breakfast cup and saucer, John Edwards, Staffordshire, England, 1890–1900; ironstone fruit bowl, Richard Alcock, Burslem, England, ca. 1890. All ironstone courtesy of Edward G. Cornwell. PAGE 160: Chromolithographed paper trade card, United States, 1880–1900. PAGE 161: Trade catalogue, Rogers, Smith & Co., New Haven, Conn., 1867. Trade catalogue, Simpson, Hall, Miller & Co., Wallingford, Conn., 1891. PAGES 164–65: Trade catalogue, Simpson, Hall, Miller & Co., Wallingford, Conn., 1891. PAGE 166: Handwritten dinner menu, 1897. Handwritten lunch menu, 1899. PAGE 169: Elizabeth F. Ellet, ed., *The New Cyclopaedia of Domestic Economy* (Norwich, Conn.: Henry Bill Publishing Co., 1873), 404. PAGE 171: Frontispiece from A Practical Housekeeper, *The American Practical Cookery-Book* (Philadelphia: J. W. Bradley, 1861). PAGE 175: *Ladies' Home Journal* 10 (September 1893): 7. PAGE 176: *Ladies' Floral Cabinet and Pictorial Home Companion* 3 (October 1876): 156. PAGE 177: Photograph of John Little dining room, San Francisco, ca. 1875; courtesy of the Society of California Pioneers. PAGE 178: Silver-plated nut bowl, Woodman-Cook Co., Portland, Maine, 1893–1914; set of silver-plated nut picks, William Rogers Manufacturing Co., Waterbury, Conn., ca. 1890. PAGE 179: Molded sugar centerpiece, United States, ca. 1870. PAGE 181: Menu of Mrs. John Pixley Munn, 26 January 1892; courtesy of the Department of Rare Books and Special Collections, Rush Rhees Library, University of Rochester. PAGE 182: Printed dinner menu, 249th Anniversary of the Ancient and Honorable Artillery Company, Fanueil Hall, Boston, 1887. PAGE 183: Dining room, Manchester, Mass., 1883–1887; photograph by Mrs. Greely Curtis; courtesy of the Society for the Preservation of New England Antiquities. PAGE 185: Photograph attributed to Horace Chandler; courtesy of the Society for the Preservation of New England Antiquities. PAGE 186: Silver-plated tea tray, Andover Silver Plate Co., Wallingford, Conn., ca. 1910; bone-china tea set, Samuel Alcock & Co., Staffordshire, England, design registered 1843; "Battenberg" lace tablecloth, probably United States, 1875–1915; embroidered linen tea-tray cloth, United States, ca. 1890; cotton damask napkin, United States, ca. 1885; silver-plated cake basket, Wilcox Silver Plate Co., Meriden, Conn., ca. 1875; pressed-glass compote, "Tree of Life" pattern, Portland Glass Co., Portland, Maine, 1865–1875; silver-plated and mother-of-pearl dessert knife, Gorham Manufacturing Co., Providence, R.I., ca. 1870; silver-plated butter pat, Tiffany & Co., New York, ca. 1890; silver-plated and mother-of-pearl fruit knife (on plate), United States, ca. 1890; butter-serving knife, "Tipped" pattern, Meriden Britannia Co., Meriden, Conn., introduced 1862. Cake basket and lace tablecloth courtesy of Edward G. Cornwell. PAGE 188: Photograph, United States, ca. 1900. PAGE 192: *Harper's Weekly* 3 (26 February 1859): 153. PAGE 194: Frontispiece from *The Successful Housekeeper* (Detroit: M. W. Ellsworth & Co., 1883); courtesy of Jean Callen King. PAGE 195: Printed supper menu, Cavalry Supper at the Clinton Hotel, Rochester, N.Y., 1881. PAGE 197: Photograph of W. L. Coggshall dining room, Groton, N.Y.; courtesy of the Dewitt Historical Society, Dewitt, N.Y. PAGE 198: *Harper's Weekly* 11 (30 November 1867): 761.

RECIPES AND INSTRUCTIONS

PAGE 203: Painted cast-iron and tin family scale, United States, patented 1865; stamped tin measuring cup, United States, ca. 1890. PAGE 207: Chromolithographed paper trade card, printed by Mayer, Merkel & Ottman, N.Y., ca. 1890. PAGE 208: Chromolithographed paper trade card, H. K. & F. B. Thurber & Co., United States, 1870–1900. PAGE 219: Lithographed paper trade card, United States, ca. 1885. PAGE 220: Gardner Egg Carrier, Winchester Box Manufacturing Co., Baldwinsville, Mass., patented 1889. PAGE 269: Painted tin spice box, United States, ca. 1880. PAGE 273: Lithographed paper fruit-crate label, printed by Schmidt Label & Lithography Co.. San Francisco, ca. 1890. PAGE 284: Cast white-metal ice-cream molds, Germany, France, or the United States, 1850–1900. PAGE 288: Silver-plated pie server, A. F. Towle & Son Co., Newburyport, Mass., 1880–1882.

NOTES, BIBLIOGRAPHY

PAGE 299: Chromolithographed paper trade card, Charles H. Phillips Chemical Co., printed by Lindner, Eddy & Clauss, New York, copyright 1891.

PICTURE
CREDITS
AND
DESCRIPTIONS

• ——— •

INDEX

About the Author

Susan Williams is Curator of Household Accessories and
Tablewares at the Strong Museum in Rochester, New York,
America's leading collection of Victoriana, where she
has worked since 1973. She was born in Rochester in
1948, and graduated from the University of Denver.